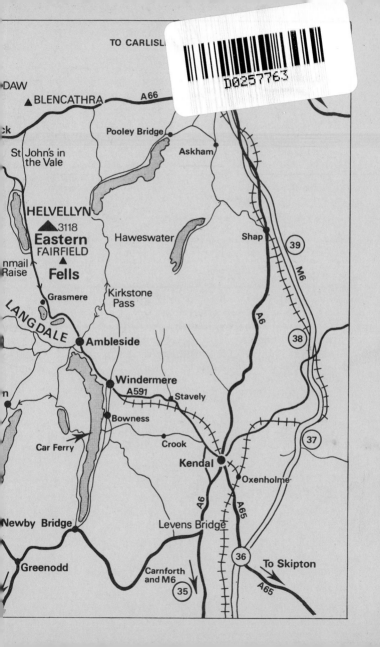

Rock climbing in the Lake District

This pictorial guide is intended for those wishing to climb in the Lake District in summer or winter

Rock climbing in the Lake District

Bill Birkett
Geoff Cram
Chris Eilbeck
Ian Roper

An illustrated guide
to selected climbs in
the Lake District

Constable London

First published in Great Britain 1975
by Constable and Company Limited
3 The Lanchesters, 162 Fulham Palace Road
London W6 9ER
Copyright © 1990 T.W.Birkett, A.G.Cram,
J.C.Eilbeck and I.Roper
2nd edition revised 1977, Reprinted 1981, 1984
3rd edition revised and extended 1987
4th edition revised 1990, Reprinted 1994
ISBN 0 09 467640 2
Printed in Great Britain by
BAS Printers Ltd, Over Wallop

Dedicated to Bill Peascod

Contents

Maps

Key to maps

●   = Stretcher box

M.R.P. = Mountain rescue post

Preface to the first edition

This guide attempts to describe, with as much pictorial aid as possible, 200 climbs selected from the 1,500 climbs currently available in the Lake District. The guide is intended to provide useful coverage for the new visitor to the area or for someone who climbs here only rarely. Nine area centres are given with general information about the local facilities.

The routes are chosen from the direct experience of the three authors over the last fifteen years. We have endeavoured to produce a balanced selection and we hope that there is something for everyone. A novel idea is the inclusion of combined climbs where these are particularly good. As far as the quality of the climbs is concerned, we have tried to indicate this by using a star system, grading each climb according to our own experience and a survey of opinion in the climbing world.

The task of selection has been a difficult one, and we have been forced to omit many excellent climbs. For example, no girdle traverses could be included, because it is so difficult to provide the detailed description required. We have given as much information as possible on winter climbing.

Geoff Cram
Chris Eilbeck
Ian Roper
Keswick 1973

Preface to the second edition

This second edition appears with the minimum of alteration. We have not made any changes in the basic format of the guide, but we have tried to correct all our errors, and to provide up-to-date information. We have included one more crag: Neckband Crag on Bowfell. We have also included a few of the large number of very hard new climbs which have appeared recently in the Lake District.

A.G.C., J.C.E., I.R. 1976

Preface to the third edition

Bill Birkett has greatly extended the information provided in the second edition, including both technical pitch gradings and E grades for the extreme climbs. Additionally, there are five new crags described, and some eighty further routes, both on the new crags and those covered already. Photographic content has also been revised and modernized.

It is intended that this guide will now cover the whole spectrum of difficulty from Moderate to E6 and provide sufficient information for you to climb some of Lakeland's finest climbs. With the addition of the new crag information (including Bowderstone notes) and winter climbing notes, it is hoped that the climber will get the best out of Lakeland – whatever the prevailing weather! Enjoy your climbing.

B.B., A.G.C., J.C.E. 1986

Acknowledgements

We are heavily in debt to a great many people for advice, criticism and assistance with both text and photographs. Thanks again to John and Stella Adams, Jill Aldersley, Bob Allen, John Burslem, Kay and Stuart Charlton, Dave Cook, Jean Cram, Tony Greenbank, John Hartley, Bill Lounds, Peter Lucas, Paul Nunn, Al Phizacklea, Ian Williamson and Bill Young.

The photographs were taken by: R.F. Allen (pages 34, 36, 136, 169, 177, 225, 231, 246); T.W. Birkett (pages 28, 38, 46, 66, 83, 117, 126, 151, 153, 155, 158, 175, 182, 189, 196, 206, 207, 218, 221, 284); A.G. Cram (pages 6, 8, 145, 248, 256, 271, 274, 278); J.C. Eilbeck (pages 54, 62, 186, 198, 204, 215, 223, 230, 260, 263, 270, 281); C. Hall (page 209); J. Hartley (page 192); P. Lucas (pages 19, 56, 57, 141, 280); A. Phizacklea (pages 10, 13, 86, 111, 190, 212, 286); I. Roper (pages 2, 11, 15, 16, 19, 23, 24, 31, 41, 42, 44, 47, 52, 64, 69, 73, 75, 80, 90, 91, 95, 102, 105, 106, 108, 119, 124, 129, 131, 139, 150, 166, 167, 172, 184, 234, 237, 242, 244, 253, 264, 272, 276); and R. Wightman (page 160).

Authors' note

We have endeavoured to check all the information in this book but inevitably some mistakes may have crept in and others will appear as the passage of time changes the details of routes and general information. The authors would be grateful if those readers with corrections or criticisms would send them to Chris Eilbeck, Maths. Dept., Heriot-Watt University, Edinburgh EH14 4AS.

Introduction

The Lake District is one of the most beautiful areas in the country, and offers a fine selection of climbs of all standards of difficulty from the mist-enshrouded bastions of Scafell to the highly popular pitches of Shepherd's Crag. In common with other areas, the climbing population is ever increasing, and queuing for the most popular climbs is now a frequent occurrence. However, to the discerning climber there are always alternatives, and the remote valleys of the Eastern Fells or the combes of Buttermere are frequently empty while the crowds swarm over the Napes or the Langdale crags. One reason for the area's popularity: Tyneside, south Lancashire, the Midlands and industrial Yorkshire are all now linked to the Lake District by fast roads or motorways, and there is a good rail service to Windermere from the south. Bus services operate through the national park from the south to Keswick, and the Mountain Goat minibus service is expanding rapidly.

For the purposes of this book, the area is divided into geographical sections, usually by valley, in an anticlockwise order, starting from Wasdale. Each section also contains general information on the accommodation and other facilities available in the valleys. The crags and climbs are then described in the most convenient or logical order. The terms 'true right' and 'true left' refer to directions facing downstream. Otherwise, right and left are given for the climber facing the crag.

Grading system

We have adopted the generally accepted British adjectival/numerical grading system as below:

E   =   Easy
M   =   Moderate

D   = Difficult
VD = Very Difficult
S   = Severe
VS = Very Severe
HVS = Hard Very Severe (5a, 5b)

E1 = Extremely Severe (5b)
E2 = Extremely Severe (5b, 5c)
E3 = Extremely Severe (5c, 6a)
E4 = Extremely Severe (5c, 6a)
E5 = Extremely Severe (6a, 6b)
E6 = Extremely Severe (6b, 6c)

Occasionally sub-divisions of these grades are used, e.g.
MS = Mild Severe, HS = Hard Severe. Generally, the technical
grade has been omitted for routes below HVS in standard.

Winter climbs have been graded using the common numerical
system which ascends with the order of difficulty and, in this
guide, spans from Grade I to Grade IV.

Grade I   Straightforward snow climbs with no pitches, though
           there may be a cornice.
Grade II   Gullies with short ice pitches which can be quite
           difficult. This grade also includes buttresses under
           winter snow; these should be around very difficult
           standard.
Grade III Serious climbs with steep pitches. Buttresses around
           severe in standard.
Grade IV   Exacting climbs of the highest standard. Very severe
           buttress climbs.

Star grading
We have tried to indicate the relative quality of the routes by
giving a star grading: the more stars, the better the route! While
we hope that climbers will find *all* the routes in this book
worthwhile, obviously some climbs are better than others, and
the addition of one, two or three stars indicates good, very good
and outstanding climbs respectively.

Winter climbing
It is to be emphasized that although good ice conditions are
relatively rare in the Lake District, excellent winter climbs can
often be found. We have given a brief indication at the end of

each section of climbs of which we have experience, and we have included a description in some cases. The most reliable areas are still Great End, Gable Crag, the corries on the east side of Helvellyn and the Scafell gullies, which provide some of the hardest climbs. You *must* make sure that snow conditions are good, as avalanches are by no means uncommon.

Photographs

Many of the photographs were taken especially for this book. The action pictures have been taken to give an impression of the style of climbing on a particular crag or route, while the crag photographs were intended to yield the maximum amount of information to aid identification of climbs, and particularly the starting points and descents.

Maps

Sketch maps covering most of the area described in this guide are included in each chapter. However, these should be regarded as merely supplementary to the official Ordnance Survey 1 inch to the mile Tourist Map of the Lake District. This is being replaced by the 1:50,000 metric map. Our book is designed to be used in conjunction with the OS map, and every crag, mountain rescue point etc., has been pinpointed with the appropriate six-figure grid reference number. We recommend that every party visiting the Lake District should have a copy of this map and know how to use it. The 1:25,000 maps (approx. 2½ inches to one mile) are also most useful.

Other guidebooks

A comprehensive series of guides is published by the Fell and Rock Climbing Club, and these contain descriptions of all the routes in the area at the date of publication. New routes are collected and published in the FRCC Journal, and in interim guides (paperback).

Information

There are tourist information offices at Ambleside and Keswick, and at the Brotherswater campsite in Patterdale in the summer. Radio Carlisle (206 m.) broadcasts regular weather forecasts and tourist information. A Lake District weather forecast is available daily on a 24-hour service (tel. Windermere 5151).

Mountain safety and accident procedure

Mountain safety

Safety precautions appropriate to high mountain areas should always be taken when climbing on the higher crags of the Lake District. Carry waterproofs, spare clothing and food, map, compass, whistle and torch. In winter, an ice-axe is essential; crampons and ice-climbing gear are necessary if hard snow or ice is to be tackled. In winter or summer, rain combined with lichenous rock can create dangerously slippery conditions and increase gradings, especially on the high north-facing crags, such as Pillar or Scafell. For these conditions, socks worn over boots or PAs are an effective but expensive way of increasing friction.

Route-finding in mist requires skill and experience, and the difficulties of a complicated descent, such as that from Pillar Rock, are enormously magnified by mist, severe weather or darkness. If an unfamiliar descent in these conditions is contemplated, the route should be reconnoitred beforehand, and adequate time should be allowed for both ascent and descent.

Study the map and guide before setting out, and learn the position of mountain rescue posts. Leave word where you are going. If you change your plans and decide not to return, or if you descend into the wrong valley by mistake, inform the police immediately, to prevent the alert of a rescue party.

In winter conditions, avalanche danger should not be underestimated. Gullies, especially those with wide upper slopes or large cornices, are the most prone to avalanches, and should be avoided immediately after heavy snowfall or during a sudden rise in temperature. Central Gully on Great End, for instance, has been the scene of several avalanche accidents.

Buy the Mountain Rescue Committee Handbook and study the excellent advice and information given there.

Accident procedure

It is important to make the patient as comfortable as possible. Keep him/her warm, but do not overheat. Render first aid (see below), and in the case of exhaustion or a minor accident, move the victim to shelter. In more serious cases, a shelter of, for example, heather, stones or snow blocks, should be built round the patient until a stretcher can be brought. If there are more than two in a party, one should stay with the injured person while the others go for help. It is *very important to mark the position of the victim as conspicuously as possible*. If the victim must be left alone, he should be tied to the rock to prevent him wandering off in a shocked or semi-conscious state.

Never underestimate the dangers of shock or exhaustion if you are in any doubt whether to call out the rescue team.

Those going for help should proceed at a speed consistent with safety to the nearest manned mountain rescue post or telephone. They should carry a written message, if possible, stating the location of the victim, the time of the accident, and a description of the injuries sustained. If a telephone is reached first, ring 999 and ask for the police: they will alert the appropriate mountain rescue team.

First aid
Keep calm. This helps you and the patient. Reassure the patient. Again, this helps you as well.
Check, in the following order:
1) breathing and airway 2) bleeding 3) broken bones.

1 Maintaining an airway
1. Clear the mouth and throat of teeth, blood and other debris with a finger and rag; pull the tongue forward.
2. If the airway is still obstructed (noticed by gurgling and rattling), turn the patient gently on to his side with his head downhill and ease his head back fully to straighten his neck and therefore his windpipe.
3. If there is no spontaneous breathing, start mouth-to-mouth artificial respiration and check to see if the patient has a pulse. Open the mouth by pressing on the chin. Pinch the nose with your other hand and blow into the mouth. It takes a surprising amount of effort, so check that the chest is rising. If there are severe mouth injuries, blow up the nose.

If there is no pulse, start cardiac massage as well. Kneel by the patient's left side with your hands crossed on the lower breast bone, and lean forward sharply on to straight arms once a second. Every ten strokes, inflate the lungs as above.
4. Check for penetrating chest wounds. Try to make them airtight with a dressing (e.g. polythene bag and bandage). This is not so urgent as stages 1–3 and should be done after any bleeding has been stopped.

2) **Controlling bleeding**

1. Bleeding can be hidden by clothing, so check all over. Bleeding even from big blood vessels can almost always be stopped by firm pressure.
2. Press a hand on to the bleeding point initially (the conscious patient can do this) till replaced by a pad pressed on for about 10 minutes, then bandage the pad firmly. (The pad doesn't have to be fancy: a stone in a handkerchief will do.)
3. Elevate the injured limb.
4. A tourniquet may be used:
a) as a temporary measure till direct pressure can be applied.
b) as a last resort.
c) on complete amputation of limbs.

3) **Broken bones**

The signs are pain, swelling and deformity. Immobilization reduces pain and, therefore, shock and further damage. Formal splints will not normally be available, so improvise. Don't bind them too tightly.

Upper arm Bandage to the chest and support the forearm with an improvised sling round the neck.

Forearm Improvise a splint or use the good forearm; arms folded across the chest. Again, support with a sling around the neck.

Thigh Pull the limb straight and, with padding between the legs to fill out hollows, tie the legs together below the hips, and at the knees and ankles. Keep the good leg straight.

Lower leg Put padding between the limbs and tie them together. Loosen the bootlaces but don't remove the boot: the patient won't thank you for trying!

Dislocations and breaks at joints Immobilize in the most comfortable position: don't attempt to straighten the limb.

Spine The patient *MAY* complain of numbness and immobility. Don't move the patient with back pain till the stretcher arrives, then transfer to the stretcher with the back and neck held immobile.

General

Arrange some shelter round the patient and some insulation underneath and on top (e.g. heather, bracken, etc.). Then you can send for help. Hot sweet drinks are now called for all round.

Never assume a person is dead until first-aid measures have

been tried for 15 minutes without restoration of spontaneous breathing. These should include artificial respiration and cardiac massage. Any patient who could be suffering from exposure should be presumed alive.

Exposure

A full discussion of this common and dangerous condition is given in the BMC leaflet 'Exposure'. Stop further heat loss by shelter, dry windproof clothing and snuggling together. Give hot sweet drinks if possible, but not alcohol. Transport the patient on a stretcher, head downhill.

NB If a member of the party is suffering from exposure, then others, including yourself, may be dangerously close to it.

Reference: GARDNER, A. WARD & ROYLANCE, P.J.
New Essential First Aid (Pan Books, 1972)

A **National Register of Long Distance Paths** has been set up as a co-operative venture between the Long Distance Walkers' Association, the Ramblers' Association, and *The Great Outdoors* magazine, to help all those involved in setting up walking routes more than twenty miles long in Britain. For further information please write to Miss Sue Coles, Administrator NRLDP, 8 Upton Grey Close, Winchester, Hampshire SO22 6NE.

WASDALE

The superb climbing surrounding the valley head is approached by road from the coastal plain, along the north side of Wastwater. Opposite are the famous screes (no rock climbs – dangerously loose except for some gullies and one small buttress), while on the north side Buckbarrow (136059) and Yewbarrow (170079) offer many short climbs. At the east end of the lake, the path winding up Brown Tongue to Scafell and Scafell Pike is clearly visible. The road ends at Wasdale Head: a tiny village overshadowed by some of the highest Lakeland fells. To the north-west lie Mosedale and Pillar Mountain (Pillar Rock is on the opposite side and is described under Ennerdale), while to the north-east is Great Gable with a profusion of buttresses.

The valley is traditionally the finest centre for rock climbing, with all grades of difficulty on good rhyolite. The routes are generally well protected and possible in wet weather; while in winter, good snow and ice gullies are to be found in the area, particularly on the north face of Great End. It should be noted that routes on Gable Crag can be difficult in bad conditions, but Pikes' Crag and the south-west face of Great Gable dry very quickly and face the afternoon sun.

Access
The best approach is by road from Gosforth or Santon Bridge on the coastal plain. Apart from routes along the coast roads, Santon Bridge can be reached from Ambleside over the Wrynose and Hardknott Passes. There is a Mountain Goàt minibus service daily in the summer months on this route from Keswick, Windermere and Ambleside. The last petrol station is at Gosforth (9 miles from Wasdale Head) and closes at 6 p.m. weekdays, 4 p.m. Sat/Sun. The petrol station in Holmrook is normally open until 10 p.m. (9 p.m. winter weekends).

Rail services from north and south serve Seascale. From here it would be necessary to take a bus to Gosforth or call a taxi (tel. Seascale 28193). The only bus service which approaches Wasdale does the return journey Whitehaven – Gosforth – Strands on Thursday morning and evening only (for the market at Whitehaven).

Wasdale Head can be reached on foot from Seathwaite in

Borrowdale in 1½ hours, or even from Langdale via Rossett Ghyll and Esk Hause (about 3 hours).

Accommodation and camping
At Wasdale Head, camping is restricted to the official National Trust campsite at 183075 and a small site near the Wasdale Head Inn. A favourite spot for high camping (for those who can survive the carry up Brown Tongue!) is Hollow Stones, under Scafell Crag (206073), where there is also a bivouac boulder. At Wasdale Head there are the Wasdale Head Inn (tel. Wasdale 229) and several guest-houses. Others are found 5 miles away at Strands/Nether Wasdale, where there is also Church Site Campsite (tel. Wasdale 252). The youth hostel, Wasdale Hall, is at the west end of the lake, 4 miles from Wasdale Head (145045; tel. Wasdale 222). There is a Fell and Rock Climbing Club hut at Brackenclose (185073), and an Achille Ratti Club hut at Buckbarrow (136054).

Food and drink
At Wasdale Head, the Inn and guest-houses provide meals. At the west end of the lake there are hotels and guest-houses in surrounding villages and in adjacent Eskdale. Milk and other supplies can be bought from the National Trust campsite shop, from the Barn Door shop at Wasdale Head and from Wood How Farm, Nether Wasdale. The nearest shopping centres are Gosforth and Seascale (early closing: Saturday). Traditional climbers' drinking is at the Wasdale Head Inn, Ritson's Bar; alternatives are the Bridge Inn at Santon Bridge and the Screes Hotel at Strands, for real ale and bar meals. The local licensing hours are 11–3 p.m. and 5.30–10.30 p.m. on weekdays and 12–2 p.m. and 7–10.30 p.m. on Sundays, with 11 p.m. closing on Fridays and Saturdays.

Garages and car hire
The nearest garage is Rigg's at Gosforth, 9 miles from Wasdale Head. This is the last port of call for petrol, and closes at 6 p.m. weekdays, 4 p.m. Sat/Sun. There is a motorists' shop, and the garage does repairs until 4.30 p.m. on weekdays (tel. Gosforth 225). The nearest 24-hr. recovery services are Mitchell's at

Wastwater and Wasdale Head, showing Great Gable in the background.

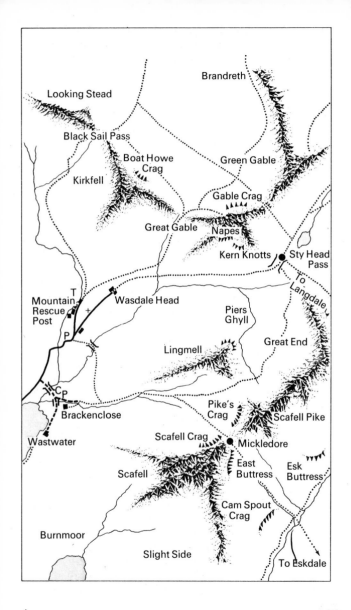

Brandreth

Looking Stead

Black Sail Pass

Boat Howe
Crag

Green Gable

Kirkfell

Gable Crag

Great Gable

Napes

Kern Knotts

Sty Head
Pass

To
Langdale

T

Mountain
Rescue
Post

Wasdale Head

Piers
Ghyll

P

Great End

Lingmell

C P

Pike's
Crag

Scafell Pike

Brackenclose

Scafell Crag

Mickledore

Wastwater

East
Buttress

Esk
Buttress

Scafell

Cam Spout
Crag

Burnmoor

Slight Side

To Eskdale

Holmrook (tel. 228; night 250) and Postlethwaite's at Eskdale Green (tel. 239). The nearest taxi service is at Seascale (tel. 28193) or Eskdale Green (tel. 239). Cars can be hired in Whitehaven (tel. 66611 or 65281) or Egremont (tel. 820144).

General services

Telephones are to be found at the Wasdale Head Inn, at Strands/Nether Wasdale and at Santon Bridge. There are public toilets at the Wasdale Head Inn and at the National Trust campsite. The Barn Door shop near the Inn at Wasdale Head sells mountaineering and camping supplies (including food) and books, maps and guides.

Mountain rescue

For assistance, ring the local police first, giving as much information as possible. They will contact the Mountain Rescue teams which are based at the Outward Bound Mountain School, Eskdale, and at Keswick and Langdale. Stretchers and first-aid kits are available at the following points: Mickledore (210069); Styhead Pass (219095); Wastwater Hotel (187088); Eskdale Outward Bound Mountain School (144002) and Seathwaite Farm, Borrowdale (235121).

SCAFELL CRAG (208068)

Four tremendous buttresses containing some of the best climbs in the Lake District rise on the north side of Mickledore. From left to right they are Central Buttress, Pisgah Buttress, Scafell Pinnacle and Deep Ghyll Buttress (standing above the Shamrock). Similarly the three main gullies are Moss Ghyll, Steep Ghyll and Deep Ghyll. The climbs are described from left to right.

Approach: From Wasdale take the well-marked path which starts from the car-park at the head of the lake and continues beside Lingmell Beck. Eventually climb the steep grass of Brown Tongue to the combe below the crags (Hollow Stones) – about 1½ hours. From Borrowdale the easiest route is via Sty Head Pass and the Corridor Route. This leads to the col between Scafell Pike and Lingmell, from which a path contours round below Pikes Crag towards Scafell Crag. Time: 2–2½ hours. From Eskdale follow the approach for Esk Buttress, then go straight up to Mickledore from the waterfall of Cam Spout. Time: 2½–3

hours. Scafell is occasionally approached from Langdale although this is rather a long walk. Ascend Rossett Ghyll and continue to Esk Hause. Follow the tourist path over Scafell Pike to Mickledore. About 3 hours.

Descent: From Central Buttress, down a well-scratched scramble towards Mickledore, the last 60 ft./18 m. requiring care (Broad Stand; Moderate). From the Pinnacle or Deep Ghyll, descend the upper part of Deep Ghyll (steep and rather loose) taking care to bear true left into Lord's Rake via the West Wall Traverse (Easy).

1 **Botterill's Slab**   ***   VS
235 ft./72 m.   *F. Botterill, H. Williamson and J. E. Grant   1903*
A tremendous, classic slab climb following the narrow slab on the left of the Central Buttress. Start up a chimney directly below the slab.
1) 50 ft./15 m. Follow the chimney and rocks above to a good stance and belay. 2) 120 ft./37 m. Cross on to the slab and follow the face and left edge, in an exhilarating position, to a small niche. Continue directly up the slab to a large ledge and belay. It is possible to traverse right a few feet above the niche to chimney – either for a runner or an easier alternative to the last part of the slab. 3) 65 ft./20 m. Easy climbing up the gully at the right.

2 **The White Wizard**   *   E3   (4b, 6a, 5c, 5b, 5c)
320 ft./98 m.   *C.J.S. Bonington and N. Estcourt (var.) 1976/Free: M. Berzins 1977/Pitch 3 by P. Botterill*
Often done; varied climbing gaining a spectacular position. Takes the wall right of Botterill's Slab.
1) 50 ft./15 m. (4b) Pitch 1 of Botterill's Slab. 2) 80 ft./24 m. (6a) Up the corner for a few feet until a long step right gains a crack leading to a ledge (peg runner). Next follow the shallow corner on the right to a ledge. 3) 65 ft./20 m. (5c) Continue straight up the groove (climbing left wall where necessary) and up the overhanging crack to the ledge. Hard to start for the short. 4) 50ft./23 m. (5b) From the right end go across and up to a distinct crack. Up to the ledge. 5) 75 ft./23 m. (5c) From the right pull round the edge (peg runner) and up a groove, to

Botterill's Slab, Scafell Crag

the right again, to a small ledge. Move up round the bulge, balancey, to easier rock. A tremendous pitch.

3   **The Nazgul**   **   E3 (4a, 5c, 5b, 5b)
285 ft./87 m.   *L. Brown and K. Jackson   1967/Free: P. Botterill, S. Clegg 1975*
This fine route takes the thin crack up the left-hand side of the Great Flake of the Central Buttress. Start up a short crack immediately right of Botterill's Slab.
1)   60 ft./18 m. Climb the crack and easy ledges rightwards to a stance and belay directly below the crack.   2)   85 ft./26 m. (5c)   Climb the crack, past an old peg runner, to a niche. Swing out left on to a narrow slab. Follow the slab to a pedestal and continue on good holds to Jeffcoat's Ledge on Central Buttress. A strenuous pitch.   3)   40 ft./12 m. (5b)   Climb the wall to the pinnacle on pitch 6 of Central Buttress and follow the latter to the large ledge and belay.   4)   100 ft./30 m. (5b)   Above on the left is a line of narrowing slabs. The first few feet are difficult but the holds improve and a good flat ledge and belay are soon reached.

4   **Central Buttress**   ***   HVS (4b, 4b, 5b, 4a, 4a, 4c, 5a, 4a,)
S. W. Herford and G. S. Sansom   1914
Probably the greatest classic climb in the whole of the Lake District. The route described actually follows the Direct Start and Direct Finish, giving a sustained climb which includes the best pitches of the normal route. Start where the Rake's Progress path crosses Moss Ghyll at a corner below a large roof.
1)   65 ft./20 m. (4b) Climb the corner then the rib to a good stance below an overhanging roof. Peg belay recommended.
2)   75 ft./23 m. (4b) Traverse left for 10 ft./3 m. to a corner. Climb this and the wall above, bearing left to the Oval. Belay at the foot of the flake crack.   3)   65 ft./20 m. (5b) Climb diagonally left to gain the crack and ascend to the large chockstone. From here either a bold layback or difficult wedging enables good holds on top of the flake to be reached. Traverse the crest of the flake to belay.   4)   45 ft./14 m. (4a) Continue along the crest to a small tower. Shortly after this descend an easy crack to a large ledge (Jeffcoat's Ledge).

Central Buttress, Scafell Crag

Scafell Crag
*R = Rake's Progress. 8 = Moss Ghyll. Route 4 shows the normal start
and finish of Central Buttress*

The Great Flake, Central Buttress

5)   60 ft./18 m. (4a) Follow the ledge and leftward slanting slab to a block belay.   6)   40 ft./12 m. (4c) Move down and traverse delicately right along a sloping ledge past a pinnacle to a corner. Climb this, then the outside wall to a large recess. There is a belay at the left end of the ledge.   7)   90 ft./27 m. (5a) From the left end of the ledge climb a short slab then follow some ledges to a gangway. This leads to an overhanging crack with an awkward finish. Belay.   8)   80 ft./24 m. (4a) Climb the mossy crack in the corner to easy ground.

5 **Saxon*****   E2 (5a, 5b, 5b)
400 ft./122 m.   *J. Eastham and E. Cleasby (var.) 1976/Pitch 1: A. Mullen and H. Thompson   1939*
A magnificent climb in a fine position. Up the wall to the right of the Great Flake. Start exactly where Rake's Progress touches Moss Ghyll.
   1)   140 ft./43 m. (5a)   Climb a short corner and then the rib to gain the ledge below the large roof (possible to belay). Traverse left to an open corner and balance up this to better holds (poorly protected). Continue leftwards up the wall to gain the Oval.   2)   130 ft./40 m. (5b)   Go over right to below a short corner (possible belay position). Up the corner, move left, then up the wall to climb across rightwards to the arête and a small ledge (junction with Moss Ghyll Grooves). Go back left to small rock ledges then go directly for the obvious crack. Up this and the continuation groove to a V-ledge. (Difficult to find a decent belay: poor on the left, better high in the corner above.)
   3)   130 ft./40 m. (5b)   Up the dirty, often wet corner and continue more or less in the same line to the top.

6 **Moss Ghyll Grooves**   ***   MVS
260 ft./79 m.   *H. M. Kelly, Blanche Eden-Smith and J. B. Kilshaw   1926*
One of the best climbs at this standard in the area, following an excellent series of grooves to the left (true right) of Moss Ghyll. Starts in the gully at the top of pitch 3.
   1)   55 ft./17 m. Climb the slanting groove to a good ledge. Surmount the overhanging block on the right to a grassy corner and belay.   2)   45 ft./14 m. Up the corner for a few feet, then

Jerry Peel on the main pitch of Saxon

traverse left (crux) on to the edge (the Pedestal). Climb the arête leading back to the groove and continue to a stance and belay.   3)   20 ft./6 m. Climb the narrowing slab until an easy traverse leads right into the next groove. Large belay.   4)   80 ft./24 m. Climb the slab above to a recess. Belay on the right in a hole or round a block on the slab above.   5)   60 ft./18 m. Ascend the left wall of the gully and move left on to a large ledge. Climb the steep wall above to the summit ridge.

7   **Slab and Groove Route**   **   VS

240 ft./73 m.   *R. J. Birkett and L. Muscroft   1948*

A very good route with interesting situations. Start at the foot of a huge slab capped by an overhang, on the left (true right) side of Moss Ghyll.

1)   110 ft./34 m. An excellent pitch. Climb the groove on the right-hand side of the slab until it is possible to traverse left to a thin crack. Go up this until a step left on to the edge can be made. Climb the edge for a few feet then traverse left to a groove. Climb the groove until level with a recess on the left, then step right and ascend a wall to a corner and block belay (above the overhang which caps the slab).   2)   80 ft./24 m. Follow the groove to a stance and belay.   3)   50 ft./15 m. Easy climbing leads to the summit.

8   **Moss Ghyll**   ***   VD

415 ft./126 m.   *J. N. Collie, G. Hastings and J. W. Robinson   1892*

A splendid and traditional gully climb between the Central and Pisgah Buttresses.

1)   30 ft./9 m. A chimney with overhanging chockstone. The Rake's Progress path crosses above this pitch.   2)   40 ft./12 m. Climb the corner on the left. Continue into the very deep chimney.   3)   40 ft./12 m. Climb the chimney from the back out on to the chockstone. A short chimney follows to ledges and a belay. (Pitches 2 and 3 can be avoided on the right if the chimney is wet.)   4   50 ft./15 m. Two short chimneys.   5)   25 ft./8 m. Easy slabs and a short walk into the gully to a recess below the Tennis Court Wall.   6)   25 ft./8 m. Climb the short steep wall to the Tennis Court.   7)   25 ft./8 m. Traverse back into the gully and continue to a large cave.   8)   30 ft./9 m. From the

On the rib after the crux of Moss Ghyll Grooves

14

back of the cave climb on to the 'window sill'. Step down and make a short delicate traverse left (the Collie Step) then climb easy slabs to belay in a recess.   9)   25 ft./8 m. An easy traverse back into the Amphitheatre. Two finishes are described; first the natural continuation of the gully, second an escape left from the Amphitheatre.   10a)   30 ft./9 m. Climb over the two chockstones to belay on the right wall.   11a)   25 ft./7 m. Back up the chimneys and go through a hole to belay on a boulder.   12a)   40 ft./12 m. Traverse out a little and climb over two strenuous chockstones.   13a)   35 ft./11 m. A rather awkward chimney is followed by scrambling to the summit.   10b)   50 ft./15 m. Climb a rib in the left-hand corner of the Amphitheatre, then a crack to ledges and block belay.   11b)   45 ft./14 m. Climb a crack above the block, then traverse left to an easy chimney. Continue to ledge and belay.   12b)   30 ft./9 m. A short corner on the left leads to easy ground.

9 **Pisgah Buttress Direct**   MS
450 ft./137 m.   *S. W. Herford and F. M. J. McConechy*   *1911*
A pleasant buttress climb. Starts below the middle of the buttress at a shallow corner.

1)   80 ft./24 m. Trend left for 40 ft./12 m., then work right and climb an awkward bulge to a little slab. An easier groove slanting up to the left leads to a ledge and belay.   2)   60 ft./18 m. Easy ledges on the left, followed by an upward traverse to the right under some loose blocks, then climb a corner to a crevasse.   3)   25 ft./7 m. The corner on the right. Block belay.   4)   30 ft./9 m. Traverse a good ledge to the left to a large ledge (the Fives Court) and thread belay.   5)   30 ft./9 m. The corner crack.   6)   40 ft./12 m. Continue up the crack, over a bulge to easy slabs. These lead to a large block on the right edge of the buttress.   7)   10 ft./3 m. A difficult pull-up to a ledge.   8)   50 ft./15 m. Follow the ridge above, then a groove followed by easier rocks.   9)   40 ft./12 m. A grass gully.   10)   85 ft./26 m. Easy slabs.

Slab and Groove, Scafell Crag

10   **Scafell Pinnacle via Slingsby's Chimney**   ***   HD

335 ft./102 m.   *W. C. Slingsby, G. Hastings, E. Hopkinson and W. P. Haskett Smith   1888*

A varied and interesting route. Start by scrambling up Steep Ghyll (between Pisgah Buttress and Scafell Pinnacle) for 200 ft./61 m. Just below a steep pitch a series of ledges on the right mark the start of the route.

1)   45 ft./14 m. Easy rocks and ledges to a terrace.   2)   35 ft./11 m. Easy slabs lead to a deep crevasse.   3)   20 ft./6 m. Cross the crevasse and climb a slab to the foot of Slingsby's Chimney.   4)   25 ft./7 m. Climb the awkward chimney.   5)   45 ft./14 m. The chimney continues more easily.   6)   55 ft./17 m. Easy rocks and scrambling to the top of Low Man.   7)   55 ft./17 m. Ascend the Knife-Edge Arête to a good stance and belay.   8)   55 ft./17 m. Easy climbing leads to High Man.

Descent: Can be awkward in wet conditions. Down the left (east) side is an easy trough. Descend this and a short overhanging wall to Jordan Gap (top of Steep Ghyll). Easy rocks leftwards lead on to Pisgah.

11   **Jones's Route Direct from Lord's Rake**   ***   S

215 ft./65 m.   *O. G. Jones and G. T. Walker   1898*

A superb route which gives excellent slab climbing on rough rock. Start on the terrace below the Pinnacle (reached via the preliminary section of Steep Ghyll) on the edge of Deep Ghyll.

1)   25 ft./8 m. An easy slab leads to some detached blocks. 2)   50 ft./15 m. Gain the sloping gangway and follow it leftwards. Then ascend steeply for a few feet before traversing left to a nich (the First Nest).   3)   25 ft./8 m. Climb the wall above going slightly left to the Second Nest.   4)   50 ft./15 m. Follow the shallow gully for 35 ft./11 m., then traverse delicately left. A short ascent leads to the Waiting Room. Thread belay 10 ft./3 m. above.   5)   30 ft./9 m. Climb up into the cave and climb on to the triangular ledge projecting at the top right side (the Mantelshelf). Traverse right along the ledge to the easier crack which leads to a good stance and belay.   6)   35 ft./11 m. The easy chimney leads to the crevasse on Slingsby's Chimney route.

Scafell Pinnacle
SG = Steep Ghyll. DG = Deep Ghyll. WW = West Wall traverse

12 **Hopkinson's Cairn Direct**   *   S
165 ft./50 m.   *S.W. Herford and G. W. Sansom   1912*
A fine open climb, rather more sustained than Jones's Route and
with less protection. Starts as for Jones's Route.
  1)   100 ft./30 m. Follow the first three pitches of Jones's Route
to the second Nest.   2)   65 ft./20 m. Climb the shallow corner
on the right, then traverse right across the slab to a flat ledge.
Climb the undercut slab (choice of lines) to a small stance, then
continue delicately, working right, to good holds. The large ledge
supporting Hopkinson's Cairn is reached by a pull-up. Belays on
the ledge are rather poor and it may be preferable to take a
stance just below. From Hopkinson's Cairn, Low Man is reached
by the following climb (D, 170 ft./52 m.). Climb the corner on
the left, then step right to a belay. Continue up until the wall on
the left can be crossed to another stance. Follow slanting
gangways, then an easy chimney and scrambling leads to Low
Man.

13 **Moss Ledge Direct**   *   MVS
335 ft./102 m.   *F. Graham and G. M. Wellburn   1925*
A good slab climb, delicate and serious. The Jones's Arête Finish
from Hopkinson's Cairn is also described. About half-way along
the Pinnacle Terrace it goes over a small buttress. Start at the
foot of this buttress.
  1)   40 ft./12 m. The face of the buttress leads to the
terrace.   2)   30 ft./9 m. A rib on the wall leads with difficulty to
a ledge. Continue to a niche and belay (the First
Nest).   3)   120 ft./36 m. Follow a diagonal fault up to the right
and round a nose of rock. Continue up slabs to some sloping
ledges which are climbed at the right-hand end. Traverse left
across the top step to reach Moss Ledge. Continue up Herford's
Slab to a stance and belay either on or just below Hopkinson's
Cairn.   4)   70 ft./21 m. Climb a small groove in the arête
between the front face and the Deep Ghyll wall to a small
overhang. Pass this on the left and follow easier rock tending
right to a ledge and poor belays in the 'Bad Corner'.   5)   20
ft./6 m. The smooth exposed slab on the right is climbed from left
to right (the Bad Corner).   6)   35 ft./11 m. Jones's Arête.
Follow the crest to belay on a large block.   7)   20 ft./6 m. An
easy crack leads to the top of Low Man.

14 **Edge Hog**   *   E1   (5a, 5b, 4c, 5a)
300 ft./91 m.   *T. W. Birkett, M. R. Myers and C. J. Richardson (alt.) 1973*
A big route hidden on the right side of the Pinnacle. Bold, even today. Start from Deep Ghyll, some way above Jones's Route, where an obvious gangway/groove drops in and about 100 ft./30 m. below the second chockstone.

1)   70 ft./21 m. (5a) Up the steep wall using the flake ledge to gain the gangway. Up this through the overhang at the top and belay over to the right (poor stance and belay).   2)   70 ft./21 m. (5b) Step left to regain the groove and continue until a move right enables the wall to be climbed directly. At the top step left to a ledge and go diagonally left to Hopkinson's Cairn.   3)   90 ft./27 m. (4c) Traverse right across stepped grooves until above line of pitch 2, then climb a corner groove to a flake runner. Traverse right then follow the edge via a shallow groove to a ledge.   4)   70 ft./21 m. (5a) Step right and (avoiding easier ground – a mossy corner, Gibson's Chimney, lies to the right) climb directly up the wall to the top knife-edge.

15 **Woodhead's Climb**   *   MS
160 ft./49 m.   *A. G. Woodhead and W. L. Collinson 1907*
A short route with a good finish. Starts at the corner where the Deep Ghyll Wall of the Pinnacle meets the wall which runs down from Professor's Chimney. (The deep-cut chimney descending from Jordan Gap.)

1)   30 ft./9 m. Get on to a slab on the Deep Ghyll Wall, move left and climb directly to a good ledge and belay.   2)   55 ft./17 m. From the left end of the ledge, climb the wall above and work right to follow the arête to a large recess. Belay.   3)   45 ft./14 m. Herford's Finish. Gain a corner on the left, then cross the slab above rightwards to a small ledge. Go straight up over a bulge then step left. Up to a stance and belay.   4)   30 ft./9 m. An awkward step is followed by easy rocks to High Man.

16 **West Wall Climb**   D
185 ft./56 m.   *J. W. Robinson, T. H. Doncaster and H. W. Blunt 1898*
A pleasant route with short pitches. The start is 50 ft./15 m. to the right of the Great Chimney (VD), a prominent landmark on the Deep Ghyll side of Deep Ghyll Buttress.

30 ft./9 m. A deep chimney.   2)   25 ft./8 m. An awkward corner leads to a ledge.   3)   .25 ft./8 m. The chimney on the left.   4)   35 ft./11 m. Climb the wide corner ahead, starting on the left and finishing to the right.   5)   10 ft./3 m. Easy rocks to the foot of an arête.   6)   40 ft./12 m. Climb arête.   7)   20 ft./6 m. A little chimney, then a small cave pitch leads to the top.

SCAFELL EAST BUTTRESS   (210068)

This magnificent barrel-shaped crag stretches for almost ¼ mile in a south-easterly direction from Mickledore. It provides a network of high-standard routes on superb rock, and this, coupled with the magnificent outlook, makes its climbs among the finest in Lakeland. Unfortunately, the cliff is frequently wet, since it takes a considerable amount of drainage, and the rock becomes abominably greasy in a very short time. As a result, the climbs are serious for their length and standard, and parties attempting any of the climbs on this crag should be capable of organizing a safe escape for themselves in the event of failure or bad weather. The climbs are described from right to left, the order in which they are approached from Mickledore, the usual base for operations in the area.

Approach: See Scafell Crag.

Descent: At the top right-hand side of the crag a short gully leads down into Mickledore chimney. Cross this to join the scrambling route down Broad Stand on to Mickledore (with a short stretch of climbing at moderate standard).

17 **Chartreuse**   **   E1   (5a, 5a)
160 ft./49 m.   *R. Smith and D. Leaver*   *1958*
A facet of the buttress rising out of Mickledore chimney yields the first climb. Start by scrambling up Mickledore chimney until it is possible to break back left to a ledge and poor belay below the large slab.
1)   70 ft./21 m. (5a) Traverse delicately left until it is possible to follow a shallow corner up the edge of the slab to a stance and belay in a corner on the left. A poorly protected pitch.   2)   90 ft./27 m. (5a) Climb the corner above to the overhang and move right on to the slab. Continue up the crack to a large overhang and traverse right to a very steep fist-wide crack. Follow this with difficulty to a large stance.

Scafell East Buttress, right flank

23

Scafell East Buttress, left flank

24

18 **Midnight Express** ** E3 (5c, 6a)
155 ft./47 m. *P. Botterill and J. Lamb 1979*
Superb eliminate climbing up the Chartreuse slabs with a bold
first pitch and an intimidating finish (RPs protect the slab). Start
at the foot of Mickledore chimney.
1) 120 ft./36 m. (5c) Up rightwards for 30 ft./9 m. then straight
up the centre of the slab to a triangular foothold. Continue
straight up to and through the overlap. Up until a diagonal crack
in a bulge, then direct to a large block. Belay in groove to
right. 2) 35 ft./11 m. (6a) Climb the wall above the block to
make a committing move left to the very top of the crack of
Chartreuse.

19 **Fulcrum** ** VS (4c, 4c, 4b)
180 ft./55 m. *J. Adams and K. Jackson 1968*
A good climb which winds its way through an impressive part of
the crag. Start up the chimney directly below the twin grooves of
Mickledore Grooves (q.v.).
1) 50 ft./15 m. (4c) Climb the chimney and the right-hand
groove to a small stance and belay. 2) 60 ft./18 m. (4c) Step
down and left on to the steep wall. Climb this then traverse left
under an overhang to enter the base of a groove. Climb up the
groove to the stance at the top of pitch 2 of Leverage. 3) 70
ft./21 m. (4b) Continue up the groove to the overhang, then take
the steep left-hand crack. Pull out right at the top, move
leftwards to an arête, then continue to the top.

20 **Leverage** * E1 (–, 5a, 4c)
180 ft./55 m. *R. Smith and D. Leaver 1958*
The crack line which splits the first pitch of Mickledore Grooves
gives a strenuous climb.
1) 25 ft./8 m. The impending crack 15 ft./4 m. right of
Mickledore Grooves is climbed on to the slab. Follow this up to
the right to a ledge and belay. 2) 75 ft./23 m. (5a) Move back
left into the crack and follow this over three bulges into a groove,
which leads more easily to a small ledge and belay on a rib.
Move right into a corner to a better stance and belay. 3) 80
ft./24 m. Follow the corner to a small overhang. Pull round this
to the right to gain a slab, and follow this to the top.

21 **Mickledore Grooves**   ***   VS

225 ft./68 m.   *C. F. Kirkus, I. M. Waller and M. Pallis   1931*

Notable for its long final pitch. Start 25 yds/23 m. left of
Mickledore chimney, where a short slab slants up to the right.

1)   85 ft./26 m. Pull on to the slab and follow it up to the right to
the foot of a pair of grooves. Climb the left-hand groove, and
after 15 ft./4 m. transfer into the right-hand groove. Follow this
to a ledge and belay in a big corner.   2)   140 ft./43 m. Step
round to the right on to a large slab and after a step up to the left,
a diagonal crack can be followed rightwards into a big groove.
Climb the groove until the angle eases and a ledge can be
reached on the right. Follow the ledge round the corner until a
short awkward wall can be climbed to the top.

22 **Dyad**   ***   E3   (6a, 5b, 4b)

210 ft./64 m. *K. Jackson and C. Read (alt.) 1968/Free: J. Lamb and P.
Botterill 1972*

Brilliant strenuous climbing. Start 15 ft./4 m. left of Mickledore
Grooves by a steep ramp.

1)   70 ft./21 m. (6a) Up the ramp pulling right to below the
crack. Continue to a small ledge and then up the thin crack, with
a hard finishing move on to a rock ledge. Belays on left
(poor).   2)   60 ft./18 m. (5b) Up into the groove and climb
until a step right is possible to gain the rib. Up for a few feet, then
pull up and back left to a slab. Continue to ledge.   3)   80 ft./24
m. (4b) Climb the crack on the right.

23 **May Day Climb**   **   E2   (5b, 4c, 5b, 4b)

270 ft./82 m.   *R. J. Birkett, C. W. Hudson and C. R. Wilson   1938/
G. Oliver and L. Willis   1959*

A strenuous climb, frequently wet, which takes the big slanting
groove in the upper part of the crag, some 30 ft./9 m. left of
Mickledore Grooves. Start at a narrow slab inset in the
impending wall some 12 yds/11 m. left of Mickledore Grooves.

1)   60 ft./18 m. (5b) Climb the slab (more strenuous than it
appears) until a traverse right leads to a small stance and belay
below a small steep groove.   2)   50 ft./15 m. (4c) Climb the
groove with difficulty until the angle eases and the big groove can
be entered. A sloping ledge and thread belay are reached on the
left.   3)   80 ft./24 m. (5b) Continue up the crack above the
belay and follow the corner on the right, using a crack in the

right wall. Move right to gain the arête and follow this to a stance above the corner.   4)   80 ft./24 m. (4b) The wide crack and easy slabs lead to the top.

24 **Overhanging Wall**   *   HVS   (5a, 4a)

205 ft./62 m.   *M. Linnell and A. T. Hargreaves   1933*

A route of some delicacy despite its steepness. Start below and left of May Day Climb on an overhung ledge.

1)   85 ft./26 m. (5a) Move up to the left to a good ledge, then ascend a little before traversing right and up to gain a 'saddle'. Step down to the right and climb a crack to a ledge; step right again and climb steeply on small but good holds until a grass ledge in a corner is reached.   2)   120 ft./36 m. (4a) Traverse left and down on to the White Slab and climb it to a large square block. Continue up the Slab until it is possible to work into a mossy corner on the right (often wet). Break back left and continue into the final gully. Belay. Scrambling leads to the top.

25 **Lost Horizons**   ***   E4 (4c, 6b, 5c)

245 ft./75 m. *P. Livesey and J. Lawrence 1976/Free: R. H. Berzins and M. Browell 1982*

The great tilted central groove. Tremendous climbing up overhanging rock. Start 20 ft./6 m. right of the lowest point of the buttress. (As for Great Eastern.)

1)   70 ft./21 m. (4c) Up slabs and a short wall and a further slab to belay below the largest corner groove.   2)   125 ft./38 m. (6b) Up the corner to a ledge. Continue to near top of the groove (peg high in groove, difficult to clip and in a poor state) from where moves left gain a crack leading to a precarious position on a rock ledge. Move back right into the groove (small wires in groove) and continue up, very strenuously, to the second and largest ramp (Great Eastern). Immediately above is a crack splitting the impending wall.   3)   50 ft./15 m. (5c) Climb the crack.

26 **Centaur**   ***   HVS (4b, 5a, 5a, 4c, 4c, 4c)

320 ft./97 m.   *L. Brown and S. Read   1960*

Sustained, exposed and varied climbing combined with difficult route-finding make this one of the finest routes on the East Buttress. Start 20 ft./6 m. right of the lowest point of the crag.

1)   60 ft./18 m. (4b) Climb the groove on good holds, passing a large ledge to a corner stance and piton belay.   2)   50 ft./15 m.

(5a) 15 ft./4 m. above the ledge, on the left edge of the corner, is a small resting place. Gain this, starting from the corner; go up then traverse back right, across the groove, to a comfortable ledge and peg belay. 3) 50 ft./15 m. (5a) Traverse right into a shallow corner parallel to the main groove and climb this for 15 ft./4 m., then traverse back left along a sloping shelf to regain the main corner and follow this to a slab stance. Piton belay. 4) 60 ft./18 m. (4c) Above is an impending wall in which is inset a thin horizontal slab. Gain this from a point about 15 ft./4 m. to the right, then traverse the slab left to a scoop (often wet, good thread runner). Climb the scoop, with an awkward finish, on to a slab, and up this. 5) 30 ft./9 m. (4c) Climb a crack on the left to a precariously perched pinnacle. Stance and belay on the far side of the pinnacle. 6) 70 ft./21 m. (4c) Leave the ledge on the left then trend back right at once and go up the steep wall to a corner of blocks. Climb the magnificent layback crack above – a spectacular finish!

27 **Great Eastern Route**   **   MVS
225 ft./68 m.   *M. Linnell and S. H. Cross   1932*
A magnificent climb with no great difficulties. Start by scrambling up an opening 20 ft./6 m. right of the lowest point of the crag and walking left to an overhung ledge.
1) 70 ft./21 m. Follow a gangway up to the left to an overhang. Continue up the crack on good holds to a hanging slab on the left. Cross the slab, pull up the corner and traverse left to an exposed rib which is climbed to a good stance and belay. 2) 30 ft./9 m. Climb the twin cracks above to a stance and belay below a roof. 3) 75 ft./23 m. Traverse the slab on the right, then go up a step before continuing the traverse to a small crevasse. 4) 30 ft./9 m. Move up a corner, then either climb a chimney on the right or the wall on the left. 5) 20 ft./6 m. Go up and round the corner on the right to a ledge at the top of the White Slab. Belay in the corner.

28 **The Yellow Slab**   ***   HVS (4b, 4c, 4c)
175 ft./53 m.   *M. Linnell and H. Pearson   1933*
This variation finish, which has very fine situations indeed, starts from the top of pitch 1 of Great Eastern Route. 2) 110 ft./33

Lost Horizons, second pitch

m. (4c) A pinnacle on the left is used as a starting point for this pitch. Step off the pinnacle and up a short crack to the foot of the Yellow Slab. Climb the centre of this to the foot of a steep wall, when a move left brings one to the foot of a jamming crack. Climb this to a small stance nd belay on the left in a superb situation.   3)   60 ft./18 m. (4c) Move left along the ledge and pull up the corner with the aid of some large, if dubious, flakes. Continue traversing left on sloping holds until a final awkward move gives access to the top of the crag.

29 **Gold Rush**   *   E2   (5b, 4b, 5b, 5a)
410 ft./125 m.   *A. G. Cram and W. Young   1969*
This route starts along the terrace, about 40 ft./12 m. left of Great Eastern Route below a wet corner.
1)   130 ft./40 m. (5b) Pull over the steep walls on the right then traverse left to the corner. Climb through the water to the overhang, which is climbed on improving holds. Continue up the slab and two short walls to the stance and pinnacle belay of Great Eastern.   2)   50 ft./15 m. (4b) Follow easy ledges horizontally left, then climb a black wall and traverse a short slab to a poor stance and peg belay below a long corner.   3)   50 ft./15 m. (5b) Climb the corner and crack direct to the top of the Yellow Slab. Stance and chockstone belays.   4)   100 ft./30 m. (5a) Continue up the crack to the big overhang. Move out left then continue up the wall and slab above to a large ledge and peg belay.   5)   80 ft./24 m. Easy rocks to the top of the crag.

30 **Ichabod**   ***   E2   (–, 5c, 5b, –)
310 ft./94 m.   *G. Oliver, G. Arkless and N. Brown   1960*
The large rightward-facing corner on the left of Great Eastern Route gives the line of this magnificent climb. Below the corner is a leftward-slanting gangway which provides the first pitch.
1)   50 ft./15 m. The gangway is followed to an overhung stance.   2)   80 ft./24 m. (5c) Pull round the overhang to the right into the corner. Climb this to a good thread then descend slightly and traverse right into a groove, which is followed until it is possible to pull out to the right. Climb directly into the groove

The Yellow Slab

above and up to good thread belay. 3) 110 ft./33 m. (5b) Climb the V-groove on small holds to a bulge. Move left with difficulty into the main corner and climb this without further incident to the foot of a final steep crack which leads to a large platform. 4) 70 ft./21 m. The easy buttress on the left leads pleasantly to the top, or walk off to the left.

31 **Phoenix** *** E2 (–, 5b, 5c)
290 ft./88 m. *R. Moseley 1957/Pitch 3: R. Matheson and E. Cleasby 1976*
The route takes the line of cracks on the left of the great prow which bounds the corner of Ichabod on the left. Ahead of its time, strenuous and spectacular.
1) 60 ft./18 m. The easy gangway of Ichabod. 2) 90 ft./27 m. (5b) Climb a crack on the left of the overhang above the stance to a resting place. A finger-jamming crack is followed then a shallow chimney leads to a hard finish on to a rounded ledge. Step left into a groove and follow this on better holds to a stance. A sustained pitch. 3) (the Arête Finish) 80 ft./24 m. (5c) Climb the crack in the rib, above the gangway, to its top. Then step right to the edge and continue steeply and boldly to the top.

32 **Hell's Groove** *** E1 (–, 5b, 5a, 4b, 4a)
265 ft./80 m. *P. J. Greenwood and A. R. Dolphin (alt.) 1952*
80 ft./24 m. left of Ichabod is a big groove guarded by a short impending crack. This sustained climb is a fine natural line up the East Buttress. Start directly below the crack.
1) 30 ft./9 m. Climb an easy slab to a stance and belay. 2) 25 ft./8 m. (5b) The crack gives a short but extremely strenuous struggle before the ledge below the main groove can be gained. 3) 80 ft./24 m. (5a) From a small ledge above the stance, step into a crack in the right wall and follow this over a series of bulges to a ledge below a steep wall. Climb to a crack above a small block at the right hand end of the ledge and gain the stance above by a final difficult move. 4) 85 ft./26 m. (4b) Climb a crack on good holds to the right of the overhang above, then trend left into an open chimney. Follow the chimney and crack above into an amphitheatre. 5) 45 ft./14 m. (4a) Move up to the left along a crevasse then move back to the right along another crevassed block when a cave pitch leads to the top.

33 **Trinity**   *   HVS (5a, 5a, 4c)
225 ft./68 m.   *D. D. Whillans and J. R. Sutherland*   *1955*
The groove parallel to Hell's Groove yields a climb of
considerable character. Start directly below the groove.
1)   100 ft./30 m. (5a) A short wall leads into the groove which is
followed past an awkward overhang to a stance and belay.
2)   95 ft./29 m. (5a) Continue up the open corner over two
bulges, the second being passed by a difficult layback. The angle
relents and good holds lead up to a rock ledge in a recess. Pull up
the short wall on the right to a big grassy ledge.   3)   30 ft./9 m.
(4c) The corner and crack above are followed on good holds to
the top of the crag.

PIKES CRAG   (210072)

Pikes Crag is the large but rather broken crag which faces Scafell
across Hollow Stones. The main crag is divided by a ridge which
falls from the highest point. This is the line of Grooved Arête.
The crag faces south-west and dries quickly, but the climbing in
general is not of the same quality as that on Scafell.
Approach: As for Scafell Crag.
Descent: The descent starts from the col joining the crag to the
Pike. Descend to the col by a steep crack on good holds, or a
broken chimney-groove on the right. Care is needed in wet
conditions. Continue down the gully on the Mickledore side
(south) of the crag, making a detour on the left to avoid a short
pitch.

34 **Grooved Arête**   *   VD
370 ft./113 m.   *C. F. Holland and G. R. Speaker*   *1924*
A good climb with much variety, providing a worthwhile
expedition in all weather conditions. Starts below the V-shaped
hollow capped by an overhang which is a prominent feature of
the bottom of the ridge.
1)   60 ft./18 m. Take the easiest line to the foot of the crack
forming the left edge of the overhanging wall above.   2)   40
ft./12 m. Climb the crack until a traverse left can be made to the
edge. Climb this to a large ledge. Belay at the back in a
chimney.   3)   70 ft./21 m. Climb the chimney and continue in
the same line to reach an angular corner.   4)   55 ft./17 m. The
crack in the corner is polished and hard to start. After reaching a
ledge, traverse left a little, then go up past some blocks and

traverse right to a prominent block on the edge of the ridge. (A pleasant alternative to pitches 3 and 4 is to follow the crest of the ridge. This gives open delicate climbing at severe standard.) 5) 60 ft./18 m. Ascend the slab above, work left and then back right to ledges on the crest. 6) 25 ft./8 m. Cross the corner on the left and continue up a slab to a ledge below a huge block. A way off can be made here, but this would miss one of the best pitches. 8) 45 ft./14 m. Traverse down the ledge to the left to gain the front of the ridge. Climb the slab above, with difficulty (especially when wet) to the summit of the crag.

35 **Sentinel** * VS
240 ft./73 m. *P. Fearnehough and J. Wright 1960*
A fine climb following the impressive crack up the centre of the large square-cut pillar about 200 ft./61 m. left of the rib of Grooved Arête. Start by scrambling up ledges diagonally left to the foot of the pillar.
1) 50 ft./15 m. Climb a shallow crack in the centre of the pillar to a good ledge and belay directly below the impressive crack. 2) 70 ft./21 m. Move up and climb the steep crack. Avoid some doubtful blocks on the right and continue up the crack on good jams to a ledge and belay. 3) 60 ft./18 m. Easier climbing to a ledge and belay below and left of an obvious overhanging crack. 4) 60 ft./18 m. Climb the groove to the overhang. Pull over this (strenuous) and continue up the easier groove to the top of the crag.

36 **Juniper Buttress** ** VD
260 ft./79 m. *H. M. Kelly and party 1924*
A good route which starts at a large block some 20 yds./18 m. right of the left bounding rib of Pulpit Rock.
1) 35 ft./11 m. Gain a small ledge then traverse right to a corner crack. Climb this to a stance and belay on the left. 2) 25 ft./8 m. A gangway up the wall to the right to a ledge. 3) 35 ft./11 m. Surmount a series of blocks finishing up a crack. 4) 50 ft./15 m. Scramble up working right to blocks on the edge of a grassy gully. 55 ft./17 m. Climb the groove above on the left followed by a short crack. 6) 60 ft./18 m. Start at a rib on the right and climb the exposed wall above using a thin crack. Easier rocks lead to the top of Pulpit Rock.

Pikes Crag, from Hollow Stones

37 **Wall and Crack Climb** ** VD

270 ft./82 m. *H. M. Kelly and party 1924*

A pleasant climb which takes the left-hand edge of Pulpit Rock.
1) 65 ft./20 m. Step round to the left of the ridge and climb to a
belay. Continue up a steep wall to another stance. 2) 50 ft./15
m. Climb a vertical crack to a rock platform. A staircase of rock
on the right leads to a terrace. 3) 70 ft./21 m. The wall above
is climbed slanting right, followed by a crack in three
sections. 4) 35 ft./11 m. Another rock staircase leads to a
ledge. Belay below a crack on the right. 5) 50 ft./15 m. Climb
the steep crack or the wall on its left. Scrambling follows to the
top.

KERN KNOTTS (216094)

This short but steep crag lies on the south-west slope of Great
Gable and overlooks the Sty Head Pass. The rock is excellent
and the routes, though short, have much character, with the
advantage that the crag dries very quickly. The Sty Head Face is
split by Kern Knotts Crack and Innominate Crack, while the
south face is divided by the deep feature of Kern Knotts
Chimney.

Approach: From Wasdale ascend Sty Head Pass then take the
Gable Traverse path which contours round the south-west face
of the mountain. Kern Knotts is reached in 5 minutes from the
top of the Pass (about ¾ hour from Wasdale Head). From
Borrowdale ascend Sty Head Pass and join the Gable Traverse.
Time about 1 hour.

Descent: The best descent from the crag is found on the west side.

38 **Innominate Crack** MVS

60 ft./18 m. *G. S. Bower, Bentley Beetham and J. B. Wilson 1921*

A much-photographed classic, sustained but not serious with
modern protection. Takes the thinner, right hand of the two
cracks splitting the Sty Head face of the crag.

1) 60 ft./18 m. Climb the crack, some use being made of a
subsidiary crack on the left in the middle third of the pitch.

Grooved Arête on Pikes Crag

39 **Kern Knotts Crack** MVS

70 ft./21 m.   *O. G. Jones and H. C. Bowen*   1897
A well-polished classic which repulses many would-be tigers.
Takes the wide, left-hand crack splitting the Sty Head face of the
crag.
1)   70 ft./21 m. Climb the crack to the sentry box. From here
climb either the polished crack (strenuous) or the right wall
(delicate) to reach the upper part of the crack. The rest of the
crack is followed with less difficulty.

40 **Buttonhook Route** HVS (5a, 4b)

100 ft./30 m.   *F. G. Balcombe and C. J. A. Cooper*   1934
A remarkable climb for its time; it is short but strenuous and
serious. Start 15 ft./4 m. left of the corner where the Sty Head
and Wasdale faces of the crag meet.
1)   75 ft./23 m. (5a) Climb a pair of twin cracks to the overhang
and by means of a long reach gain a wedged flake on the right.
Pull over the overhang and continue up a thin crack to a small
stance. Traverse horizontally left with increasing difficulty,
passing a thread runner to an open scoop: climb this on poor
sloping holds to a ledge and belay on the right.   2)   25 ft./8 m.
(4b) Finish up the rib above.

41 **Kern Knotts Chimney** * D

190 ft./58 m.   *O. G. Jones, W. H. Fowler and J. W. Robinson*   1893
An old-fashioned chimney climb, best attempted without
rucksacks. Starts below the deep chimney in the Wasdale face.
1)   70 ft./21 m. Ascend an easy staircase, then climb the
chimney past a chockstone to the top.   2)   50 ft./15 m. Go
under the bridged block to a belay, then up a polished
slab.   3)   70 ft./21 m. Easy slabs lead to the top of the crag.

THE NAPES   (211099)

Following the Gable Traverse from Sty Head, the first obvious
feature is the huge expanse of Tophet Wall. The classic Severe on
this face takes an impressive slanting line from left to right
between overhangs. Further along the traverse, the Needle can
be seen, and a higher traverse at this level can be reached by
scrambling up on either side of the Needle. Some 200 ft./61 m.

Bill Birkett on Innominate Crack

past the Needle is the Eagle's Nest Ridge, and further round is Abbey Buttress. The next big ridge along the traverse is Arrowhead Ridge. Further on, the prominent landmark of the Sphinx Rock provides an amusing problem.

Descent: By the scree slopes bounding the Napes on either side; Little Hell Gate to the west of the Sphinx Rock and Great Hell Gate to the right of Tophet Wall. The gullies between the Napes ridges are loose and wet and are not recommended in either direction except in good winter conditions.

42 **Tophet Wall**   ***   S

265 ft./81 m.   *H. M. Kelly and R. E. W. Pritchard*   *1923*

A superb climb, serious and sustained, with the most exciting moves at the end. Starts just left of the middle of the wall and slants to the right.

1)   40 ft./12 m. Climb up on the right of an overhanging crack, then step into the crack and follow it to a ledge.   2)   45 ft./14 m. Traverse up to the right to a grass ledge below a wall. This point can also be reached from the ground by an easy traverse from the right.   3)   30 ft./9 m. The wall is climbed on small holds to a ledge. Move left to a corner.   4)   25 ft./8 m. Climb the crack in the corner, then ascend the right wall to a corner and belay on the right.   5)   50 ft./15 m. Traverse right on good handholds to a corner. Climb the rib on the right to a stance.   6)   30 ft./9 m. Climb a small pinnacle then move back left and follow the steep crack on good jams to a ledge.   7)   45 ft./14 m. Easier climbing leads to the top. A short distance further on is an easy gully on the right for the descent.

43 **Incantations**   **   E5   (5a, 6b, 6b)

300 ft./91 m.   *P. Whillance and D. Armstrong (var.)*   *1984*

Climbs a thin crack leading through some steep ground. Start as for Tophet Grooves.

1)   80 ft./24 m. (5a) Up the nose and follow an easy groove rightwards to a sizeable sloping ledge.   2)   120 ft./36 m. (6b) Up the crack above to holds on the left. Up to a peg runner and on up the overhanging wall to reach a thin rightward-slanting crack in the slab. Continue to ledges then right through a bulge to step right on to the Great Slab. Up to the traverse left and

Tophet Wall, Great Gable

follow this to belay in a grassy groove.   3)   100 ft./30 m. (6b)
Up the rib then step right to below a thin rightward-slanting
crack, leading through the overhanging wall. Up this (peg
runner high on left – tricky to clip) to gain the groove above.
Climb this, up the right-hand branch, to the top.

44   **Tophet Grooves**   **   HVS (5b, 5a. 4c, 4a)
225 ft./68 m.   *R. J. Birkett and V. Veevers   1940*
The route follows the big groove up the left edge of the Tophet
Wall. Start directly below the main groove up a smaller one.
1)   55 ft./17 m. (5b) The groove is awkward to start and leads to
a juniper ledge and belay, below the main groove.   2)   50 ft./15
m. (5a) Climb the open groove to the overhang (care needed
with a doubtful block) then traverse right across a mossy scoop
before climbing up to a belay in the groove on the left.   3)   70
ft./21 m. (4c) Step right and climb a mossy wall to a good ledge.
Then follow a grassy crack on the right to a large belay.   4)   50
ft./15 m. (4a) Climb the crack above to the top.

45   **The Needle**   **   HVD
W. P. Haskett Smith (solo)   1886
This famous pinnacle gives an interesting and nowadays very
polished climb with some exciting moves. The following pitches
all lead to the Shoulder beneath the top block.
1a)   40 ft./12 m. The crack splitting the Wasdale face provides a
safe but strenuous struggle: easier in descent (if you don't get
stuck!).   1b)   50 ft./15 m. From the foot of the Wasdale crack
traverse right to the arête and climb this direct.   1c)   60 ft./18
m. Climb the crack on the side facing Lingmell.   2)   15 ft./4 m.
From the Shoulder, mantelshelf with difficulty on to the polished
ledge on the right-hand edge of the top block. Toe-traverse to the
left, then an awkward step up leads to the top. A belay can be
arranged by looping the rope round the overhangs of the top
block. The descent is not quite as difficult as the ascent, and the
last man can be protected by running the rope over the top block.

46   **Needle Ridge**   **   D
325 ft./99 m.   *W. P. Haskett Smith (solo)   1884*
A justifiably popular climb up the ridge behind the Needle.

On Tophet Wall, Great Gable

Starts from the gap behind the Needle. The first pitch is much the hardest on the climb.

1)   35 ft./11 m. Climb a polished slab to a chimney, trending left to a stance.   2)   50 ft./15 m. A short but steep wall leads to easier rocks. Climb a broken wall to a stance, then walk 25 ft./8 m. to the rib.   3)   240 ft./73 m. Follow the scratched and obvious route up the ribs and corners; frequent belays.

47 **Crocodile Crack**   HVS (5a, 4a)
185 ft./56 m.   *G. Oliver, G. Arkless, P. Ross and N. Brown   1960*
All the interest is concentrated into one long pitch. Start from the Dress Circle (the large ledge overlooking the Needle) about 15 ft./4 m. to the right of Eagle's Nest Direct.

1)   140 ft./43 m. (5a) Climb a flake-crack for 25 ft./8 m. before moving left on to a steep wall. Climb this and the crack above to an overhang at 50 ft./15 m., which is surmounted facing left. Continue up the crack with good situations to a large ledge.   2)   45 ft./14 m. (4a) Grassy chimneys lead up to the ridge.

48 **Eagle's Nest Ridge Direct**   ***   MVS
120 ft./36 m.   *G. A. Solly and party   1892*
A sustained and delicate pitch with little protection. Takes the arête at the left edge of the face overlooking the Needle.

1)   50 ft./15 m. Climb up steep rock, trending right, to a ledge.   2)   70 ft./21 m. Traverse left to the edge, using two parallel cracks. Climb the edge to a small platform (the Eagle's Nest). A second platform (the Crow's Nest) is reached after a further 15 ft./4 m. A slab with sloping holds is climbed to reach easy ground on the ordinary route.

49 **Eagle's Nest Ridge via the West Chimney**   **   HD
355 ft./108 m.   *G. A. Solly and M. Schintz   1892*

Opposite : Napes Needle

Overleaf left : Abbey Buttress

Overleaf right : Eagle's Nest Ridge Direct, Great Gable

A popular climb and justly so. Start up the battered chimney on the left of Eagle's Nest Ridge.

1)   70 ft./21 m. (Can be split.) Easy scrambling and then good holds in the chimney lead to a large platform.   2)   25 ft./8 m. Continue up the chimney with more difficulty to a crevasse.   3)   40 ft./12 m. Traverse right through the crevasse to a polished slab, which leads with some difficulty to a rock ledge in a corner.   4)   40 ft./12 m. The strenuous chimney is climbed on to a slab. Continue up this to a level crest.   5)   60 ft./18 m. The chimney on the left or any of several well-scratched variations lead to the next crest.   6)   120 ft./36 m. Continue up the crest. Difficulties can be chosen or avoided at will. Stances and belays at frequent intervals.

50 **Abbey Buttress**   **   VD

180 ft./55 m.   *F. Botterill and J. de V. Hazard   1909*
A good buttress climb. Starts from the crevasse which is an obvious landmark on the traverse along the foot of the napes, about 150 ft./46 m. left of Eagle's Ridge.

1)   60 ft./18 m. Climb to a ledge, then step right and ascend a steep crack to a ledge and belay.   2)   65 ft./20 m. Go up steep rock for 15 ft./4 m. to a wide ledge. Traverse left for 15 ft./4 m., then go straight up for 25 ft./8 m. Traverse right below an overhang, then climb the arête on good holds to a large ledge.   3)   30 ft./9 m. Climb a crack on the left corner of the buttress.   4)   25 ft./8 m. Continue up the left edge to join Eagle's Nest Ordinary Route.

51 **Arrowhead Ridge Direct**   * VD

225 ft./68 m.   *W. C. Slingsby and party   1892/G. A. Solly and party   1893*
One of the best of the Napes ridges. Takes the obvious ridge on the left of the Napes with an unmistakable arrowhead-shaped pinnacle near the top. Starts at the bottom of the ridge.

1)   80 ft./24 m. Follow the ridge for two pitches.   2)   40 ft./12 m. Ascend the slab to the base of Arrowhead, which is climbed on good holds. Belay round the top of the Arrowhead.   3)   35 ft./11 m. Cross the gap and follow the horizontal section of the

ridge to a slabby face which leads to a belay.   4)   80 ft./24 m. Scrambling along the easy upper part of the ridge.

GABLE CRAG   (213105)

Situated on the north face of Great Gable and overlooking Ennerdale, the crag offers excellent climbing after several days of dry weather. In poor conditions, however, the rocks can be exceedingly greasy. The main interest is concentrated on two buttresses: the wall, called Engineer's Slabs (!), which lies just right of the centre of the face below the summit; and Mallory's Buttress, which lies on the left side of the face and right of a wide scree gully.

Approach: From Wasdale leave the Sty Head path just beyond the bridge and follow a path up the steep south-west ridge of Great Gable (Gavel Neese). Then continue diagonally left to gain the col between Kirk Fell and Great Gable (Beckhead) from which a faint path contours round below Gable Crag. Time – about 1½ hours. From Borrowdale (the easiest approach), it is best to start at the top of Honister Pass. Follow the footpath towards Green Gable, then traverse the Ennerdale flank of the mountain, via the Moses Trod path, to a point below Gable Crag. About 1 hour. A longer alternative from Borrowdale would be to ascend Sty Head Pass and then cross Windy Gap between the two Gables. The Crag can be reached easily from Ennerdale, and from Buttermere by first ascending Honister Pass then following the route above.

Descent: A descent from Engineer's Slabs is described after the route. From the Slant, descend towards Windy Gap.

52 **Sledgate Ridge**   *   MVS

240 ft./73 m.   *A. H. Greenbank, J. Wilkinson and A. E. Wormell   1958*

An excellent approach to Engineer's Slabs. Start from the path below and to the left of Engineer's Slabs.

1)   70 ft./21 m. A difficult crack is followed by a water-worn groove on the right. After 30 ft./9 m. ascend a wall on the left to a large ledge.   2)   60 ft./18 m. From the left-hand end of the ledge, get on to the wall above and traverse boldly rightwards across the slabs to a large grass ledge.   3)   110 ft./33 m. The

wall above is climbed to the centre one of three cracks. Follow
this to the top. (Descend on the right to reach Engineer's Slabs.)

53 **Engineer's Slabs**   ***   VS
180 ft./55 m.   *F. G. Balcombe, J. A. Shepherd and C. J. A.
Cooper 1934*
A magnificent climb, steep and sustained, but much harder in
poor conditions. Starts below the middle of the wall which is
reached by a steep scramble from the foot of the face, or via
Sledgate Ridge.
1)   80 ft./24 m. Climb a wall on small holds, just left of a short
groove, to a ledge at the top of the groove. Continue up a crack,
then reach a pair of steep cracks which lead to an obvious
chimney. A few feet higher is a sentry box and nut belay.
2)   55 ft./17 m. Traverse right from the sentry box to another
crack, which is climbed for 25 ft./8 m. to a stance. Continue up
the crack by layback to another stance and piton belay below a
groove.   3)   45 ft./14 m. The groove is started from the left and
then followed direct with difficulty to the top. If the groove is wet
the crack on the left can be climbed, followed by a short arête to
the top of the crag.
Descent: Follow a rake slanting down to the right (looking out) to
the top of the chimney which forms the east edge of the Slabs.
Traverse round to the right and descend a steep grass slope.
Traverse back left to a small col by a pinnacle, then down a gully
to the foot of the Slabs.

54 **Sarcophagus**   **   E3   (4c, 5c, 5b)
215 ft./65 m.   *P. Whillance and D. Armstrong (var.) 1977*
Lies between the Tomb and Engineer's Slabs. A good route
starting as for the Tomb, just 10 ft./3 m. right of the Engineer's
Slabs.
1)   60 ft./18 m. (4c) Follow the Tomb to the sentry box, then up
and move right to a grass ledge and pinnacle belay.   2)   75
ft./23 m. (5c) A poorly protected pitch. Step up leftwards to a
block at the right end of a grassy ledge. Move up off the block
and climb the wall above to join the Tomb at the end of its
traverse. Go left to a thin crack and up this, passing an overlap,
to gain a narrow ledge on the right. Small nut belay.   3)   80

Looking down the impressive final groove of Engineer's Slabs

ft./24 m. (5b) Up and left to a groove/crack. Climb this and the jam crack to finish up a groove. (This is left of the final groove of the Tomb.)

55 **The Tomb** ** E2   (4c, 5b, 5a)
235 ft./72 m.   *A. G. Cram and W. Young   1966*
An impressive climb which ascends the wall on the right of Engineer's Slabs. Start 10 ft./3 m. right of the latter route.
1)   60 ft./18 m. (4c) Traverse right to gain a small sentry box, then climb straight up to a ledge and belay.   2)   65 ft./20 m. (5b) Move left and climb the wall for 20 ft./6 m. on small holds. Then either move right and climb directly up the wall or traverse left and climb the edge of the wall until it is possible to traverse back right. Both routes lead to a good runner. Traverse right to a crack which is climbed to a good stance.   3)   110 ft./33 m. (5a) Continue up the groove to an overhang then move left across the wall to gain a bottomless groove. Climb this to the top.

56 **The Slant**   HVS (5a, 5a)
150 ft./46 m.   *M. Burbage, L. J. Griffin, P. L. Fearnehough and G. Oliver   1968*
A short but well-worthwhile climb. It lies on the small, steep buttress well to the left of Engineer's Slabs. It is best reached by scrambling up a scree gully 100 yds./91 m. to the west of Windy Gap and striking rightwards when the buttress comes into view. Start below the left-hand end of the prominent rightwards-sloping slab.
1)   100 ft./30 m. (5a) The short steep wall and cracked bulge give access to the slab. Follow this on good holds to the foot of a steep crack. This leads via a difficult move into a V-groove, which is left for a slab on the right. A stance and thread belay are reched below a large overhang.   2)   50 ft./15 m. (5a) Traverse left below the overhang to reach a deep-cut groove, and follow this strenuously to the top.

WINTER CLIMBING
If good snow and ice conditions are to be found, then this area has some very good climbs to offer. Because of the possibility of

On the crux of the Tomb, Gable Crag

variable conditions, the grades given below are only approximate.

Scafell: There are four classic winter gullies: Mickledore Chimney (Grade I), Moss Ghyll (Grade III/IV) with the Collie Step as the normal crux, Steep Ghyll (Grade III/V) usually with a long hard pitch and Deep Ghyll (Grade I/II).

Pikes Crag: Exceptionally can give good gully climbs in the range Grade I/II. After heavy snowfall Pike's Crag may come into condition sooner than Scafell.

Great End: See Borrowdale section.

The Napes: A selection of easy gullies, very rarely in good condition because of the lower altitude and the southerly aspect.

Gable Crag: Often in good condition as the crag faces north, with a variety of worthwhile gullies and ridges in the range Grade I/II. The summer descent from Engineer's Slabs can be a good winter climb (Grade II). The first large gully to the right of Engineer's Slabs, Central Gully (VD), also gives a good winter climb at about Grade II.

Opposite: Winter climbing on Gable Crag

Overleaf left: Starting Deep Ghyll, Scafell, with the Pinnacle looming above

Overleaf right: Deep Ghyll, Scafell

ESKDALE AND DUDDON

These two quiet valleys have much in common and it is convenient to describe them jointly. Both valleys form convenient bases for the southern and western Lake District, since with motor transport it is possible to reach Wasdale, Langdale and Coniston in about half an hour. As well as these centres, Eskdale itself has two major crags and several smaller ones; whilst Duddon has one crag which is quick drying and near the road, offering good climbing when the higher crags are out of condition. Duddon has also many short buttresses giving some pleasant outcrop climbs.

Access
Eskdale and Duddon are two roughly parallel valleys separated by a relatively low area of higher ground. The two are connected by Hardknott Pass (1 in 3: no caravans or nervous drivers!) and by the road over Birker Fell between Ulpha and Eskdale Green. Access by road is via the coast road to the south-west or via Wrynose Pass from the east. In the summer months, a picturesque miniature railway runs between Ravenglass (BR station) and Dalegarth, near Boot in Eskdale. The nearest railway station to Duddon is Foxfield, also on the coastal line. There is a Mountain Goat minibus service daily from Easter to October) from Keswick or Windermere via Ambleside over Wrynose and Hardknott, and to Duddon via Coniston. There is a post-bus service between Cockley Beck and Broughton.

Accommodation and camping
There is a campsite at Boot, and at Brotherilkeld Farm at the head of Eskdale; in Duddon, sites can be found at Hall Dunnerdale (215955) and at Turner Hall (233964). Those prepared to carry their tents some distance will find some excellent sites in upper Eskdale below Esk Buttress. There are several inns, guest-houses, and farmhouses offering accommodation in both valleys. Youth hostels can be found at Black Hall Farm (283011) in Duddon and near the head of Eskdale (195010). The Outward Bound have a school in Eskdale Green, and there is a Rucksack Club hut near Turner Hall in Duddon.

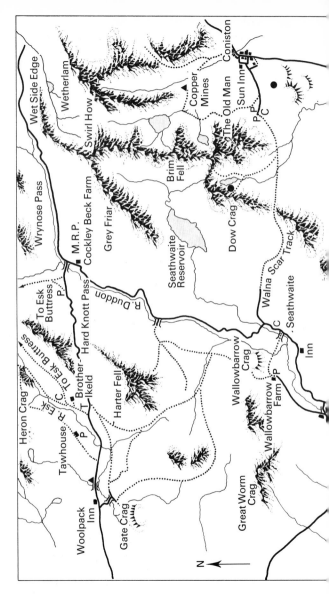

Coniston
Sun Inn
P
C
The Old Man
Copper Mines ▲
Wetherlam
Swirl How
Wet Side Edge
Wrynose Pass
Brim Fell
Grey Friar
Seathwaite Reservoir
Dow Crag
M.R.P.
Cockley Beck Farm
Hard Knott Pass
P
To Esk Buttress
Heron Crag
To Esk Buttress
R. ESK
R.C.
Brother-ikeld
Tawhouse
P
T
Harter Fell
R. Duddon
Walna Scar Track
C
Seathwaite
Inn
Wallowbarrow Crag
Wallowbarrow Farm
P
Great Worm Crag
Wallowbarrow
Woolpack Inn
Gate Crag
N ←

Food and drink

Many of the farms and guest-houses in the area serve meals and snacks, and food and drink can be found at the Woolpack Inn (190010) in Eskdale and the Newfield Inn (227960) in Duddon, the latter being especially recommended. In addition, there are other inns in Boot and Eskdale Green (licensing hours 11–3, 5.30–10.30; Sun. 12–2, 7–10.30) and a licensed restaurant at Boot. There are shops and a PO in Boot, Eskdale Green (early closing: Sat.) and Ulpha, with larger shops in Gosforth and Broughton.

Garages and car hire

Postlethwaite's Garage at Eskdale Green (tel. 239) operates 24-hr. recovery and taxi services, but the nearest petrol station is at Holmrook (closing 10 p.m.; winter weekends 9 p.m.) or at Broughton. Car hire is available at Whitehaven (tel. 66611 or 65281), Egremont (tel. 820144) or Ulverston (tel. 53962 or 55428).

General services

Public telephones in Boot, Eskdale Green, Ulpha, Hall Dunnerdale, also one at the head of Eskdale at the foot of Hardknott Pass. Public toilets at Eskdale Green and Broughton. Broughton has also a climbing-equipment shop (open on Sundays).

Mountain rescue

For assistance, telephone the police. There is an MR post at Eskdale Outward Bound School (143002; tel. Eskdale 281). In addition, there is a first-aid post at Cockley Beck Farm (247017; Thomas Stretcher; no telephone) and an unmanned post at the top of Mickledore on Scafell (210068) for Esk Buttress.

Esk Buttress   (223064, called Dow Crag by the Ordnance Survey)

This fine crag lies on the south flank of Scafell Pike. A combination of sound clean rock, southern aspect, and relatively low altitude, make this crag an attractive prospect at most times of the year. Despite its isolated position, the crag has become very popular in recent years. There is an excellent selection of climbs and the crag is well known for its incut holds.

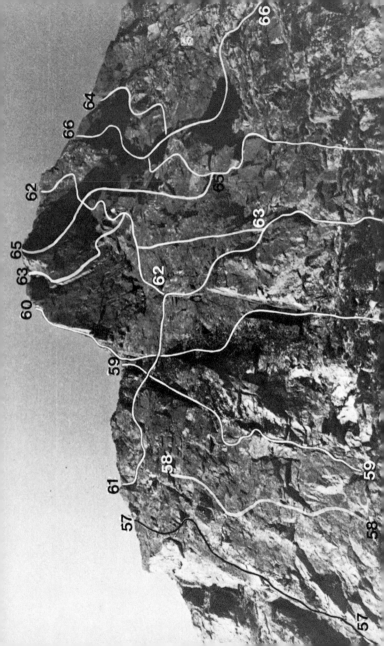

Approach: The easiest approach is from Eskdale. Park near the foot of Hardknott Pass and follow either the Taw House Farm track on the west bank of the river, or the Brotherilkeld path on the east bank and cross the river by a footbridge to join the west bank path past Taw House. Immediately after crossing Cowcove Beck (stone bridge), strike up the fellside via a good zigzag path. The path continues across a pleateau and after some miles Upper Eskdale is reached. Continue up the valley past some large boulders (excellent bivouac sites) and the waterfall of Cam Spout to reach the crag. A fairly fit party will do this in 1½ hours or less. In mist, stick to the path which follows the Esk Valley; slightly longer.

The approach from Wasdale is common with the Scafell approach to the top of Mickledore, then descend the Eskdale side for 500 ft./152 m. and slant left across the fell side to the top of the crag; 1¾ hours, with a steep ascent on the return journey.

From Duddon or Langdale, it is usual to motor to Cockley Beck Bridge and walk up Mosedale. From the head of Mosedale descend slightly and cross Lingcove Beck, then contour round under Gait Craigs and across the marshy Esk valley to the foot of the crag. This takes about 1¾ hours.

Finally, the approach from Seathwaite in Borrowdale up Grains Ghyll and over Esk Hause takes about 2 hours.
Descent: Slant down the left side (south-west). Various routes, some involving scrambling, join the stream which bounds the Cam Spout side of the crag.

57 **The Red Edge** ** E1 (5a, 4c)
240 ft./73 m. *J.A. Austin, N. J. Soper and E. Metcalf 1962*
A steep and exhilarating climb with sufficient holds and adequate protection. The route lies up the shallow groove in the rib bounding the central wall on the left. Start up the well-defined chimney.
1) 40 ft./12 m. Steep climbing to the foot of the chimney. Belay. 2) 130 ft./40 m (5a) A magnificent pitch. Pull on to a chockstone in the bed of the chimney then move right to the arête. Gain a small ledge a few feet higher with difficulty and continue up the shallow groove to a small overhang. Difficulties, though not excessive, are relentless, and there are no resting

Esk Buttress

places. Ether climb the overhang, or cross the wall to a hidden spike on the arête and climb this until the groove above the overhang can be regained. Continue up the groove on improving holds to a stance in a corner. 3) 70 ft./21 m. (4c) The twin cracks are climbed for 10 ft./3 m. Move left round the corner then diagonally up large but dubious flakes to the top of the crag.

58 **Humdrum** ** E3 (5c, 4b)
180 ft./55 m. *M. Berzins and R. H. Berzins 1977*
A superb, bold and technical wall climb taking a line between Red Edge and Black Sunday. Scramble up to a small bush beneath the right-hand end of the wall, then traverse left to a flake belay.
1) 120 ft./36 m. (5c) Steeply up a vague corner to an overlap. Pull over leftwards, first taking the edge then the groove, and continue up to a poor resting ledge. Go across diagonally leftwards to the top of a groove. Move up and after a few feet traverse the wall to the right to a flat hold in the middle of the wall. Continue straight up, gaining a groove and a crack through the final bulge to reach ledges. 2) 60 ft./18 m. (4b) Up the slab on the left to the top.

59 **Black Sunday** * HVS (–, 5a, 4a, 4a)
305 ft./93 m. *J. A. Austin, E. Metcalf and N. J. Soper 1962*
A good climb, which is rather strenuous and needs dry conditions. The route follows an obvious line up a crack and groove between Red Edge and Square Chimney. Start at the foot of the arête below the Red Edge.
1) 115 ft./35 m. Easy climbing to a bilberry ledge. Move up to a belay below and left of the overhanging crack. 2) 90 ft./27 m. (5a) Climb the strenuous crack, with an exit to the right on to a glacis. Move back into the crack for a few feet until a long step left enables a thin slanting crack to be reached. Climb this with difficulty to a resting place under an overhang. Traverse back right and make an awkward pull round the overhang on to the wall on the right. Follow this to a ledge and belay. 3) 55 ft./17 m. (4a) Ascend the corner crack, then continue to a stance and belay on the left. 4) 45 ft./14 m. (4a) The wall on the left of a mossy groove leads to top of crag. Belay 30 ft./9 m. back.

The Cumbrian, Esk Buttress

60 **Square Chimney/Medusa Wall**   **   VS

480 ft./146 m.   *R. J. Birkett and L. Muscroft   1947*

A good direct route with exposed and exciting situations. The Square Chimney is a prominent feature of the crag on the lower half of the Central Pillar, just left of centre. Starts at the foot of steep broken rock and vegetation directly below the Chimney.

1)   170 ft./52 m. Scramble up via ledges, little walls, and steep vegetation to reach a ledge just to the right and below the start of the chimney proper. Many belays *en route.*   2)   100 ft./30 m. A sustained pitch. Climb easily to the foot of the Chimney, which is climbed with difficulty for 40 ft./12 m. Medium-sized climbers will be able to adopt a back-and-foot position (just) but shorter men will have to bridge (much harder). At this point the left side of the chimney falls away. Fix a good runner in the crack (it is possible to belay here, no stance) and gain a small sloping ledge on the left by an awkward move. Traverse left and up a delicate mossy slab into the corner. Climb this to a small stance and belay.   3)   30 ft./9 m. Continue up the corner groove, or the rib on the left, to reach a belay on the traverse of Bridge's Route.   4)   40 ft./12 m. Climb the easy gully above and move out right to a rock ledge below the final tower. Belay on left.   5)   45 ft./14 m. Take the central of three grooves above to the top of the pinnacle, then move right and up to a good belay and stance in a superb position at the edge of the tower overlooking the central wall.   6)   95 ft./29 m. Climb the groove above for 15 ft./4 m., then move right to the rib and climb this to a ledge and belay. Continue up easier rocks, trending right, to the top of the crag.

61 **Bridge's Route**   ***   HS

410 ft./125 m.   *A. W. Bridge and party   1932*

A superb route, one of the best of its standard in the Lakes, with sustained and exposed climbing. The rock is clean and the route 'goes' without too much difficulty in the wet. Starts more or less directly below the Square Chimney.

1)   170 ft./52 m. Scrambling up vegetation and occasional steep little walls leads to a ledge just below and to the right of the base of the Square Chimney. This pitch can be split.   2)   45 ft./14 m. Take a line of weakness in the steep wall above, about 30 ft./9

Bob Wightman on Humdrum, Esk Buttress

m. right of the line of Square Chimney. A grass ledge is reached with belay.   3)   25 ft./8 m. Climb the crack on the left and follow the flake to a ledge and belay.   4)   45 ft./14 m. Gain the steep groove above and climb it to the level of a jammed spike. Move right and continue straight up on good holds to a ledge and large belay.   5)   40 ft./12 m. Make an exposed traverse left to a mossy ledge. Climb the groove on the left to a stance and belay.   6)   40 ft./12 m. Continue the line of the traverse to a pile of flakes on the corner of the buttress. Small belay.   7)   45 ft./14 m. Climb the steep mossy groove above to a grassy shelf and belay at the top.

62 **Central Pillar**   **   E2   (5a, 5b, 5b, 4c)
495 ft./151 m.   *P. Crew and M. Owen   1962*
The route attempts a direct line up the Central Pillar and is forced on to the right-hand arête at the top. A climb with small exposed stances and poor protection. The first four pitches are shared with Bridge's Route.
5)   70 ft./21 m. (5a) Climb the thin crack above the belay for 15 ft./4 m., then traverse horizontally right for 25 ft./8 m. or so, when the steepening wall can be climbed, slightly leftwards with increasing difficulty until a hard move right leads to a poor stance and belays.   6)   40 ft./12 m. (5b) Climb the shallow groove above, swing across right to a small ledge then step back left. A hard move over a small overhang is then made to gain a slab. Move right and across this and up to a small stance and sundry spike and piton belays below a corner where all roads seem to end.   7)   70 ft./21 m. (5b) Traverse right in a most exposed position and pull up to a small uncomfortable ledge. Above on the left a large dubious block sticks out of the overhanging wall. Surmount the block and wall above to gain a traverse line which leads rightwards to a grassy bay.   8)   30 ft./9 m. (4c) The wide crack in the corner, or alternatively the rib on the left, leads to the top.

63 **The Cumbrian**   ***   E5   (5a, 5a, 6a)
270 ft./82 m.   *R. Valentine and P. Braithwaite (alt.)   1974/Free: M. Berzins and R. H. Berzins   1977/Pitches 1 & 2: R. Graham and A. Hyslop   1977*

Central Pillar, Esk Buttress

A brilliant route which climbs the sensational hanging corner dominating the upper wall of Esk Buttress.

1)   100 ft./30 m. (5a) Take pitch 1 of Bridge's Route to the top of the crack. From the pinnacle take a thin crack for 30 ft./9 m., then step left to a continuation crack. Up this to a narrow ledge.   2)   60 ft./18 m. (5a) Straight up the slab above to join the traverse of Central Pillar; follow this to a ledge on the rib.   3)   110 ft./33 m. (6a) Go left, working up into a corner below the impending headwall. (Poor tiny wire runners.) Step down left and move left into the groove directly below the Corner. Move up groove/crack to an excellent runner and make a difficult few moves (crux) to gain the wall and rib immediately right of the corner. Transfer into the corner (very awkward position and crack size to place gear) and bridge and layback for 30 ft./9 m. or so until a rest can be had. Continue up, surmount the bulge and move rightwards to a ledge below the final short corner. Climb directly up this, making some awkward moves, and finally step left before a last pull leads to the top. (Possible to escape final corner by moving on to the left arête.)

64 Great Central Climb   VS

525 ft./160 m.   *R. J. Birkett and T. Hill   1945*

Another very long route which attempts to ascend the Central Pillar: this time the climb is forced rightwards. Start directly below the Central Pillar.

1)   180 ft./55 m. Scramble up rock and vegetation to a pinnacle leaning against the bottom of the Pillar proper.   2)   125 ft./38 m. From the top of the pinnacle, move diagonally right to finish on a trio of blocks below a small overhang. Move left below the overhang to gain a groove which is climbed to a small ledge. Continue straight up to a ledge on the left (possible belay), then climb up until it is possible to traverse right to the nose of the buttress. Move up to a stance and belay below twin grooves.   3)   20 ft./6 m. Move up the left-hand groove, then traverse right with difficulty to enter Trespasser Groove above pitch 3.   4)   50 ft./15 m. Either do pitch 4 of Trespasser Groove (HVS) or abseil 15 ft./4 m. from the belay to gain a traverse line on the right wall. Cross this to a grass ledge and move up to another grass ledge and thread belay.   5)   70 ft./21 m. Climb straight up to a juniper ledge. An overhanging crack is then climbed to the Waiting Room on Bower's Route.   6)   50 ft./

15 m. Frankland's Crack. The impending crack leads via an awkward finish to slabs. Go up to a belay below a wide corner crack.   7)   30 ft./9 m. The crack.

65 **Fallout**   **   E4   (4b, 4b, 5a, 5b, 6a)
360 ft./110 m.   *T. W. Birkett (Pitch 5) and A. Hyslop   1979/Pitches 3&4: R. O. Graham   1978*
The crucial final pitch traverses and ascends the big wall right of the Cumbrian. Magnificent climbing and possibly the loneliest lead in the Lake District.
1)   80 ft./24 m. (4b) Pitch 1 of Great Central Climb.   2)   50 ft./15 m. (4b) Pitch 2 ditto.   3)   70 ft./21 m. (5a) Traverse left to climb a groove and up to a very shallow grassy groove which leads to a block belay on the right.   4)   70 ft./21 m. (5b) Take a series of short grooves in the arête to belay on the left of the ledges.   5)   90 ft./27 m. (6a) Up above the belay there is a peg in a horizontal crack and it is advisable to clip this. Step down left, to the edge of the verticality, and make some moves up to a sloping ledge. Now make an ascending traverse leftwards to the arête. An *in-situ* wire (doubtful even when placed in 1979), which can be clipped by reaching down from the traverse, constitutes the only runner. Move up the edge until a horizontal crack offers respite and security. Continue up the edge to the top or move left into the top of the Cumbrian.

66 **Trespasser Groove**   **   HVS   (–, –, 4c, 5a, 5a, 5a)
435 ft./132 m.   *A. R. Dolphin and D. Hopkin (alt.)   1952*
The route takes the large rightward-facing groove which bounds the Central Pillar on the right. The climbing is fairly strenuous, with several long reaches, but difficulties are well protected. Starts as for Bower's Route.
1)   100 ft./30 m. The slabs are climbed from left to right. Finish up a grassy shelf to a sloping heather terrace and block belay.   2)   85 ft./26 m. Traverse diagonally left to a small ledge. Climb a groove slanting up to the right to grass ledges at the foot of the main groove. Piton belay.   3)   90 ft./27 m. (4c) Climb the slab until it is possible to move left into the corner, which is ascended to a recess. The bulge above is awkward, but by bridging up as far as possible on the left, it is possible to reach good holds. Spike belay.   4)   40 ft./12 m. (5a) The steep right wall of the groove is climbed with difficulty, starting with an

awkward mantelshelf. A traverser right from a flake leads to a good ledge and belays.   5) 40 ft./12 m. (5a) Move back left and climb the corner to the overhang. Make a long reach right to a small hold and swing across on this to better holds. Ascend to a large ledge (the Waiting Room).   6)   80 ft./15 m. (5a) Frankland's Crack. Climb the slightly overhanging crack on the left with an awkward finish. Above, easy slabs lead left and a steep crack leads strenuously to the top of the crag.

HERON CRAG   (222030)
A superb and impressive crag with 250 ft./76 m. of steep compact rock. The right wall, although appearing mossy, offers routes of high quality. All the routes, except those on the right flank, dry quickly after rain, and the low altitude means the crag is often in condition when the high crags are not.
Approach: Park near the foot of Hardknott Pass and follow the farm tracks on either side of the river. If the west bank path is taken, keep to the Throstle Garth path, and when the path begins to dip down towards the river, follow a narrower track on the left which leads eventually to the foot of the crag (½ hour).
Descent: Down the slopes at the left-hand (south-west) end of the crag.

67 Side Track   *   VS
180 ft./55 m.   *R. B. Evans and I. F. Howell   1960*
The buttress to the left of Gormenghast is seamed with grooves and slabs and has a conspicuous line of overlaps slanting left from near the foot of the deep chimney immediately left of Gormenghast (Babylon HS). This delicate climb follows the slab under the overlaps. Start below the tree-filled chimney of Babylon.
1)   35 ft./11 m. Easily up to a tree at the foot of the chimney.   2)   75 ft./23 m. Move up to a ledge on the left then traverse left below the overhangs until it is possible to move up into a groove (runner). Traverse left out of the groove on to the rib and ascend this to a small stance.   3)   30 ft./9 m. Continue straight up to a large oak belay.   4)   40 ft./12 m. The very steep wall is climbed via a shallow scoop. Exit right from the scoop on small holds and finish up a loose groove.

Heron Crag, Eskdale

73

68 **Gormenghast** *** HVS (4c, 5b, 5a)
250 ft./76 m. *L. Brown and A. L. Atkinson 1960*
A superb route which takes the impressive central pillar of the
crag. One of the best climbs of its grade on sound, clean rock.
Starts to the right of the tree-filled groove which bounds the
central pillar on the left.
1)   40 ft./12 m. (4c) Climb the steep wall directly to a good
ledge and piton belay below an obvious overhanging
crack.   2)   110 ft./33 m. (5b) Move 10 ft./3 m. left and ascend
the impending wall on widely spaced holds until it is possible to
traverse back into the crack. Climb the crack and continue up
the groove above to a stance and belay on a holly.   3)   100
ft./30 m. (5a) Move right from the tree and ascend on good holds
past a block. Follow a crack, then go straight up the wall on
small holds until better holds lead right to a good ledge. Climb
the bulging rock above on good holds to the top.

69 **Bellerophon** ** VS
185 ft./56 m. *O. R. D. Pritchard and B. S. Schofield 1958*
A highly enjoyable climb, which follows the deep groove on the
right of the central pillar. Although rather mossy, it can be
climbed in wet conditions.
1)   40 ft./12 m. Climb the arête on the left of the chimney to a
good ledge and belay.   2)   40 ft./12 m. Move right and climb
the steep crack to enter the big groove. Belay on a large grass
ledge.   3)   45 ft./14 m. Climb the mossy corner until a step left
leads to a stance and belay on top of a pinnacle.   4)   60 ft./18
m. Go straight up for 20 ft./6 m. then traverse left to an
enormous bird's nest. A shallow groove, slanting left, finishes the
climb.

70 **Spec Crack** E1 (5b, 4b, 5a)
215 ft./65 m. *P. Walsh, J. A. Austin and E. Metcalf 1961*
A route up the mossy wall to the right of Bellerophon. The
overhang is hard and strenuous but well protected: the rest is
delicate, steep climbing up mossy rock. Starts 30 ft./9 m. to the
right of Bellerophon.
1)   80 ft./24 m. (5a) Climb the wall to the overhang (runner)
and pull over into the crack above with difficulty. Continue up

Pulling over the overhang on Spec Crack, Heron Crag

the crack to a holly tree belay.   2)   40 ft./12 m. (4b) Ascend the
crack on the right to a small stance below an overhanging
crack.   3)   65 ft./20 m. (5a) Climb the crack until it is
necessary to break out on the left wall. Go up this to a small
stance.   4)   30 ft./9 m. Continue up another crack to the top.

71 **Mean Feat/Assassin** **   E3   (5c, 5c)
200 ft./61 m.   *T. W. Birkett and R. O. Graham   1977/79*
A surprisingly clean and technical route up the large mossy wall.
Start in the scooped groove about 20 ft./6 m. right of Spec Crack.
1)   90 ft./27 m. (5c) Up to a ledge at 20 ft./6 m. then move left
into a scoop (very poor protection). Gain the overhanging wall
and move up left to the edge. Continue steeply up until easy
ground leads leftwards to Spec Crack. Continue straight up the
obvious crack to the horizontal traverse line and peg
belay.   2)   110 ft./33 m. (5c) Up the wall left of the belay,
stepping right to climb a bulging section (poor peg runner).
Continue to a resting place and good peg runner. Take the
obvious traverse line (crack) left to a groove and crack. Follow
this directly up the wall above the overhang. Near the top, step
left into a short chimney and finish up this.

WALLOWBARROW CRAG   (222966, called Low Crag by
the Ordnance Survey)
This pleasant crag has a variety of short but interesting routes.
Some important points in its favour are that it dries out very
quickly after rain, faces south-west, and lies at a low altitude.
Many a wet weekend at Wasdale has been saved by a sudden
change in the weather and a visit to Wallowbarrow on the way
home.
Access: By road from the bridge over the River Duddon, about
one mile south-west of Seathwaite. Take a narrow lane and park
near High Wallowbarrow Farm. From here it is 10 minutes walk
to the crag. On foot from Seathwaite, take a path starting near
the church and cross the Duddon by a footbridge (note the first
crossing is Tarn Beck) to High Wallowbarrow Farm.
Descent: The crag is split into two buttresses, West and East, by a
dirty loose gully. Descend from the West Buttress to the left
(west) and from the East Buttress to the right.

72 **Bryanston**   *   VS

180 ft./55 m.   *J. Smith*   *1956*

A good climb up the centre of the West Buttress with a steep and exhilarating final pitch. Starts in the centre of the foot of the buttress.

1)   80 ft./24 m. Climb a broken rib to a stance and large flake belay in a recess on the left.   2)   55 ft./17 m. Move right and ascend diagonally rightwards for 30 ft./9 m. Traverse horizontally right and go up to a small stance and belay below and right of a steep crack.   3)   45 ft./14 m. Climb the crack. The initial move is awkward and the rest steep, but the holds are excellent. When the crack ends, move left and continue to the top on large holds.

73 **Thomas**   HS

160 ft./49 m.   *W. F. Dowlen and D. Stroud*   *1955*

Another good climb which takes the clean rib on the right-hand side of the West Buttress. Starts just left of the foot.

1)   70 ft./21 m. Ascend a groove slanting right, then straight up to below some perched blocks. Step right and climb to a ledge with a tree belay on the left.   2)   60 ft./18 m. Move back right on to the face and go up the steep cracked wall to a large ledge at the top of the ridge.   3)   30 ft./9 m. Traverse the wall on the right for a few feet, then ascend the steep and awkward wall direct to the top.

74 **Digitation**   MVS

175 ft./53 m.   *D. G. Heap, J. R. Amatt and C. B. Greenhalgh*   *1963*

An enjoyable route up the slabs on the right side of the East Buttress. Starts at a block lying against the face and directly below a large oak.

1)   35 ft./11 m. Climb the block and the slab above to a ledge and belay on the right.   2)   80 ft./24 m. Step left and ascend the shallow groove to a small overhang (runner). Pull over leftwards (awkward) and continue up on better holds to a large grass ledge and oak tree.   3)   60 ft./18 m. Climb the steep wall behind the ledge until it is possible to move easily into the corner on the left. Follow the corner to the top.

75 **Cornflake**   *   VS

200 ft./61 m.   *M. Thompson, F. Draper and J. Lindsey*   *1966*

A good route, continuously steep and exciting despite the break at half height. Lies on a buttress below and to the east of Wallowbarrow, about 100 yds./91 m. upstream from the footbridge across the Duddon between Wallowbarrow Farm and Seathwaite. Starts at a block below a cleaned rib.

1) 30 ft./9 m. Step off the block and climb the rib to a ledge and tree belay.   2)   70 ft./21 m. Climb the slab right of the corner and continue up past a ledge and an oak on steep rocks until it is possible to traverse left to the foot of an impending V-groove. The lower section of the groove is rather blank, but good holds are soon reached and the top gained. Scramble up an extra 20 ft./6 m. to a belay. Walk 50 ft./15 m. right along the terrace to the foot of a wide flake crack curving up to the left.   3)   100 ft./30 m. Climb the crack and make an exciting hand traverse along the crest of the flake to a niche. Gain the top of the flake and step into the groove above. Follow this to a grassy ledge, then cross a mossy slab to the right and continue up easier ground to the top. Descend the crag to the west.

WINTER CLIMBING

Due to the relatively low altitude of the crags in this area, there is little of interest except in a very hard winter. There are short gullies on the crags overlooking Seathwaite Tarn in the Duddon valley, and in the Eskdale the crags below the ridge joining Slight Side to Scafell may offer some short climbs. The head of Little Narrowcove on Scafell Pike may also have some short routes.

CONISTON

Coniston is a useful centre for the southern Lake District but tends to get very crowded at peak holiday times. The main climbing attraction here is Dow Crag, with a variety of big mountain routes and many shorter problems. In addition, there are several smaller crags round Levers Water and elsewhere which offer numerous shorter climbs in pleasant surroundings, despite the old mine workings and the expanding quarry activities. The area is shown on the Eskdale and Duddon map.

Access

By road from Greenodd to the south, Ambleside to the east, and from Duddon (via Wrynose Pass) from the west. There is a frequent bus service from Ambleside and weekday service from Ulverston, the nearest railway station. Those on foot approaching from the Duddon valley can take the pleasant Walna Scar road.

Accommodation and camping

The official camp is at Lands Point, south of Coniston village near the lake (304964), but some good sites can be found below Coniston Old Man on the Walna Scar road (up the steep hill behind the disused station, then follow an unmetalled road for about half a mile to just past the point where a steep road goes up to a quarry on the right (282968). A good bivouac site can be found in some large boulders in the scree below Dow Crag.

There are many hotels and guest-houses in Coniston village and also some inns and guest-houses in Torver to the south. There is a youth hostel in the village (Far End, 302980) and another in the Coppermines Valley (289986). In addition, there are many small club huts in the area.

Food and drink

Coniston is well equipped with hotels, cafés and pubs. The nearest bar to the crags is in the Sun Inn (300975). Licensing hours are 11–3, 5.30–10.30; Sun. 12–2, 7–10.30. There are several shops in Coniston; early closing days: Thurs. and Sat. Torver has some pleasant inns.

Garages and car hire

Hellens Garage, Broughton Road, Coniston (tel. 41253), is open until 9 p.m. (winter 8 p.m.) for petrol, and runs a taxi service. Hadwin's Garage, Torver (tel. 41317 or 41494), runs a 24-hr. breakdown service. The nearest car hire is at Ulverston (tel.

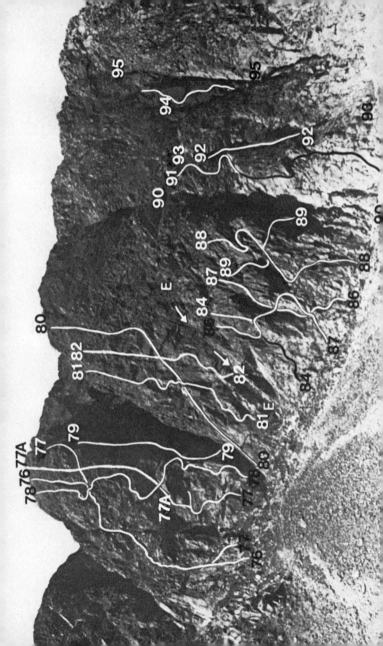

53651; after hours 57712) or Windermere (tel. 2000 or 2839). In addition to Hellens Garage, there are taxis at Ambleside (tel. 3003 or 33172), Windermere (tel. 2033, 2355 or 3439) and Ulverston (tel. 53962 or 55428).

General services

Public toilets can be found in Coniston. There are public telephones in Coniston and Torver. The nearest equipment shops are in Ambleside, 7 miles away.

Mountain rescue

There is a manned post in Coniston at Dow Crag House (305976; tel. Coniston 330). In addition, there is an unmanned post at the foot of Dow Crag (263979). For assistance, go to the rescue post or telephone the police, whichever is quicker.

DOW CRAG   (263978)

Dow Crag is the most readily accessible big mountain crag for those approaching the Lake District from the south. Since it has a good variety of long climbs, it has always been a popular pilgrimage for those aspiring to higher things. The rock is sound and compact and gives enjoyable climbing in good conditions, but when wet can resemble verglas in texture and temperature. If the prevailing wind is from the north, the crag feels much colder than its altitude would suggest.

Access

From Coniston, take the road up the steep hill behind the disused railway station and follow the unmetalled road (the Walna Scar road) below Coniston Old Man. Shortly after passing through two rock gateways, a path leaves the track on the right. Follow this, passing below some old quarries on the west flank of the Old Man, and round a rocky spur to reach Goat's Water. The crag lies above the tarn and is reached by a steep diagonal ascent up the scree. The crag can also be reached from Torver by a path crossing the Walna Scar road just above the rock gateways. From the Duddon valley, follow the Walna Scar road to the watershed, and take the ridge over Brown Pike and Buck Pike to the top of the crag.

Descent: For those climbs which finish at the top of the crag, the best descent is on the left (south) down a slanting scree rake to

Dow Crag
E = Easy Terrace, used for descent

the south of Easy Gully. Easy Gully, which bounds 'A' Buttress on the left, is another possible descent route but one not recommended in the presence of other parties, due to the danger of rockfall. Most of the routes on 'B' and 'C' Buttresses finish on Easy Terrace, and the best descent from this is on the left (some scrambling, awkward in the dark or in bad conditions).

76 Arête, Chimney and Crack   MS

360 ft./110 m.   *T. C. Ormiston-Chant, T. M. G. Parker and S. H. Gordon   1910*

A long and interesting route, marred slightly by a broken middle section. Start at the lowest point of the left-hand side of 'A' Buttress.
1)   70 ft./21 m. Climb the Arête on good holds to a rock ledge. Continue up the wall with increasing difficulty to an overhung ledge.   2)   35 ft./11 m. Move left and up a crack to large block belays.   3)   70 ft./21 m. Easy grass and rock slanting right to a recess of blocks.   4)   25 ft./8 m. Move right to below the Chimney.   5)   30 ft./9 m. The Chimney, passing an awkward chockstone.   6)   40 ft./27 m. The exposed ledge is traversed to the right to below a chimney-crack.   7)   90 ft./27 m. The Crack is exposed but furnished with good holds all the way to the top.

77 Gordon and Craig's Route   **   HVD

310 ft./94 m.   *S. H. Gordon, A. Craig and party   1909*

A very good climb of its standard, tracing the easiest way up the buttress. Care is required in the choice of belays, as there has been at least one serious accident on the upper section of the climb. Start at a scoop sloping left some 40 ft./12 m. up to the right from the start of Arête, Chimney and Crack. Many scratches hereabouts.
1)   45 ft./14 m. The scoop leads to a good belay.   2)   35 ft./11 m. Step left and move up to ledges leading to join Arête, Chimney and Crack.   3)–6)   165 ft./50 m. As for the same pitches of the previous climb.   7)   20 ft./6 m. Follow a slab from the right-hand end of the traverse into a niche.   8)   40 ft./12 m. Continue up to the right to a ledge of blocks and climb an exposed crack to a ledge. This pitch is the hardest on the climb. Scramble up left to the summit ridge.

Rick Graham pulling out of the Cave on Samba Pa Ti

77A **Isengard/Samba Pa Ti**   ***   E2   (4b, 5b, 5b, 4b)

350 ft./107 m.   *L. Brown and R. McHardy   1962/A. Hyslop and R. Graham   1977*

An excellent way up this big buttress, with two contrasting but equally difficult pitches. It takes a vague crackline to gain the cave of Eliminate A, then pulls boldly through the roof. Start 15 ft./4 m. left of Eliminate A below the obvious short corner-crack.
1)   30 ft./9 m. (4b) Up the crack, then move right to a stance and awkward belay.   2)   130 ft./40 m. (5b) Climb the steepening slab, bearing left, until a hard move through a bulge leads to a long horizontal ledge. Move right a few feet to a bulging crack. Climb it to the overhang and pull through this at its weakest point to gain the slab. Up to belay in the large cave.   3)   100 ft./30 m. (5b) Climb the right edge of the slab to overhang and pull straight over on good holds. Continue up the impending groove, trending rightwards, to the next bulge. Pass it on the right, then move leftwards to belay on a ledge below the obvious crack (Gordon and Craig's).   4)   90 ft./27 m. (4b) Take a line 10 ft./3 m. right of this crack.

78 **Eliminate 'A'**   ***   VS

375 ft./114 m.   *H. S. Gross and G. Basterfield   1923*

A magnificent route, wending its way up the walls and overhangs of the right-hand side of the buttress. All difficulties are adequately protected. Start at a grassy ledge at the foot of the right-hand side of the buttress overlooking Great Gully.
1)   45 ft./14 m. A spiral ascent to the right is made until a crack containing a loose spike can be climbed on to a grass ledge with belay 8 ft./2 m. above.   2)   60 ft./18 m. Mantelshelf on to the belay, and continue up a line of scoops and grooves to a recess under an overhang. Move awkwardly left on to a slab and up on better holds to a good ledge and belay.   3)   15 ft./4 m. Move round to the right and up to an overhang block ledge.   4)   50 ft./15 m. The Rochers perchés pitch. (The blocks which gave the pitch its name have long since disappeared.) Move left on to the wall and make an awkward move on to a small ledge in the corner. Step down to the left to a good thread to protect the second, and cross a slab to a belay in the Cave.   5)   55 ft./17 m. Follow the exposed flake up to the left and up a short chimney to a good ledge and belays.   6)   65 ft./20 m. An exposed pitch. Traverse right across a delicate slab to the foot of a shallow

groove which leads on good holds to the Gordon and Craig traverse.   7)   85 ft./26 m. The crack is climbed to the top, or, more difficult but distinctly artificial, climb a shallow groove 12 ft./4 m. left of the crack and step right to a flake almost in the crack. Climb the overhang and a shallow groove leading leftwards to the top.

79 **Sidewalk**   *   E2   (5b, 5a, 5b, 4b, 5a)
305 ft./93 m.   *L. Brown and B. Stevens   1960*
This formidable climb traces a line up the right-hand arête of 'A' Buttress overlooking Great Gully. Although the first pitch is the hardest, the climb remains serious and exposed right to the top. Start in Great Gully.
1)   55 ft./17 m. (5b) Climb the crack on the left of the boulder. Move left into an impending scoop and climb up to a small ledge.   2)   30 ft./9 m. (5a) The corner crack is smooth and strenuous but short. A good ledge on Eliminate 'A' is reached.   3)   50 ft./15 m. (5b) Move right below the steep wall and pull over a tiny overhang to gain a shallow corner (runners). Step out right into the prominent dogleg crack and move up to an exposed ledge.   4)   70 ft./21 m. (4b) Go up easier ground above, trending first right then left, to a belay below the shallow groove. Care is required with loose blocks on this and the next pitch.   5)   105 ft./32 m. (5a) Climb the shallow groove to the overhang and follow the slanting crack out to the left to the top of the crag.

80 **Giant's Crawl**   **   D
420 ft./128 m.   *E. T. W. and D. T. Addyman and X. Stobart   1909*
A fine climb which takes the band of slabs which crosses the steep upper half of 'B' Buttress in a diagonal line from the foot of Great Gully. Starts immediately right of the foot of the Gully.
1)   60 ft./18 m. Climb easy slabs and traverse left along a narrow ledge to the foot of a crack.   2)   80 ft./24 m. Go up the crack for 30 ft./9 m., then continue up the slab to a good rock ledge. Walk up to the right to reach belays.   3)   30 ft./9 m. Easily up for a few feet then more slab climbing on the left to another ledge and small belays.   4)   90 ft./27 m. Continue up the slabs above, taking a central line and passing ledges with poor belays. A large grass ledge overlooking Easy Terrace is reached (possible escape by traversing down to the right to reach

the Terrace). 5) 40 ft./12 m. Traverse a ledge to the foot of an overhanging corner. 6) 60 ft./18 m. Climb the difficult crack up the corner to a good ledge. Walk round to the left to another crack in a steep groove, which has better holds and leads to a belay on the right. 7) 60 ft./18 m. Easier climbing and scrambling leads to the top.

81 **Nimrod** ** E1 (5a, 5b, 5c)
250 ft./76 m. *D. Miller and D. Kirby 1962*
Although artificial in its line, the climbing on this varied route is both hard and sustained. The first two pitches lie up the steep walls below the slab of Giant's Crawl. Start up a shallow groove at the left end of the wall and above the foot of Easy Terrace.
1) 100 ft./30 m. (5a) Gain the groove from the right and climb it to a small overhang. This is overcome using doubtful flakes and a long delicate traverse is then made to the right to the foot of a shallow groove. The best stance is 10 ft./3 m. below. 2) 50 ft./15 m. (5b) Climb the right wall of the groove until the wall steepens, then make a committing move into the groove. More hard moves then lead to the slab of Giant's Crawl. 3) 100 ft./30 m. (5c) Move across the slabs to the foot of an open corner. Climb this with difficulty to a small ledge and continue up a thin crack to a very small spike. Traverse left to an arête and move up to a small ledge. Turn an overhang on the left and move up to easy ground. Continue to a good stance on the right. Descend rightwards to Easy Terrace.

82 **Holocaust** *** E4 (6a, 5a, 5b)
240 ft./73 m. R. Matheson, G. Fleming and J. Poole *1971/Free, as described: R. Matheson 1977*
Brilliant technical wall climbing, taking steep ground right of Nimrod. Start from the embedded boulders on a grass ledge/ramp above Easy Terrace, right of Nimrod's second pitch.
1) 120 ft./36 m. (6a) Take the shallow groove to a recess. Trend right up the steepening rib until moves rightwards across the overhanging wall enable a hidden pocket to be reached. (This move is often jumped!) Pull directly up steep ground to the obvious recess. Go up diagonally rightwards to a runner below steeper ground. Move delicately left and up to a ledge leading to

Rob Knight on the crux of Holocaust

87

the large slab of Giant's Crawl.   2)   70 ft./21 m. (5a) The clean
overhanging wall above is taken on its right by a groove. Up this
until a swing left gives access to a quartz-marked gangway slab.
Follow this to a recessed grass ledge.   3)   50 ft./15 m. (5b)
Climb the crack on the left of the ledge to a further good ledge.
Descend diagonally right to reach Easy Terrace.

83 **Pink Panther**   **   E3   (5c)
140 ft./43 m.   *R. and M. R. Matheson   1973*
Another delectable wall climb taking an eliminate line left of
Leopard's Crawl. Protection is spaced and requires thought.
Start from an embedded flake above and left of Leopard's
Crawl.   1)   140 ft./43 m. (5c) Step on to the wall from the
sharp spike and follow a scoop running up slightly rightwards
until stopped by bulging rocks. Traverse right until it is possible
to stand on a stunted flake. Pull up and right into a groove.
(Lower variations traversing right with hands at flake level are
harder.) Follow the groove, then the wall on the left, to gain a
large slab. Traverse right under the overhangs to a scoop; this is
followed to the top.

84 **Leopard's Crawl**   *   HVS   (5a, 4c)
160 ft./49 m.   *R. J. Birkett, L. Muscroft and T. Hill   1947*
This very open climb takes the steep wall below the final crack of
Murray's Route. Poor protection and sustained climbing
combine to make it unusually serious for its length. Start at a
bridged block midway between the stretcher box and the foot of
Easy Rake.
1)   90 ft./27 m. (5a) Pull on to the wall above the block, make a
slightly descending hand traverse to the right and move up into a
shallow groove (poor runners). Traverse very delicately across
the slab to a niche below a shallow groove, and go up this to a
good ledge below the last pitch of Murray's Route.   2)   70
ft./21 m. (4c) Traverse right for 15 ft./4 m. and climb a shallow
groove to the top of the crag, and Easy Terrace.

85 **Tarkus/Catacomb**   **   E1   (5b, 4c, 5a, 5b, 5b)
390 ft./119 m.   *R. B. Matheson and M. R. Matheson   1972*
A good combination which is both delicate and strenuous.
Protection is adequate but not always easy to arrange. Starts just
below the bridged block of Leopard's Crawl.

88

1) 110 ft./33 m. (5b) The objective is a hidden flake crack 15 ft./4 m. to the right. This is best reached by moving up, then making a descending traverse with the aid of a small flake. Go up the wall, slightly leftwards, to a horizontal break and better holds. Traverse right to a sentry box, then climb the impending groove to a spike. Continue straight up the delicate wall and easier crack to join Murray's Route. 2) 70 ft./21 m. (4c) Traverse right for 15 ft./4 m. and climb a shallow groove to the top, and Easy Terrace (pitch 2 of Leopard's Crawl). Scramble over easy ledges to below an obvious traverse line beneath the overhangs, high on the steep wall well right of Nimrod. Start at the foot of a wide crack at the upper end of the upper terrace (Hyacinth Terrace). 3) 120 ft./36 m. (5a) Climb the crack, steep then overhanging, then move left using good flake holds to an overhung gangway. Follow this, then hand-traverse to a ledge. Go diagonally left to a horizontal fault leading to Giant's Crawl. Belay 30 ft./9 m. up on the right. 4) 40 ft./12 m. (5b) A leftward-slanting line leads to a grass ledge in the centre of the upper wall. 5) 50 ft./15 m. (5b) Climb the overlaps to the right and then broken cracks to the top. Descend diagonally right to Easy Terrace.

86 **Murray's Route** *** S
250 ft./76 m. *D. G. Murray, W. J. Borrowman and B. L. Martin 1918*
A magnificent route, one of the best of its standard in the Lakes. It takes a generally leftward-trending line up 'B' Buttress, starting just left of the stretcher box.
1) 65 ft./20 m. Climb the deep V-chimney to the overhang. Move out left across a very polished slab (good fingerholds in the crack) to a resting place, then move up to a position below the overhang. Pass this on the left with difficulty and move up into the big corner. 2) 55 ft./17 m. Go diagonally right over a perched flake and move up the arête to the left of a chimney. Step into the chimney and climb up to a deep cave. 3) 35 ft./11 m. make a steep pull up a crack above the chimney and cross a big flake to a ledge in the corner, above the first stance. 4) 35

Overleaf left : Eliminate 'A', Dow Crag

Overleaf right : Murray's Route, Dow Crag

ft./11 m. The V-chimney on the left is followed by an exposed traverse along another flake to a stance below the final crack.   5)   60 ft./18 m. The very smooth crack leads to the top.

87   **Murray's Direct**   **   VS

155 ft./47 m.   *Various parties   1922–45*

A series of variations on Murray's Route which gives a sustained direct route up the buttress. Starts at a vertical embedded flake 40 ft./12 m. left of the start of Murray's Route.

1)   40 ft./12 m. Tiger Traverse. From the top of the flake move on to the wall and traverse round to the right until the slanting slab can be gained. Follow this delicately to the right to ledges, belay on higher ledges on a large flake on the right.   2)   35 ft./11 m. Climb the steep wall above the large flake, moving left to a stance below a vertical layback crack.   3)   80 ft./11 m. Move up into the corner and climb the crack for 15 ft./4 m. to good footholds. Continue up the crack to below the large overhang and traverse right to the foot of another crack. Climb this to a grass ledge, then scrambling leads to Easy Terrace.

88   **Abraham's Route**   S

255 ft./78 m.   *G. D. and A. P. Abraham and F. T. Phillipson   1903*

A pleasant route with an interesting final pitch. Starts up a grassy groove at the foot of the buttress.

1)   45 ft./14 m. Climb the groove, past grass ledges, to a recess with a belay on the right.   2)   35 ft./11 m. Step back across the groove and continue until it is possible to traverse 10 ft./3 m. left to a belay below a steep wall.   3)   45 ft./14 m. Ascend the open groove in the steep wall above. The climbing eases after 20 ft./6 m. and eventually the left end of a long ledge is reached.

4)   60 ft./18 m. Climb slabs on the right; continue to below an impending wall, with a large belay on the right.   5)   70 ft./21 m. Descend to the left for about 30 ft./9 m., until a difficult move can be made to cross the sloping rib on the left to reach a sloping foothold. Continue up the slab above to reach a small spike, then move left again and climb an easier slab and broken ground to reach Easy Terrace.

89   **Woodhouse's Route**   *   HVD

190 ft./58 m.   *G. F. and A. J. Woodhouse   1905*

A polished and strenuous route, especially in wet conditions.

Fortunately the pitches are short and the stances large. Starts by scrambling up towards Central Chimney for 100 ft./30 m. to the foot of a wide groove below and to the left of the large pinnacle set in the left wall of the Chimney.

1)   30 ft./9 m. Climb the groove to the foot of the pinnacle. Follow the wide crack on the left to the crevasse behind the pinnacle.   2)   35 ft./11 m. Move back left and enter a chimney with difficulty. Climb this with good holds on the left to a ledge and belay. Move left and traverse on grassy ledges to reach a deep recess.   3)   30 ft./9 m. Climb the polished wall on the left with some help for the right foot from a deep crack. A problematical pitch, leading to a ledge on the left.   4)   45 ft./14 m. Ascend the easy arête above the ledge to a large grassy terrace. Walk right to a large block belay below a steep crack.   5)   30 ft./9 m. Climb the crack, with a difficult start, or alternatively the delicate easy-angled slab running diagonally right below the wall. Follow a crevasse to the right to another steep wall with a projecting block and recess.   6)   20 ft./6 m. Climb the wall left of the block with difficulty.

90 **Central Chimney**   *   MS
130 ft./40 m.   *O. G. Jones and G. Ellis   1897*
Takes the corner crack between 'B' Buttress and 'C' Buttress, with a steep left wall and a slabby right wall. Scramble up broken ground for 100 ft./30 m. from the path to the foot of the corner proper.

1)   35 ft./11 m. The first 20 ft./6 m. is climbed using large wedged flakes. The remainder of the pitch is much smoother and is climbed with the left foot in the crack. Traverse right from a recess for 10 ft./3 m. to a ledge and flake belay.   2)   40 ft./12 m. Move back and climb the Chimney, using the right wall, to reach another recess with small belays on the right.   3)   55 ft./17 m. Take to the rib on the right and climb on good holds to a small flat ledge, then continue up to the cave with more difficulty. Bridge up the cave until the left wall can be gained and good holds lead to the top. Easy Terrace can be reached by scrambling up to the left.

91 **'C' Ordinary Route**   ***   D
360 ft./110 m.   *G. F. and A. J. Woodhouse   1904*
A worthwhile route in all weather conditions, particularly

suitable for beginners. Starts just left of the foot of 'C' Buttress.
1) 50 ft./15 m. Climb the crest of the buttress to a narrow ledge on top of a large flake. 2) 55 ft./17 m. Go up to a small ledge and follow the polished slabby scoop above to easier ground and ledges. A good ledge with a fallen flake is reached. 3) 35 ft./11 m. Climb an open scoop, starting from the left end of the ledge, to another ledge on the right. 4) 35 ft./11 m. Ascend easy rocks leftwards to a ledge on the corner of the buttress. 5) 25 ft./8 m. Climb corner of buttress or an easier groove on the right to a ledge. 6) 50 ft./15 m. Move right and ascend to a smooth slab, which is followed to a large ledge. A ledge with better belays is reached up on the right. 7) 45 ft./14 m. Traverse left for 10 ft./3 m. and climb the wall on the left of the crack above. Move left to below a small cave and climb a wide crack to the top of a large flake to the left of the cave. From the top of the flake, step up left then back right to a small stance and good belay 10 ft./3 m. above the flake. 8) 65 ft./20 m. Traverse slabs to the right to a good ledge. Continue rightwards, following a gangway round a bulge to a ledge. A short wall on the left followed by a horizontal traverse leads easily to Easy Terrace.

92 **Eliminate 'C'** MVS
150 ft./46 m. *H. S. Gross and G. Basterfield 1922*
A good climb in grand surroundings following a line parallel to Intermediate Gully. Start at the top of the second pitch of that climb (the horrors of its first two pitches can be avoided by scrambling on the right).
1) 85 ft./26 m. A diagonal crack leads out to the left to a small ledge. Step down to the left and then make a delicate move up the arête to a good ledge. Step right and continue up the arête on good holds to a fine stance overlooking the gully. 2) 65 ft./20 m. On the right is a fine slab, undercut at its base. Climb the corner on the left for a few feet, then cross the slab on small holds to a very prominent spike. Climb the arête on good holds and finish up a leftward-slanting groove.

93 **Intermediate Gully** ** HS
170 ft./52 m. *E. A. and J. H. Hopkinson and X. Campbell 1895*
One of the finest gully climbs in the district, offering both

Eliminate 'C', Dow Crag

94

sustained and strenuous climbing throughout its length on perfect rock. Scramble up the gully for 100 ft./3 m. until the walls close in. Usually wet.

1) 30 ft./9 m. A strenuous crack and short chimney, climbed by its right wall, leads to a comfortable recess and belay.   2) 25 ft./8 m. Awkward bridging is used to overcome the smooth chockstone.   3) 70 ft./21 m. Step left into the steep crack which leads strenuously to easier rock. When this steepens, climb the left wall to a recess below a large chock.   4) 15 ft./4 m. Struggle over the jammed stone to gain a cave.   5) 30 ft./9 m. Move up to the right then step left to gain a crack in the left wall which is followed to Easy Terrace.

94 **Great Central Route**   *   HVS   (4c, 5a, 5b, 4a)
205 ft./62 m.   *J. I. Roper, G. S. Bower and party   1919*
Above the wide funnel of Easter Gully is an amphitheatre dominated by an imposing pillar. Great Central Route ascends this pillar. Start by scrambling up Easter Gully into the amphitheatre to a point just left of the nose of the pillar.
1) 45 ft./14 m. (4c) Climb the nose and the slabs above to a ledge below a vertical crack (South America Crack).   2) 35 ft./11 m. (5a) Gain the crack from the right, and layback to reach the wider part. Easier climbing leads to the Bandstand.   3) 60 ft./18 m. (5b) The difficult wall above. Start just left of a slight nose, then, after a step right, climb to a tiny ledge. Continue up a crack to a good ledge (runner under overhang). Traverse left across the slab and move up Broadrick's Crack to belay.   4) 65 ft./20 m. (4a) Move right on to the wall and climb up until it is possible to gain a ledge on the right. Traverse to the right-hand end, then step down and move round the corner to a slab. Follow this on good holds to the top.

95 **Hopkinson's Crack**   **   HS
150 ft./46 m.   *C. Hopkinson and O. Koecher   1895*
A classic crack climb, up the right-hand corner of the amphitheatre, on clean sound rock. Start by scrambling up Easter Gully, with one moderate cave pitch, into the amphitheatre.
1) 50 ft./15 m. Climb the crack to a good ledge on the left. Thread belay below the steep crack on the left.   2) 40 ft./12 m. Move back into the corner and climb up on decreasing holds

until another ledge on the left leads to a belay.   3)   60 ft./18 m.
Re-enter the crack and climb it to the top. Belay 10 ft./3 m. up to
the right.

The best descent is to traverse left on grass ledges to the easy
upper half of Intermediate Gully, which is descended to Easy
Terrace.

WINTER CLIMBING

Despite its cold reputation, Dow Crag is not often in good
condition for winter climbing. When conditions are suitable Easy
Gully, to the left of 'A' Buttress, gives a relatively easy route, and
the other gullies give climbs of varying degrees of difficulty. Some
of the easier summer climbs, such as Giant's Crawl, can be
exciting winter routes.

GREAT LANGDALE

This easily accessible valley runs in a westerly direction from
Ambleside. Famous for its trio of Pikes, it ranks as the most
popular area in the Lake District for both climbing and walking.
Because of this popularity the crags are often overcrowded, and
those preferring peace and quiet are advised to go elsewhere at
peak holiday times. There is a good selection of both high
mountain crags and valley outcrops, with climbs in all grades. In
general, the rock is sound and the protection good, and as many
of the crags face south, they are quick to dry. The more remote
Deer Bield Crag is described in this section also, although it does
not lie in Great Langdale itself.

Access

There is a regular bus service from Ambleside to Langdale. Cars
are still allowed up the valley, though the road is heavily
congested in the summer months and the official car-parks
(285061, 285059, 295064) cannot cope, filling up very quickly.
Langdale can also be reached from Duddon by car, via Wrynose
Pass and the Blea Tarn road.

Accommodation and camping

Camping is allowed on the official site a the head of Langdale
(285059) and at Chapel Stile (315053), and there are several
climbing huts (FRCC, Wayfarers, Achille Ratti) about a mile
from the valley head at Raw Head (304067) and one (Yorkshire
Ramblers) in Little Langdale (309029). Langdale is well served
with guest-houses and hotels, although it is necessary to book
well in advance for peak holiday times. Many more hotels and
guest-houses can be found in Ambleside, 7 miles away. There are
youth hostels at High Close (338052) and Elterwater (327046)
and in Ambleside. There is an accommodation bureau in Church
Street, Ambleside (tel. 2582).

Food and drink

Langdale and Ambleside are well provided with places to eat
and drink. There are bars at the head of Langdale at both the
Old and New Dungeon Ghyll Hotel, and the Stickle Barn, which
has a large ground-floor bar (bar meals) and a first-floor
cafeteria (open late in summer). In Ambleside, the Golden Rule
is strongly recommended (near the Ambleside Climbing Wall).
Normal licensing hours 11–3, 5.30–10.30; Sun. 12–2, 7–10.30.
There is a small shop on the Langdale campsite; a PO/general

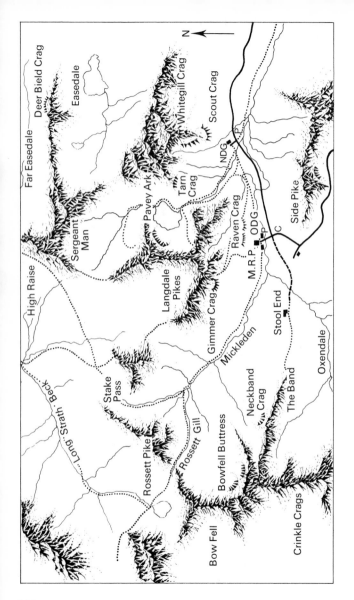

store (open all day Sat. and Sun.) and a Co-op (early closing: Sat.) in Chapel Stile; and shops at Elterwater (early closing: Sat.) and Ambleside (early closing: Thurs.)

Garages and car hire

There are petrol-pumps at Chapel Stile (Langdales Hotel, closes 11 p.m.) and an AA garage with 24-hr. breakdown service in Ambleside (tel. 33273 or 32025). Taxis are available at Ambleside (tel. 32205, 32474, 33003 or 33172) and car hire at Windermere (tel. 2000 or 2839).

General services

There is a tourist advice bureau in the centre of Ambleside, and most general services, including equipment shops. Public toilets can be found at Chapel Stile and telephones at Chapel Stile, Elterwater and Skelwith Bridge.

Mountain rescue

For assistance ring the local police (999). There is a MR post at the Old Dungeon Ghyll Hotel (286061; tel. Langdale 272), and first-aid boxes at the New Dungeon Ghyll Hotel (295065) and at the Co-op in Chapel Stile.

WHITE GHYLL CRAG (298071)

This easily accessible crag lies some 800 yds./730 m. NE of the New Dungeon Ghyll Hotel, and is very obvious as a notch in the skyline. It provides a number of climbs of about 150–250 ft./46–76 m. in length, mainly in the higher standards.

Approach: Use the car-park opposite the New Dungeon Ghyll Hotel. A footbridge behind the hotel is crossed to reach Mill Ghyll Farm. A path leads first steeply up the hillside then right over a stile to a wood. Pass below this to gain the stony bed of the Ghyll. Follow this to the crag.

Descent: The crag is divided by a series of ledges into an upper and lower section. The ledges (Easy Rake) provide a convenient means of descent from climbs on the lower crag and the right-hand section of the upper crag.

96 **Slip Knot** *** MVS
150 ft./46 m.   *R. J. Birkett and L. Muscroft   1947*
An interesting climb with very good holds. Starts on the lower crag directly below a corner, capped by a large overhang, opposite a sycamore.

1)   85 ft./26 m. Easy climbing leads to the foot of the corner

White Ghyll, Lower Crag

102

proper. Follow this for 20 ft./6 m. then a line of good holds leads out up the right wall to a good ledge below the overhang.

2)   65 ft./20 m. Traverse left below the overhang into the corner. Move delicately on to the arête and climb this, with an exhilarating move over the bulge, to a niche on the left. A steep wall leads to easy climbing. Easy Rake can be reached by traversing shattered ledges to the left.

97   **Laugh Not**   *   HVS (5a)
115 ft./35 m.   *J. Brown, R. Mosley and T. Waghorn*   *1953*
This is the open corner to the right of Slip Knot. It is not as steep as that climb, but what it lacks in height and steepness, it makes up in smoothness. The protection is very good. Start by scrambling up to the right from the foot of Slip Knot to the foot of the corner.

1)   115 ft./35 m. (5a) The first few feet of the corner are easy. After a small overhang, a finger-jamming crack is followed strenuously to a narrow ledge on the left wall. Above this the crack widens and is climbed more easily to a rapidly vanishing tree stump. A few feet higher, a crack leads out up the right wall to a ledge below the overhang. From here, either step down and cross a blank slab to the arête on the right, or make an alarming hand-traverse on the lip to the same point. Take a belay immediately to avoid rope drag. The top of Slip Knot is reached by scrambling up to the left.

98   **Man of Straw**   *   E1   (5a)
95 ft./29 m.   *J. A. Austin and D. G. Roberts*   *1965*
Takes the groove up the right arête of the Laugh Not wall. From the foot of Laugh Not, scramble right to below a wide crack.

1)   95 ft./29 m. (5a) The crack leads to a ledge below a smooth groove. Bridge up the groove to just below the overhang, then step left on to the rib. Pull up this to a small foot-ledge. Toe-tap right to the arête and up to belay (low) in a little corner.

99   **Hollin Groove**   S
150 ft./46 m.   *R. J. Birkett and L. Muscroft*   *1945*
A varied and interesting climb taking the conspicuous V-groove 50 ft./15 m. to the left of the sycamore. Start at the foot of a short steep crack.

1)   40 ft./12 m. The crack is strenuous. At its top move left and

up to a stance below a steep wall. 2) 30 ft./9 m. Move left and up into a groove below a holly. A very steep move to the right on good holds leads to a stance below the main groove. 3) 80 ft./24 m. The groove is followed to Easy Rake. Scramble up to a belay. The climb can be extended above Easy Rake by climbing the ridge above at VD standard.

100 **White Ghyll Wall** ** MVS

205 ft./62 m. *R. J. Birkett, L. Muscroft and T. Hill 1946*

A fine route, exposed in its upper section. This climb is on the upper crag and starts near a triangular cave some 35 ft./11 m. left of where Easy Rake runs into the ground.

1) 50 ft./15 m. The rib on the right of the cave leads to a ledge below a large overhang. (Perhaps Not, a loose HVS, leads across the overhung slab to the left.) 2) 30 ft./9 m. Traverse right to a block belay. (This point can be reached by an easy traverse left from the highest point of Easy Rake, thus providing a useful extension to the climbs on the lower crag.) 3) 50 ft./15 m. An undercut scoop is climbed past a difficult overhang to a good spike. Move diagonally left up the steep wall until a delicate traverse can be made into a hidden groove – belay 10 ft./3 m. above. 4) 95 ft./29 m. A diagonal ascent of the slab on the left is followed by easier climbing on good holds to the top of the crag.

101 **Gordian Knot** ** VS

200 ft./61 m. *J. W. Haggas and Miss E. Bull 1940*

A magnificent route, breaking through the central overhangs via a hanging corner. Start at the first obvious break to the left of White Ghyll Wall.

1) 60 ft./18 m. The steepening slab is climbed with increasing difficulty to a niche. Opposing spike belays. 2) 50 ft./15 m. Traverse easily right to the foot of a steep corner. The first few moves are problematical and lead to a small ledge on the right wall. Good holds lead back into the corner which is followed to a chockstone belay. 3) 80 ft./24 m. The wide crack is climbed to a good ledge on the right. Continue up the wall above on good holds to the top of the crag.

102 **Haste Not** *** VS

190 ft./58 m. *R. J. Birkett and L. Muscroft 1948*

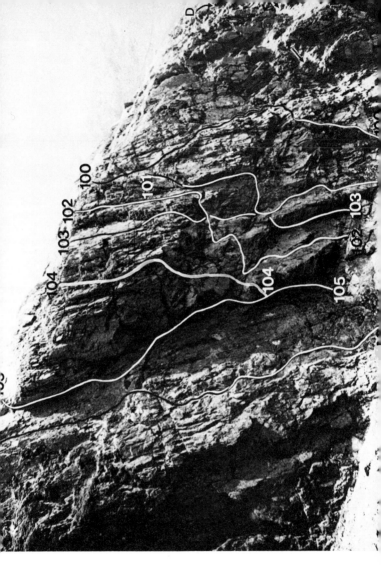

White Ghyll, Upper Crag
D = Descent route

A climb of sustained interest and spectacular situations. A recess immediately left of Gordian Knot marks the start of the climb.

1)   70 ft./21 m. The left-hand corner of the recess is climbed to the overhang. Cross the wall on the left, with difficulty, to reach a groove in the slab. The groove is followed, via an awkward bulge, to a large platform and block belay.   2)   50 ft./15 m. An exposed traverse is made to the right to a prow. Climb the slab to an overhang (runner) then make a series of sensational moves along a narrow gangway into a groove. Swing round the rib on the right to the ledge above the second pitch of Gordian Knot. Move along the ledge to a belay.   3)   70 ft./21 m. Move back left and climb the wall above past an inverted-V overhang. Easier climbing leads to the top of the crag.

103 **Haste Not Direct**   **   E2 (5a, 5c, 4a)
Pitch 1:   P. Allison and N. Smithers   1962/Pitch 2:   J. A. Austin and C. E. Davies   1965/Pitch 2 (last 30 ft./9 m.):   J. A. Austin and R. Valentine   1971
Two fine pitches become increasingly difficult. Starts up the long corner on the right of the normal route.

1)   70 ft./21 m. (5a) Climb the corner to a large roof. Move out right on to the rib and belay on the right as for Gordian Knot.   2)   85 ft./26 m. (5c) Enter the narrow groove above on the left with difficulty, pullng out left to a resting place and peg runner after a few feet. Continue up the slab and overhang to the traverse of Haste Not. Climb the very strenuous bulging crack above.   3)   60 ft./18 m. (4a) Continue up walls and slabs to the top.

104 **Paladin**   **   E3   (–, 5c)
155 ft./47 m.   *R. Matheson   1970/Free: 1971*
Takes an improbable and impressive groove rightwards through the overhangs right of White Ghyll Chimney. Start at the Chimney.

1) 45 ft./14 m. Up the Chimney to a ledge and block belay.   2)   110 ft./33 m. (5c) Up directly above the belay, pulling on to a wall. Step right into the groove and climb this until stopped by a bulge. Pull leftwards and up the wall. Continue directly to the top.

The Gordian Knot, White Ghyll Crag

105 **White Ghyll Chimney** * S

185 ft./56 m. *H. B. Lyon, J. Herbert and H. P. Cain 1923*

An impressive climb, for its standard, up the big cleft which separates the overhangs of the central mass from the more amenable slabs to the left.

1) 40 ft./12 m. Easy climbing up the cleft to the belay at the top of pitch 1 of Haste Not. 2) 100 ft./30 m. Scramble up into the chimney proper and climb this (often wet) with difficulty until a groove out on the left can be gained (arrange protection for the second after this move). Follow the groove to a terrace and block belay. If the chimney is very wet, it can be avoided on the left wall. 3) 45 ft./14 m. Make an awkward diagonal ascent to the right to regain the chimney, and follow this steeply to the top.

106 **White Ghyll Slabs** * S

225 ft./68 m. *G. Barker and A. T. Hargreaves 1930*

A fine open route on good holds. Start about 25 ft./8 m. left of White Ghyll Chimney.

1) 90 ft./27 m. Good holds lead diagonally leftwards to a ledge below a shallow groove. Go up this to a fine spike belay on the right. 2) 55 ft./17 m. The steep wall, a few feet left of the belay, is delicate at first. Better holds then lead rightwards to a terrace and block belay. 3) 80 ft./24 m. The grooved arête leads to the top of the crag.

PAVEY ARK (286080)

Situated in a magnificent position overlooking Stickle Tarn, this large cliff rivals Gimmer Crag as the central rock-climbing attraction of the Langdale Pikes. It gives a number of climbs between 200 ft./61 m. and 300 ft./91 m. in length and of all standards. Despite its vegetated appearance, most of the climbs are on sound clean rock which is a delight to climb.

Approach: From the New Dungeon Ghyll Hotel, a direct ascent of Mill Ghyll to Stickle Tarn is the obvious approach. From the Old Dungeon Ghyll Hotel, it is best to take a traversing path from the Dungeon Ghyll Beck alongside a wall when the Mill Ghyll Path is joined about a third of the way up. Another alternative is the ascent of Middlefell Buttress (q.v.) followed by a traverse of the hillside below the summit crags of Harrison

Pavey Ark. JR = Jack's Rake

Stickle to reach Stickle Tarn.

Topography and descents: The cliff is divided into two sections by an oblique series of ledges (Jack's Rake) which runs from the bottom right-hand side of the crag to the top left. Jack's Rake is graded as an easy rock climb, but this does not prevent hordes of tourists from ascending it (and sometimes descending it at speed!) and kicking loose rocks down the crag below. It is, therefore, even more necessary than usual to wear a helmet and keep an alert look-out for falling objects, animal or mineral. The Rake provides a convenient descent from climbs below it or those ending close to the summit. Care should be exercised when descending in wet weather if wearing PAs or similar footwear. Above the foot of the Rake rises Rake End Chimney which marks the left-hand boundary of the third section of the cliff, the East Wall, which extends to the right of Rake End Chimney until the cliff fades out in grassy ledges and shallow vegetated chimneys.

Climbs below Jack's Rake

Two gullies to the left, Little Gully and Great Gully (with its great chockstone, well seen from below), provide Moderate and Difficult climbs respectively. To the right of Great Gully rises Stony Buttress, then a shallow vegetated gully separates this buttress from a sweep of slabs capped by a bulge and curving ledge system, the Crescent.

107 Crescent Climb/Gwynne's Chimney   M/D

410 ft./125 m.   *H. A. Gwynne and party   1892/F. Botterill and W. E. Palmer   1907*

A good combination suitable for most weather conditions. Start right of Stony Buttress, up a rib to the right of a dirty chimney. 1) 180 ft./55 m. Climb the rib to belay at the left end of the Crescent. 2) 50 ft./15 m. Traverse right, under the Crescent. 3) 100 ft./30 m. Scramble up to Jack's Rake. Over to the right is an obvious chimney. 4) 55 ft./17 m. Climb the chimney to belay on a yew tree. 5) 25 ft./8 m. Continue directly or, better, step right and climb the rib. It is usual to scramble off up the obvious weakness, from here. Care is required as it is a long way down.

Arcturus, pitch 3: Arthur Glencross and Tony Roberts

110

108 **Arcturus**   **   HVS   (5a, 4c, 4c)
270 ft./82 m.   *J. A. Austin and E. Metcalf   1963*
To the right of Crescent Slabs, the cliff steepens, with a
prominent overhang at half weight. This wall is defined on the
right by a grassy, rightward- slanting break with a holly at its
foot. This break is taken by Deception: a vegetated S. The route
described here takes the steep slabs and walls to the left. It is a
magnificent climb, with impressive and varied situations on
perfect rock. Start directly below the holly of Deception.
1)   120 ft./37 m. (5a) Up the wall and move left of the holly
until it is possible to get established on the impending wall which
protects the slab above. Climb the wall to a foothold on the slab
and step left, or step left below the slab and go up. Neither way is
easy. Climb the slab above, bearing slightly left to a good ledge
below the overhangs.   2)   105 ft./32 m. (4c) Step right from the
ledge and climb a shallow corner, with difficulty at first, to a
ledge on the left. Step right and follow a crack to another ledge
(good nut runner on the right). Traverse right to a small and
very exposed slab. Cross this with difficulty to a good spike, and
step down to an excellent ledge and belay.   3)50 ft./15 m. (4c)
The rib above is harder than it appears. Follow it to Jack's Rake.
A suitable continuation is Golden Slipper.

109 **Cruel Sister**   ***   E2   (5a, 5c, 5a)
230 ft./70 m.   *R. Matheson and S. Colvin   1972/Free: J. Lamb and
P. Botterill   1975*
A modern classic, taking the prominent hanging nose right of
Arcturus. Start as for Arcturus.
1)   100 ft./30 m. (5a) As for Arcturus to the small ledge above
the initial overlap. Step up on to the wall and climb slightly
rightwards to a shallow groove. Up this to the horizontal fault
and move right to belay below the overhang.   2)   80 ft./24 m.
(5c) Pull directly over the overhang and up a few feet to a peg
runner. Moving up slightly, traverse right to a block on the edge.
Move up, then bear leftwards across the wall to an overlap.
Continue over this to a steep crack leading to a good ledge at the
end of the Arcturus traverse.   3)   50 ft./15 m. (5a) Go left
across Arcturus to pull over an overlap on spaced holds. Step left
and take the obvious corner to grass ledges. Move up steeply
right, then gain a belay on the second ledge on the left.

Climbs above Jack's Rake

Above Jack's Rake, the cliff is less continuous than that below, with large ledges and easier angled rock. Above the finish of Crescent Slabs is Gwynne's Chimney, a good 80 ft./24 m. D. The first climb starts from Jack's Rake, some 20 yds./18 m. left of Gwynne's Chimney.

110 **Golden Slipper** * HVS (4c, 5a, 4c)

180 ft./55 m. *J. A. Austin and R. B. Evans 1958*

This aptly named route takes the front of the slender pillar to the left of Gwynn's Chimney. The delightful second pitch, on perfect rock, is remarkable for its lack of protection!

1) 40 ft./12 m. (4c) A short wall guards the foot of the pillar. Follow a gangway up to the right to a small ledge. A series of strenuous layback moves leads to the ledges below the pillar.   2) 80 ft./24 m. (5a) Climb the steepening slab on small holds to a nut runner where the slab approaches wall angle. Move right and up to a ledge and belay. A sustained pitch.   3) 60 ft./18 m. (4c) The rib on the left to the top.

111 **Cook's Tour** VD

295 ft./90 m. *J. W. Cook and G. B. Elliot 1943*

A devious route on good rock. It takes the easiest break midway between Rake End Chimney and Gwynne's Chimney, a leftwards-facing chimney-crack. Harder in wet conditions.

1) 20 ft./6 m. The open groove to a good belay.   2) 30 ft./9 m. The steep slab above is followed by a traverse right to a large pinnacle.   3) 45 ft./14 m. Easy climbing on the left leads to ledges below the rectangular slab.   4) 75 ft./23 m. Traverse left along ledges to a flake belay.   5) 20 ft./6 m. Climb a shallow gully and move right to a grass ledge and pinnacle belay.   6 40 ft./12 m. Traverse right and up to a corner with an ash, then follow the crack behind the tree to a belay up on the left.   7) 60 ft./18 m. The slab above is climbed to a stance (but poor belay), and the wall above gives good holds for the ascent to the top.

112 **Rake End Chimney** ** D

165 ft./50 m. *G. W. Barton 1898*

A fine climb on good rock. The obvious chimney above the foot of Jack's Rake gives an all-weather climb of continuous interest.

113

1) 100 ft./30 m. (Can be split.) The chimney is followed over several chockstones to a large ledge. Good belay at the point of arrival. Walk up to another belay in a cave. 2) 65 ft./20 m. Climb on to a large chockstone at the back of the cave. Pass through an opening on to the right wall. A small cave is passed on the left to the top.

THE EAST WALL

This formidable wall gives the finest climbs on the crag. The climbs are in two groups: those on the area immediately to the right of Rake End Chimney, and those on the East Wall proper: the steep wall overlooking the scree gully running up to the right from the foot of Jake's Rake. Descent from all these climbs, including Rake End Chimney, is best made by traversing well to the right, and descending the tourist route for about 30 yds./27 m., when the top of the scree gully can be gained by the descent of a short but awkward chockstone pitch.

113 **Rake End Wall** ** VS
210 ft./64 m. *H. A. Carsten and E. Phillips 1945*
This magnificent climb takes the steep pillar immediately right of Rake End Chimney. It is a sustained climb with varied technique, good protection and perfect rock. Start 15 ft./4 m. right of Rake End Chimney.
1) 70 ft./21 m. Climb the steep wall past a prominent flake until it is necessary to make a traverse to the right to a stance on the right of a large block. 2) 35 ft./11 m. Mount the block and go up the overhanging crack above. A hidden side-hold on the left wall is of material assistance. Thread belay on the right. 3) 65 ft./20 m. From the lower left-hand end of the ledge, step left to gain the foot of the steep slab. Climb the slab into a small groove on the right of a small overhang. After a few feet, quit the groove on the left and climb the arête to the large terrace. 4) 40 ft./12 m. Walk up to the next section of the wall. Climb the arête on the right of the last pitch of Rake End Chimney to the top.

114 **The Brackenclock** * E2 (5a, 5c, 5b, 4a, –)
345 ft./105 m. *J. A. Austin, N. J. Soper and A. Faller 1970/Free: R. Valentine 1971*
An eliminate-type wall climb whose two main pitches give

114

excellent climbing. Start about 50 ft./15 m. lower than Rake End Wall, near enough in the centre of what constitutes the lowest wall of the buttress.

1)   60 ft./18 m. (5a) A shallow groove leads to the right end of a grass ledge.   2)   50 ft./15 m. (5c) This pitch is distinguished by its very rough, brown rock (almost gritstone-like). From the left end of the ledge, climb up the slab, stepping left to a niche. Continue straight up to a horizontal break beneath steep walls. Belay on the left.   3)   70 ft./21 m. (5b) Go right for 10 ft./3 m. to a small ledge below a bulging wall. Climb straight up, then right to a groove. Continue up this to a ledge below a scoop.   4)   80 ft./24 m. (4a) Up the scoop to a ledge. From the right end of the ledge, climb a slabby wall trending right to a grass ledge. Continue up slabs to a further ledge.   5)   85 ft./26 m. Take the rib 20 ft./6 m. left of the belay to the top.

115   **Stoat's Crack**   *   HS

345 ft./105 m.   *B. R. Record and J. R. Jenkins*   *1933*

Above the point where Jack's Rake runs into the ground, a subsidiary buttress lies against the main mass of the crag. The crack thus formed on the right provides the initial pitch of this varied climb.

1)   25 ft./8 m. Climb a wet groove to the foot of the crack.   2)   30 ft./9 m. Scramble up to a terrace at the foot of the crack proper.   3)   25 ft./8 m. Walk left to the foot of the crack.   4)   85 ft./26 m. Traverse left into a groove and climb this, not without interest, to an overhung ledge.   6)   80 ft./24 m. Move left along the terrace and climb an open groove to another ledge. Move left along this to an easy groove which leads back rightwards to a ledge and small belay.   7)   90 ft./27 m. Climb the slabs on the right of the belay, first straight up, then bearing left to the top.

116   **Brain Damage**   ***   E3   (6a, 6a)

225 ft./68 m.   *E. Grindley, G. Higginson and P. Long*   *1973*

Deceptively steep, giving exhilarating climbing. Follows two hanging grooves up the left end of the East Gully Wall. Scramble up from the gully and start by a large spike below the black streaks issuing from an overlap.

1)   75 ft./23 m. (6a) Move up left on to jammed blocks. Climb the wall to below a downward-pointing flake. Move left and pull

up from its left-hand side (crux) to gain the bottom of a steep green groove. Follow this to a horizontal break and secure ledge. 2) 150 ft./46 m. (6a) Sustained strenuosity makes up for any lack of technical difficulty. Enter the steep groove above, place a tape over a flake on the right wall and stand on the flake. Move right around the rib and climb steeply to the overhang. Pull straight over the overhang and up the vertical wall above until, finally, the angle relents.

117 **Astra** *** E2 (4a, 4a, 5b, 5a)
295 ft./90 m. *E. Metcalf and J. A. Austin 1960*
A superb slab climb on good rock, with magnificent situations. About half-way up the scree gully to the right of Stoats' Crack, a conspicuous slab slanting right, forming the right wall of a huge open corner, will be seen. Start almost directly below this at a small break giving access to an area of less steep slabs.
1) 60 ft./18 m. (4a) Gain the slabs and make an ascending traverse left to a grassy terrace. 2) 35 ft./11 m. (4a) The wall above leads into the corner and the start of the difficulties. 3) 70 ft./21 m. (5b) Traverse right below the steep wall to the arête (runner in a thin crack just to the left). Move round the arête, with difficulty, on to the slab, where the angle eases but the holds diminish alarmingly. Move across the slab to a flake which provides a welcome respite. This is left reluctantly for the uncertain security of a sloping ledge some 15 ft./4 m. higher to the left. The short wall on the right is crossed and a stance reached immediately. 4) 130 ft./40 m. (5a) Continue up the slab above to a ledge below a V-groove. This is often wet and always awkward. Climb it to a ledge and then take the 15 ft./4 m. crack above.

118 **Fallen Angel** ** E4 (4a, 6a, 5a, 4a)
260 ft./79 m. *E. Grindley and I. Roper 1972*
This hard climb takes the slanting overhanging groove immediately right of Astra. A fine natural line. Start at the same point as Astra. (The first pitch can be avoided by coming in from the right.)
1) 80 ft./24 m. (4a) Gain the slabs and go up the right edge, overlooking the gully, to a grass ledge. Move left and up a short

Rake End Wall, Pavey Ark

corner to a rock ledge and belays.   2)   75 ft./23 m. (6a)
Traverse left to the groove and climb this until it slants up to the
right. Continue up the groove with difficulty until the groove
opens out. Transfer on to a slab on the right and climb this on
small holds to a good foothold and piton belay. A very sustained
pitch.   3)   80 ft./24 m. (5a) Climb the thin crack above for 20
ft./6 m. and step right to gain another crack, slanting right to a
pedestal on the arête. Step left into a V-groove and climb this on
small holds, passing an awkward overhang, to a ledge and
belay.   4)   25 ft./8 m. (4a) The slab above leads to the top.

119   **Cascade**   **   HVS   (–, 5a, 5a)
230 ft./70 m.   *J. A. Austin and R. B. Evans*   *1957*
Another fine climb taking the last clean, rightward-slanting slab
on the crag. Like the other routes on this wall, it gives sustained
and interesting climbing on sound compact rock. Small runners
only protect the crux. Start at the same point as Astra and Fallen
Angel.
1)   80 ft./24 m. As for Fallen Angel.   2)   60 ft./18 m. (5a) The
steepening slab on the right is climbed with increasing difficulty.
After 40 ft./12 m. a series of difficult bridging moves in the corner
leads to a loose spike 5 ft./1.5 m. below a grass ledge at the top of
the slab. Move right to gain a stance and belay.   3)   90 ft./27
m. (5a) The short wall above the point of arrival is climbed to the
foot of a prominent chimney. Climb this and continue in the
same line to the top of the crag.

GIMMER CRAG   (277069)

This imposing buttress is one of the finest and most popular cliffs
in the Lake District, with a wide range of climbs of all standards,
except the easiest, on rock that is nearly always perfect. The cliff
has a southerly aspect and dries quickly after rain.
Approaches: From the New Dungeon Ghyll Hotel, the Dungeon
Ghyll path is followed up the left bank of the Dungeon Ghyll
stream. After a series of zigzags, the path emerges on a plateau
below the cliffs of Harrison Stickle. Gimmer Crag's south-east
face is visible to the left, recognizable by the narrow cleft of

Gimmer Crag, south-east face
A = Ash Tree Ledge   B = Approach via Bilberry Chute   C = Amen
Corner   D = Descent via south-east Gully

Gimmer Chimney. After crossing the plateau, the path starts to rise and swing away to the right. At this point a level trod, indefinite at first, branches left, crossing a small beck *en route*, to the foot of the south-east face. 1¼ hours. The Old Dungeon Ghyll Hotel is the more usual starting point. The path from the New Hotel can be gained by a steep ascent of the scree gully slightly east of the Old Hotel, or by the ascent of Middlefell Buttress (q.v.) and the steep hillside above. A third alternative is to follow a path which goes up the hillside, just west of Middlefell Buttress, directly above Middlefell Farm. At the top of a wall on the left, a scree chute is entered and ascended until the path breaks out on to the hillside above. It then leads a good deal more pleasantly to the crag. It is usual to go to the crag by one of the other routes and descend by the last. Time in ascent: 1¼–1½ hours.

Topography and descent: The cliff has three faces, South-east, West and North-west, the divisions being two rather indefinite arêtes. The main cliff is separated from the hillside by two deep-cut gullies, South-east, obvious from the point of arrival, and Junipall, which cleaves the North-west face and separates it from Pallid Buttress. Both gullies provide convenient descents, although a rope should be used by parties of limited experience, and care should be exercised to avoid knocking down loose stones as there may be more than one party in the gully at the same time.

The climbs on the South-east Face start at the point of arrival, while those on the West-Face commence from a terrace (Ash Tree Ledge) some distance up the cliff. This terrace is reached by a well-scratched scramble which commences at the end of a small terrace which cuts into the cliff at the point of arrival. A short flaky rib (the Bilberry Chute) gives access to a long terrace, above which a series of ledges and short walls gives access to Ash Tree Ledge. The north-west face can be reached by climbing the Bilbery Chute to the first terrace. This is crossed to its left end, and an easy traverse followed to the top of a 30 ft./9 m. chimney which is descended with some difficulty into North-west Gully. A much easier alternative is to walk round the toe of the buttress and scramble up North-west Gully.

120 **Gimmer Chimney** * VD

260 ft./79 m. *E. Rigby, J. Sanderson and A. S. Thompson 1902*

The long crack bisecting the south-east face gives a climb of sustained interest. Start directly below the crack line.

1) 45 ft./14 m. Climb a broken rib to a stance and belays. 2) 25 ft./8 m. Continue up an easy chimney to a grass ledge and good belay. 3) 30 ft./9 m. Easy rocks are climbed, after an awkward move, to a good stance on the right. 4) 55 ft./17 m. Move left into a groove. This is difficult and leads to a sentry box with a small spike runner. The deep crack above is followed to a large stance below twin chimneys. 5) 35 ft./11 m. Move right and climb the right-hand chimney into an open gully. Good belay. 6) 70 ft./21 m. A few feet in the gully bed, followed by an ascent of the right-hand rib, leads to the top.

121 **Bracket and Slab Climb**   * HS
295 ft./90 m.   *H. B. Lyon and J. Herbert*   *1923*

A varied climb taking a parallel line to Gimmer Chimney, including the chimney to the left of pitch 5 of that climb. The omission of this chimney renders the climb a good deal easier. Start at a flake belay 20 ft./6 m. above the point where the path meets the crag.

1) 35 ft./11 m. Step off the top of the flake and go up an awkward slab to a bilberry ledge. 2) 65 ft./20 m. Traverse right to gain a rib which is followed to a grassy rake. Go up this to a rocky corner at the top. 3) 40 ft./12 m. The Bracket. On the right a series of blocks project from the wall. These are traversed to gain an awkward groove. Go up this to a belay at its top. 4) 40 ft./12 m. Diagonally right over easy rocks to a small belay at the foot of a steep wall. It is probably better to fix a runner and press on. 5) 25 ft./8 m. The Neat Bit. A footledge leads diagonally leftwards to the foot of a short crack. This leads to a slab below an impending wall. 6) 25 ft./8 m. Walk 25 ft./8 m. right to a belay at the foot of a smooth chimney. Climb this appallingly smooth and strenuous cleft to a belay in the gully above. (Those who avoid it for the easier one of Gimmer Chimney 15 ft./4 m. to the right will be forgiven.) 7) 65 ft./20 m. Work leftwards then back to the right, up pleasant slabs to the top.

THE WEST FACE

As mentioned earlier, the climbs on this face start from Ash Tree Ledge. A complex network of routes exists on the right-hand side of the face, of VD-HS in standard. In general, the routes take shallow groove lines connected by short traverses. Most of the lines are indistinct, however, and often difficult to follow, so only one route is described on this section of the crag.

122 **'B' Route** ** MS
180 ft./55 m. *H. B. Lyon, J. Stables and A. S. Thompson 1907*
This interesting route takes a line close to the right-hand edge of the west face. Start at the right-hand end of Ash Tree Ledge. 'A', 'B' and 'C' Routes are arrowed and have a common start up a line of cracked blocks.
1) 30 ft./9 m. Diagonally right over the blocks to a large platform. 2) 15 ft./4 m. Move right to a short crack which leads to another platform (Thompson's Ledge). On the right is a belay at the foot of Amen Corner. 3) 15 ft./4 m. The crack in the corner is strenuous but short and safe with a well-used landing platform below. Emerge on the gangway and belay on the left. 4) 70 ft./21 m. The gangway curves up to the left to the foot of Green Chimney (a misnomer if ever there was one: it is an open groove). Follow the chimney until it is possible to cross the right wall to a finely situated ledge – the Crow's Nest. 5) 50 ft./15 m. Step right and ascend pleasant slabs to the top.

The next six climbs on the west face include routes on the lower and higher sections of the north-west face, since in combination they give sustained climbs of respectable length. Kipling Groove, 'F' and 'D' Routes, Whit's End Direct and Springbank can be started fron Ash Tree Ledge.

123 **Crystal** E1 (5b)
130 ft./40 m. *T. W. Birkett, A. Atkinson and D. Lyle 1981*
A very pleasant route leading up to Ash Tree Ledge and the upper face. The route starts on the north-west face of the lower buttress, up a slender wall immediately right of a prominent corner (Ash Tree Corner), some 50 ft./15 m. above a huge detached flake (approximately where the path first touches the crag).
1) 130 ft./40 m. (5b) From the foot of Ash Tree Corner, scramble up right for a few feet to below the wall. Climb up, trending left at first, then directly up the centre of the wall.

124 **Ash Tree Slabs/'D' Route** ** HVD/S

255 ft./78 m. *G. S. Bower and A. W. Wakefield 1920/G. S. Bower and P. R. Masson 1919*

A pleasant combination of slabs and a good crack. The route starts on the north-west face of the lower buttress, up slabs on the left wall of a prominent corner, some 50 ft./15 m. above a huge detached flake.

1) 50 ft./15 m. Move up the corner then traverse left on good holds to the edge. Follow this to a good ledge and belay. 2) 55 ft./17 m. Move up left to a large ledge, then climb a groove leading up to the right. 3) 50 ft./15 m. Continue up to the left to a ledge midway between Ash Tree Ledge and an overhanging, triangular recess marking the start of the crack line of 'D' Route. 4) 40 ft./12 m. Climb a groove to enter the recess, then make a delicate traverse left for 15 ft./4 m. Follow a groove back right to a good stance and block belay. 5) 45 ft./14 m. Climb the 'Forked Lightning Crack' to belays on the left wall. 6) 15 ft./4 m. Move up to a sloping corner on the left, when a delicate balance move leads to the finishing holds.

125 **Intern/Kipling Groove** *** HVS (5a, 5a, 4a, 4c, 5a)

330 ft./100 m. *P. Fearnehough, G. Oliver and J. Hesmondhalgh 1963/A. R. Dolphin and J. B. Lockwood 1948*

Although these two climbs make a good combination, Kipling Groove is of course an excellent climb in its own right and can be started from Ash Tree Ledge (at the left-hand end, 50 ft./15 m. below the large overhangs). Intern starts on the lower buttress, some 20 ft./6 m. left of Ash Tree Slabs, at an overhanging groove.

1) 60 ft./18 m. (5a) The groove slants up to the right and is awkward. From a small stance at its top, swing down to the left on to a leftward-slanting slab. Follow this up to the left, using holds over the bulge (when they appear!) into a bulging corner. Move up this on to a sloping ledge on the left, when another easier corner leads to a stance with a belay up to the left. 2) 55 ft./17 m. (5a) From the belay spike, step right on to the steep wall and go up this over an awkward overhang into a groove which is followed without difficulty to a small stance and belay. 3) 40 ft./12 m. Step left on to the arête and go up this, using a thin flake crack in the last few feet, to Ash Tree Ledge, and the start of Kipling Groove. 4) 40 ft./12 m. (4a) Climb the wall at the left-hand end of the ledge to a small belay but

123

good stance below the overhangs.   5)   35 ft./11 m. (4c) Move up to the overhangs and traverse left using the undercut crack, with difficulty at first, to the foot of a thin crack. Go up this to a stance at the foot of the overhanging groove.   6)   100 ft./30 m. (5a) A superb pitch. Climb the groove, passing a dubious block with care, until forced on to the arête on the right. Climb the thin crack until it is necessary to step right again below a bulge. This is split by a crack running up to the right. A strenuous traverse is made along this crack for 15 ft./4 m. to a welcome resting place below a narrow crack, which leads, still with some difficulty, to the top of the crag.

126 **North-west Arête/'F' Route**   ***   VS
295 ft./90 m.   *R. J. Birkett and V. Veevers   1940/1941*
The start of this route lies some 20 ft./6 m. left of Intern at a grassy slab sloping up to the left. This route provides an interesting contrast, with the open wall and rib climbing of its lower half, and the strenuous crack in its upper section.
1)   30 ft./9 m. Climb up to the slab and follow it up to the left to a flake belay.   2)   135 ft./41 m. Step right on to the steep wall and climb it for a few feet until it is possible to traverse right again to a short crack leading up to an overhang. The overhang is split by a short groove on the left. This is climbed strenuously to a good spike, and excellent holds are then followed diagonally rightwards to an airy rib. Follow the rib, with a short diversion to the right, until a short crack leads to Ash Tree Ledge.   3)   25 ft./8 m. Scramble up to the right to belay directly below the huge corner line of 'F' Route.   4)   35 ft./11 m. Move up to a small ledge, then climb a bulge on the left to reach a small stance and belay below the overhangs.   5)   70 ft./21 m. A fine, strenuous pitch. Move up right and climb the corner, with increasing difficulty, to the top of the crag.

127 **Springbank**   **   E1   (5c)
150 ft./46 m.   *M. G. Mortimer, E. Cleasby (var.), M. Allen, M. Lynch and J. Lamb   1979*
To the right of the great hanging corner of 'F' Route, there is a clean attractive wall with a long rectangular overhang at about two-thirds height. It is climbed by two technically interesting

Gimmer Crack, Gimmer Crag

climbs. The right-hand one, taking the overhang direct, is Springbank. Start on the terrace, just above Ash Tree Ledge, below the wall.

1)   150 ft./46 m. (5c) Climb a groove on the right, then move left into the thin crack. Follow this up the wall and over the roof (the well-protected crux) to the top.

128 **Whit's End Direct**   **   E1   (5b)
150 ft./46 m.   *J. A. Austin and R. Valentine   1972*
The other route up the wall, taking the left end of the overhang. Start near Springbank.

1)   150 ft./46 m. (5b) Follow a thin crack, slanting leftwards, until it is possible to climb directly to the left end of the rectangular overhang. Pull up and right to pass the overhang, then continue directly to the top.

129 **Midnight Movie**   ***   E4   (5b, 6b, 6a)
250 ft./76 m.   *R. O. Graham and T. W. Birkett (alt.)   1982*
A natural line – the most direct on Gimmer. Start as for the Crack (see 131).

1)   80 ft./24 m. (5b) Climb the Crack for 40 ft./12 m., then keep straight on up the twin cracks in the impending wall. Belay on a grass ledge.   2)   50 ft./15 m. (6b) Climb the thin crack in the middle of the slab direct. When the crack dries, go for the traverse on Kipling Groove 15 ft./4 m. above. Take a hanging belay or, better, move right and down to the ledge.   3)   120 ft./36 m. (6a) Pull directly over the middle of the overlap and up a scoop for 20 ft./6 m. Step right and follow a bulging crack leading to the crux of Kipling Groove. Finish as for Kipling Groove.

130 **Gimmer String**   **   E1   (4c, 5a, 5b)
250 ft./76 m.   *J. A. Austin, D. Miller and E. Metcalf   1963*
This magnificent climb takes the arête separating the north-west and west faces. Fine positions and good protection make it the most popular climb of its standard in the area. Start at the foot of Gimmer Crack, the obvious corner crack running up the right-hand side of the face.

1)   110 ft./33 m. (4c) Climb the corner crack to a small ledge,

Gimmer Crag North West Face (upper). A = Ash Tree Ledge

then traverse left into a groove. Follow this more easily to an area of ledges. Above on the right is a monolith below a large overhang. Scramble up to a stance just beneath this.   2)   60 ft./18 m. (5a) Climb the monolith and step right to the foot of a wide crack. This is followed, not without difficulty for those of more than average girth, to the stance below the groove of Kipling Groove.   3)   80 ft./24 m. (5b) Bridge up the groove until good holds permit a short hand-traverse to a niche on the arête. A steep shallow groove is climbed with difficulty until a move left can be made on to the wall overlooking Gimmer Crack. Good holds then give a pleasant interlude before the final wall is reached. This is climbed by precarious bridging moves (crux) to reach ledges at the top of the crag.

131   **Gimmer Crack**   ***   VS

240 ft./73 m.   *A. B. Reynolds and G. G. MacPhee*   *1928*

A superb natural line up the obvious corner at the left-hand side of the north-west Face. One of the best climbs of its standard in the District. Starts at the same point as Gimmer String at the foot of a narrow corner crack.

1)   85 ft./26 m. Scramble up to the crack and follow it to a small ledge. Cross the wall on the left with difficulty, keeping as low as possible, to a ledge below a shallow groove which is climbed on improving holds to a pedestal belay.   2)   25 ft./8 m. The pedestal provides the take-off for a fierce little mantelshelf. Follow a sloping ledge up to the left to a good stance and belay.   3)   45 ft./14 m. After a strenuous move, follow the arête above until it is possible to traverse back right into the crack.   4)   15 ft./4 m. The sentry box is climbed on to the bower, a fine gathering point from which to view the antics of the leader on the next pitch.   5)   70 ft./21 m. Go straight up the crack to a small overhang, which is only overcome with considerable expenditure of energy. A small ledge provides a welcome resting place before the ascent of the final awkward chimney.

132   **Hiatus**   *   VS

325 ft./99 m.   *G. S. Bower, A. B. Reynolds, A. W. Wakefield and G. G. MacPhee*   *1927*

Gimmer Crag, north-west face A = Ash Tree Ledge

128

The climb follows grassy slabs on the left of the Crack, and turns the huge overhangs by a long traverse left. The situations improve as height is gained. Start 6 ft./2 m. left of Gimmer Crack.

1)   40 ft./12 m. A steep wall leads to a terrace. Traverse up and left to a corner and belay.   2)   35 ft./11 m. An awkward scoop on the right is followed by a ridge to the pedestal belay on the Crack.   3)   30 ft./9 m. Move across to a mantelshelf on the left. Follow the slab to a grass ledge.   4)   55 ft./17 m. A grassy gully for 30 ft./9 m. followed by a traverse left.   5)   50 ft./15 m. Another terrace leads back to the gully. Move up and traverse left across a mossy wall to ledges and belays.   6)   70 ft./21 m. Move up into a corner, then step across a large block and make a delicate traverse left up the slab below overhangs. Climb a steep corner for 10 ft./3 m. then continue the traverse to the second of two ribs. Climb this to a good niche and belay.   7)   45 ft./14 m. The slab on the left is followed by an awkward groove.
Grooves Traverse finish: A very fine alternative.
6b)   55 ft./17 m. Move up into the corner, then traverse right across the steep wall to gain a groove. Follow this to a small stance and good belay.   7b)   55 ft./17 m. Climb the mossy groove for 10 ft./3 m. then traverse delicately right for 15 ft./4 m. below a small overhang. Continue up right on good holds to the top.

RAVEN CRAG   (285065)
This easily accessible crag can be reached in 15 minutes' steep ascent from the Old Dungeon Ghyll Hotel, and in a slightly longer time from the New Hotel. It is useful as a quick-drying alternative to the higher crags in inclement weather, or for an evening or half day. Additionally, in the modern idiom, it has hard, good-quality routes only a few minutes from the car.

133   **Middlefell Buttress**   *   D (first pitch S but can be avoided)
250 ft./76 m.   *J. Laycock, S. W. Herford and A. R. Thompson   1911*
Hundreds of beginners must have taken their first steps on rock on this climb. The route lies on the clean left-hand buttress of Raven Crag, directly above the left-hand boundary of the enclosure. (The climb is a useful approach to Gimmer Crag or Pavey Ark.) The climb starts at a steep crack at the toe of the buttress.

1)   50 ft./15 m. The crack has been polished to a high gloss by myriads of sweating palms and flailing boots, and proves strenuous. A platform is reached at 40 ft./12 m. and a higher ledge reached without further difficulty. Easier alternatives lie to left or right, or the pitch may be avoided entirely.   2)   30 ft./9 m. A polished slab at the back of ledge is climbed by a variety of routes. Good belays.   3)   120 ft./36 m. A groove in the nose of the buttress is entered with some difficulty from either left or right. Big holds then lead to a large boulder on another platform. Stances and belays *en route* as required.   3)   50 ft./15 m. The steep wall above is quite difficult, a small overhang being surmounted by traversing in from either left or right. Descend via the gully on the left.

134   Evening Wall   *   S

155 ft./47 m.   *A. Gregory, J. W. Tucker and J. Woods*   1947
Start from Raven Gully, 20 ft./6 m. left of a large tottering pinnacle.
1)   35 ft./11 m. Up the wall for 15 ft./4 m. then move right to a corner. Step right and up to a small stance.   2)   50 ft./15 m. Move up for 10 ft./3 m. to a ledge, then traverse left to climb the weakness in the steep wall, to gain a ledge, and belay on the left edge of the wall.   3)   70 ft./21 m. Step awkwardly right on to the wall and pull up to better holds. Continue to the top on good holds.

135   Holly-tree Traverse   VD

170 ft./52 m.
A popular route, very polished and now without holly. Start by scrambling up to and behind the aforementioned pinnacle.
1)   45 ft./14 m. From the ledge behind the pinnacle, climb the wall for about 10 ft./3 m. until a well-worn ascending traverse leads rightwards to a niche.   2)   75 ft./23 m. Continue traversing rightwards to a groove (this was the site of the holly). Then up the rib to the right of the gully and traverse to a rock ledge below a right-angled corner.   3)   30 ft./9 m. Finish up this.

136   Trilogy   **E4   (6a)

100 ft./30 m.   *J. Lamb and E. Cleasby*   1979
A tremendous route taking the distinct corner marking the left

edge of the impressive central wall. The first 30 ft./9 m. are very badly protected, and hard. Thereafter it is usual only to utilize the *in-situ* pegs for protection (approx. 15 pts.). It is advisable, hoever, to carry a few nuts as the *in-situ* gear is old. Scramble up to the starting ledge directly below the corner, either rightwards from Raven Gully via the tottering pinnacle or, more directly, up a few cracks (Severe).

1) 100 ft./30 m. (6a) Climb the corner, peg low on the left, to a further peg in the right wall. A friend 1½ runner can be placed high in the corner before the second peg is reached (crucial). Continue up the corner to a ledge capped by more overhanging rock. Up the crack and move right under the overlap, then pull straight over (high hidden jug). Continue directly up the little chimney parting the final overhang.

137 **Pluto**   **   HVS   (4c, 4b, 5a)
225 ft./68 m.   *Pitch 1: A. L. Atkinson   1958/Pitch 2: P. Woods   1958/Pitch 3: E. Metcalf and J. Ramsden   1957*
An excellent way up the crag, offering continually interesting climbing at a reasonably consistent standard. Start from the path directly below the central wall by scrambling up to the prominent clean-cut corner crack.

1) 50 ft./15 m. (4c) The crack is climbed directly to the ledge. Belay on the large pinnacle on the terrace to the right. (Trilogy is directly overhead.)   2) 90 ft./27 m. (5a) Traverse the wall rightwards, then up via a groove to the overhang. (Care is required with shattered rock.) Traverse right under the curving overhang until a step down (blind but on good holds) enables a crossing of an overgrown groove. Belay on the ledge on the right (as for Bilberry Buttress).   3) 85 ft./26 m. (5a) On the left is a groove. Climb its right rib until a steep pull, up and right, gives access to the front of the wall (crux). Climb up, continuing over an overlap, to a traverse line. Move left to a groove. Up this, stepping left at its top, and straight up the final few feet to the top.

138 **Centrefold**   **   E6   (6c)
120 ft./36 m.   *T. W. Birkett, I. Cooksey and R. Graham   1984*
Climbs the great central wall directly. Serious, strenuous and technical. Start as for the second pitch of Pluto.

1) 120 ft./36 m. (6c) Traverse right, then up to the overhang.

Pull straight through this (*in-situ* peg to the right). Move left, then back right to an old bolt in the middle of the wall. Straight up to an old peg (eye cracked, so necessary to loop a wire over). Straight up to clip a further *in-situ* peg (bent over and cracked). Then make harder moves up (RP4 placement recommended) to gain a traverse line to the right. The obvious flake on the skyline is the objective. From the top of this, pull up leftwards through a final wall to gain a slab and nut belays. (About 40 ft./12 m. of scrambling leads to the top.)

139 **Bilberry Buttress**   VS

255 ft./78 m.   *C. F. Rolland and J. F. Renwick   1941*

Although artificial in its line, this route gives a sustained series of crack pitches unusual in Langdale. The main buttress of Raven Crag is guarded by large overhangs in the centre. Just right of these, a ridge projects downwards, separating the south and east faces of the buttress. Start at the lowest point of the right-hand side of the crag.

1)   25 ft./8 m. Easy climbing leads to the foot of the first crack.   2)   40 ft./12 m. Climb the crack by fist jams to gain an open scoop. Follow this up to the left to a ledge and flake belays.   3)   55 ft./17 m. The steep wall above is capped by a bulge, and split by a thin crack. Step right off the belay flake into the crack and climb this with difficulty to a hidden jug. Easier climbing up the arête on the left leads to a long shattered ledge. Thread belay at point of arrival.   4)   40 ft./12 m. Move along to the right to the foot of the first feasible-looking crack in the wall above. Climb this on widely spaced holds to a stance behind a large block.   5)   50 ft./15 m. Climb down to the left of the block until it is possible to traverse left in an exposed position below a line of overhangs into a recess. Move left from the recess to gain easy ground and the top of the crag.

Descent: Best made by following an airy path to the right (east) until a short descent over some split blocks gives access to a ledge. (Oak Tree Terrace)which slants down to the foot of the crag.

Above the aforementioned descent is a dirty gully and right of this a clean buttress of rock. This buttress holds a rather superb little climb.

140 **Centipede**   **   MS

300 ft./91 m. A. Gregory and C. Peckett   *1948*

Start just right of a pinnacle about centre of the buttress.
1)   60 ft./18 m. Up the front until possible to move left to a
crack. This leads to a good ledge.   2)   100 ft./30 m. Steeply up
to the overhang, then traverse left, spiralling round towards the
gully. Up the gully wall to a crack on the right. Move across,
below the crack, to the arête. From a litle rock ledge, climb
straight up the edge to a larger ledge (nut belay high on
left).   3)   150 ft./46 m. Climb the wall via a crack on the left.
Continue straight on up until it eases into scrambling.

BOWFELL   (245069)

Approach: This cliff lies just north of the summit of Bowfell and
faces east. It is reached by the ascent of the Band to where the
tourist path bears left. Continue straight ahead here, then bear
right to reach the start of a horizontal track (the Climbers'
Traverse) which leads along below Flat Crags to a spring at the
foot of the Cambridge Crag. Cross a scree chute to the foot of
Bowfell Buttress.
Descent: Down the scree gully on the left (south).

141   **Bowfell Buttress**   ***   VD
305 ft./93 m.   *T. Shaw, L. J. Oppenheimer and party   1902*
This well-polished classic takes the general line of the nose of the
buttress and starts just left of the lowest point of the crag. On the
left of the Buttress is a broad scree fan, then a steep crag with
three prominent grooves. The following route takes the right-
hand and largest groove.
1)   45 ft./14 m. Up the ridge to a good belay.   2)   30 ft./9 m.
The smooth chimney on the right is not without interest.
Continue more easily to a terrace.   3)   40 ft./12 m. Climb
diagonally left to a sentry box.   4)   60 ft./18 m. Climb the
chimney above for 40 ft./12 m. to a good belay. Easy ledges then
lead to a broad platform. Go down this to the right to a belay
below a steep crack.   5   55 ft./17 m. Climb the crack (smooth
and awkward), then slabby rocks (crux in winter) sloping
leftwards to a pinnacle.   6)   40 ft./12 m. Move left and up a
slanting groove to a chimney and follow this to a flake
belay.   7)   20 ft./6 m. The wall above followed by a move left to
a belay of impressive proportions.   8)   60 ft./18 m. Step back
right and continue up the groove to the top.

135

142 **Sword of Damocles** * E2 (4a, 4a, 5b, 5a)
180 ft./55 m. *A. R. Dolphin, P. J. Greenwood (alt.) and D, Hopkin 1952*

A famous climb, with good situations, unfortunately rather lichenous. Starts from a grass ledge below and just left of the large groove and beneath a prominent curved crack.
1) 30 ft./9 m. (4a) Traverse up and right along the curved crack to a groove, which leads to a stance and belay behind a large pinnacle. 2) 30 ft./9 m. (4a) Climb the groove on the right until a long step right can be made to a ledge and belay on the ledge. 3) 60 ft./18 m. (5b) Go up until it is possible to traverse across the groove to the left wall. Continue up the groove with difficulty until a move right leads to easier rock and a stance and belay. 4) 60 ft./18 m. (5a) Climb the steep and impressive flake-crack above to the summit.

NECKBAND CRAG (261062)

Approach: This small cliff (Earing Crag on the OS map) lies due north of the summit of the Band and is reached by following the path as for Bowfell Buttress (q.v.) until the col just beyond the summit of the Band is reached. The crag lies to the north-east of the col and is reached by descending until it is possible to contour below broken crags.

Topography: The principal features of the crag are three great corners split by equally fine arêtes. The four climbs described are all of great character and are on superb rock, which is unfortunately rather mossy, and therefore slow to dry.

Descent: The climbs finish on a terrace above which another 100 ft./30 m. or so of climbing can be constructed. It is, however, without interest and it is normal practice to traverse left to descend well to the left of the crag.

143 **Cravat** VS
120 ft./36 m. *H. and N. Drasdo 1950*

The climb lies at the extreme left-hand end of the crag and starts at the foot of the short grassy corner. It is steep and not too well protected.
1) 120 ft./36 m. Climb the corner to a grass ledge, then step right and climb a thin crack by long reaches until a line of holds

On Bowfell Buttress

leads out right to a niche on the arête. Continue the upward traverse round the arête and so into the big groove on the right, which leads on good holds to the top.

144 **Mithrandir** *** HVS (5a)
110 ft./33 m. *J. Hartley and R. Sager 1972*
This fine climb takes the first big corner to the right of Cravat. It is sustained with good protection.
1) 110 ft./33 m. (5a) Climb the groove directly to the top, with a steep finish.

145 **Gillette** * E2 (5c)
115 ft./35 m. *K. Wood and J. A. Austin 1968*
This climb should appeal to the technician, requiring finesse rather than strong-arm tactics. The climb starts about 20 ft./6 m. right of Mithrandir at an impending flake crack.
1) 115 ft./35 m. (5c) Climb the crack to the overhang (good thread) then step left and climb the long, thin gangway overlooking the corner of Mithrandir. Difficulties are continuous to the finishing jug.

146 **Razor Crack** ** E1 (5a)
120 ft./36 m. *J. A. Austin and K. Wood 1966*
The fourth route described adds yet another dimension to the climbing on this crag. The wall crack, on the right-hand side of the arête taken by Gillette, gives a strenuous and sustained route. Start as for Gillette.
1) 120 ft./36 m. (5a) Climb the crack to the overhang, then traverse right and pull over the overhang into the main crack. This is followed past another overhang at 75 ft./23 m., after which difficulties ease somewhat.

DEER BIELD CRAG (303087)
The crag is small but very steep, with smooth rock that gives either enormous jugs or nothing at all; thus the climbing, in general, is strenuous. The central buttress of the crag is completely detached, forming a fissure on either side: Deer Bield Crack on the left and Deer Bield Chimney on the right. The latter is a loose S and is not recommended.

Deer Bield Crag, Far Easedale

Approach: This cliff does not lie in Langdale at all, but in the lonely valley of Far Easedale above Grasmere. The best approach is from Grasmere up the Greenup Edge path. The cliff is the only one of any size on the left-hand side of the valley (1 hour). Alternatively, from Langdale ascend Mill Ghyll to Stickle Tarn, then strike north-eastwards, passing above Easedale Tarn, to the top of the crag (1½ hours).

Descent: Best made round the left (SE) side of the buttress.

147 **Deer Bield Crack** *** HVS (4a, 4a, 4a, 5b, 4a, 5a)
170 ft./52 m. *A. T. Hargreaves and G. G. MacPhee 1930*
A remarkable climb for its antiquity! This is not a climb to be taken lightly, as strong parties have been known to fail. Start at a prominent flake 15 ft./4 m. left of the lowest point of the buttress.
1) 35 ft./11 m. (4a) The crack above the flake is soon quitted for a niche on the right. Continue up the crack to a recess. The slab on the left is then climbed on good holds to a ledge on the right wall. Thread belay. 2) 25 ft./8 m. (4a) The chimney on the left to a large block belay. 3) 20 ft./6 m. (4a) Continue up a shallow chimney, passing some loose blocks with care, to a belay in a pear-shaped chimney. 4) 35 ft./11 m. (5b) A very strenuous pitch! Climb the chimney facing right, and as deeply inside as possible, to a chockstone runner in the roof. Traverse right under the roof and continue to a resting place and chockstone belay. 5) 40 ft./12 m. (4a) The narrower crack above eases after 10 ft./3 m., and leads to a belay below a super-Amen Corner. 6) 15 ft./4 m. (5a) Summoning all reserves of energy (and, if *in extremis*, the second man's shoulders too!) climb the corner.

148 **Deer Bield Buttress** E2 (4c, 5a, 5a, 5b)
185 ft./56 m. *A. R. Dolphin and A. D. Brown 1951*
The nature of this climb has been changed due to an extensive rockfall affecting the upper part of the buttress. It is now generally considered to be potentially dangerous because of the looseness of the remaining rock. The climb takes a groove line immediately to the right of Deer Bield Crack, and provides difficulties of both strenuous and delicate nature maintained at a high standard. Start at the lowest point of the crag.

Over the first crux on Deer Bield Buttress

1) 45 ft./14 m. (4c) A layback crack slants up to the left to join Deer Bield Crack. Follow it to a recess below an impending crack. 2) 15 ft./4 m. (5a) The crack is climbed on fist jams to the belay at the end of pitch 1 of Deer Bield Crack. 3) 35 ft./11 m. (5a) The first crux. Step right from the stance and make a difficult layback move to gain a tiny ledge on the wall. Move up with even more difficulty to a resting place and good nut runner. A very steep crack then leads to a stance below a long groove. 4) 90 ft./27 m. (5b) Climb the groove to a small overhang, above which the groove forks. Pass the overhang with difficulty to gain the right-hand groove and follow this until it is necessary to move delicately right to a scoop. Climb up left to a pinnacle (poor stance) and from this traverse left on very small holds to climb the wall directly to the top.

WINTER CLIMBING

Bowfell is the most popular area, where the gullies near Bowfell Buttress provide interesting Grade I climbs, and the Buttress itself is much more serious. With a covering of snow and ice, it is generally Grade III/IV. The gullies and Jack's Rake on Pavey Ark have provided good sport, although the crag does catch the sun. The nearest reliable winter climbing is on Great End, which is reached in about two hours after the ascent of Rossett Ghyll. See Borrowdale section.

PATTERDALE AREA

Often described as the most scenic valley in the Lake District, the area around Patterdale is also the most crowded, especially in the summer months. Patterdale is the centre for climbing in Grisedale, Deepdale and Dovedale. The crags in these three valleys are usually approached from the east, and offer a good variety of climbing. None of the crags is near the road; the nearest (Eagle Crag, Grisedale) is reached in about 30 minutes. The crags are shown on the Thirlmere map.

Access

From the M6, via the Penrith junction and the A592 through Pooley Bridge. From the south, via Kirkstone Pass from Ambleside or Troutbeck. The nearest railway station is at Penrith, and there is a bus service between Penrith and Patterdale. There are regular daily Mountain Goat minibus services (from Easter to October) over Kirkstone Pass from Ambleside and Windermere.

Accommodation and camping

There is a campsite near the Brothers Water Hotel, ½ mile south of the lake (401119), and also at Glenridding (380167). Hotels and guest-houses are found in Patterdale, Glenridding, Low Hartsop, and at the south end of Brothers Water and the summit of the Kirkstone Pass. There is a youth hostel at Patterdale (399156) and one at Glenridding (366173). Elsewhere there is an Outward Bound School (438212) and a Sheffield University Club Hut (355135) in Grisedale.

Food and drink

There are several excellent restaurants in the hotels mentioned above, and cafés in Glenridding and Patterdale. Typically, the café in Patterdale opens from Easter until the end of September. Most of the hotels have bars, the most popular being the White Lion at Patterdale, the Travellers Rest at Glenridding or the Brothers Water Inn. Normal licensing hours are 11–3, 5.30–10.30; Sun. 7–10.30. Shops and PO at Patterdale and Glenridding (early closing: Fri.).

Garages and car hire

Petrol, repairs and taxi service are available at the Ullswater Garage, Brown Howe (tel. Glenridding 213), closing at 7 p.m. in summer and 6 p.m. in winter. The nearest AA garage with 24-hr. breakdown service is in Ambleside (tel. 33273 or 32025).

There is a tourist information office at the Brothers Water campsite in the summer. Telephones at Patterdale and the north end of Brothers Water (Low Hartsop junction). Public toilets at Patterdale. The nearest equipment shops are in Ambleside (10 miles) or Keswick (17 miles).

Mountain rescue

For assistance, first ring the local police (999). There are manned rescue posts at the Patterdale Hotel (394160; tel. Glenridding 231) and at the Ullswater OB School (438213; tel. Pooley Bridge 347). There is a first-aid post at the YH in Glenridding (366174; tel. Glenridding 269), and an unmanned post by the wall at the foot of Striding Edge (359155).

EAGLE CRAG, GRISEDALE (357143)

Although there are in fact two sections to Eagle Crag, the routes described are all on the south (left-hand) crag. The crags look very broken from below but the routes are all much better than they appear. The rock is good and gives incut holds, but the crag is rather lichenous and is slippery in wet conditions. The routes are generally well protected.

Approach: From the bridge ½ mile north of Patterdale, it is possible to drive about 1 mile up Grisedale. Then follow the track up the valley eventually crossing the stream below Eagle Crag, which is approached directly. About 30 minutes in all.

Descent: Easily down the left-hand (west) side of the crag.

149 **Kestrel Wall**   *   HS

165 ft./50 m.   *R. J. Birkett and A. H. Griffin*   1954

A good steep climb on good holds. Start about 30 ft./50 m. left of the 40 ft./12 m. slab at the foot of the West Buttress: there are two cracks directly above.

1   25 ft./8 m. Climb to the rock ledge. Nut belays.   2)   50 ft./15 m. Climb the left-hand crack, moving left at the top to belay behind a large perched block.   3)   30 ft./9 m. The wall above to the large grass ledge.   4)   20 ft./6 m. A steep slab, on the right, to the upper ledge.   5)   40 ft./12 m. Pull into a groove above the right-hand end of the ledge. Move up, then step right and finish up a fine rib.

Eagle Crag, Grisedale

Sobrenada   *   VS

205 ft./62 m.   *M. A. James, G. A. Leaver and K. A. Brookes*   *1957*
An excellent and well-protected climb which is much better than
it looks. Start up a 40 ft./12 m. slab at the foot of the West
Buttress.

1)   45 ft./14 m. Climb the slab direct to a stance and
belay.   2)   80 ft./24 m. Move right and pull up into the cave.
Pull out left into a short corner. Climb this, then step right and
ascend a wall, followed by a rib to a large grass ledge and block
belay.   3)   80 ft./24 m. From a point just right of the blocks,
traverse right and upwards for 20 ft./6 m. Make an awkward
traverse left into a corner which is climbed on to a slab, the exit
being even more awkward. Move left, then gain a higher slab
which is followed to the top.

Doctor's Grooves   HS

235 ft./72 m.   *F. Fitzgerald and G. A. Leaver*   *1956*
Quite a long climb with a mountaineering atmosphere and
plenty of variety. Start just right of the toe of the buttress at the
right-hand end of the crag.

1))   40 ft./12 m. Pull up left on to a slab, then climb up and
right to belay on an ash tree.   2)   50 ft./15 m. Ascend the steep
corner above to a grass ledge.   3)   30 ft./9 m. Move up grass
ledges on the left into a corner.   4)   30 ft./9 m. Traverse the
steep wall on the right, then climb straight up to grassy ledges.
Scramble up 60 ft./18 m. to a large block belay at the foot of a
steep groove.   5)   65 ft./20 m. Climb the rib on the right of the
groove, then cross the groove to the arête on its left. Pull on to a
slab; traverse across to a corner which leads to a ledge and
belay.   6)   20 ft./6 m. A fine steep chimney-crack to finish.

HUTAPLE CRAG   (367120)

The long valley of Deepdale cuts deeply into the Fairfield Massif.
At its head are two combes, Sleet Cove and Link Cove, to the
north and south respectively of the spur of Greenhow End.
Hutaple Crag, a big, rather grassy cliff, occupies a commanding
position in Sleet Cove facing St Sunday Crag. The crag gives
long mountaineering routes, but dries slowly after rain.
Approach: Directly up Deepdale, bearing right into Sleet Cove.
Scramble up to the foot of the crag on the left (2 hours).

Topography: The cliff is bounded by East and West Hutaple Gullies, and a shallow gully splits the face of the crag itself (Curving Gully, VD). The two climbs described below are both based on the big recess or corner to the left of Curving Gully.
Descent: To the right, cross the grassy funnel above West Hustaple Gully and descend a grassy groove to the west of the rock ribs which bound the West Gully.

152 **The Amphitheatre** * VS
325 ft./99 m. *A. D. Marsden and G. Batty* *1955*
Start directly below the big corner at the left-hand side of a triangle of grassy slabs.
1) 85 ft./26 m. The slab is climbed until it is necessary to move right to a shallow groove. Go up this to a ledge and cross this to a broken groove on the right.   2) 90 ft./27 m. A fine pitch. Climb up the wall to the right of the groove. Move left then up to the right on to a slab. A delicate move is made up to the right and an obvious line taken through the overhangs to a stance and piton belay.   3) 70 ft./21 m. Step left into a steep corner, and follow this to a long terrace. Move right to the right-hand side of the prominent buttress.   4) 80 ft./24 m. Move up into a niche, then traverse left and climb the buttress to easy ground. Scramble up to cairned ledges. Descent is down a rake into the wide gully to the right of the crag.

153 **Sleet Wall** * S
330 ft./100 m. *J. C. Duckworth and G. Batty* *1952*
A clean, sound route of continuous interest. Start about 30 ft./9 m. left of the Amphitheatre at a gangway above 30 ft./9 m. of scrambling.
1) 35 ft./11 m. Follow the gangway and move back left to a small stance.   2) 25 ft./8 m. Move left then, slant rightwards to an overhung ledge.   3) 65 ft./20 m. Traverse right and follow the impressive line back leftwards to a big ledge.   4) 30 ft./9 m. Above are two cracks. The right-hand one is followed to a grassy corner.   5) 35 ft./11 m. Traverse right and up round the rib. Easier climbing then follows to a grass ledge.   6) 90 ft./27 m. Scramble to the left end of a steep wall. Move up to a ledge, then step left to a block belay.   7) 40 ft./12 m. The rib and groove lead pleasantly to the top.

SCRUBBY CRAG (367115)

This fine steep crag stands at the head of Link Cove (see Hutaple Crag) and has a sunny south-easterly aspect. Unfortunately it lies in the main drainage line of the fellside above and takes several days to dry after rain. Despite this, and the long approach, the crag is well worth visiting as it has some of the best routes in the Eastern Fells.

Approach: One of the most daunting approach marches of any crag in this guide, either by way of Deepdale or by the north ridge of Hart Crag. Allow at least 2 hours. The crag can also be reached from Ambleside via Low Pike, High Pike, and the summits of Dove Crag and Hart Crag (2½ hours, leave sacks on the col between Hart Crag and Fairfield: the crag is just north of the col).

Topography: The cliff is a steep grooved wall of excellent rock standing above a plinth of vegetated rocks. A terrace crosses the cliff above this lower wall and provides access to the first two routes. In the centre of the crag are two fine V-grooves, Grendel on the left and Hrothgar on the right. At the left end of the crag is a steep corner (Juniper Crack, 165 ft./50 m., S). Just right of this corner is a curving crack splitting overhangs, which gives the line of Beowulf.

Descent: Down the slanting rake to the left, or traverse left to the col.

154 **Beowulf** ** VS

200 ft./61 m. *N. J. Soper and P. E. Brown* *1959*

Starts about 30 ft./9 m. right of Juniper Crack directly below the curving crack mentioned above.

1) 20 ft./6 m. A short wall is climbed to a grass ledge. 2) 70 ft./21 m. The steep wall above is climbed on small incut holds, first trending right over a slight bulge then back left into a shallow groove. Follow this to small stances below the crack. 3) 110 ft./33 m. Ascend to the overhang, pull into the crack and climb it to a spike. Traverse right on dubious flakes to the top of the crag. A fine exposed pitch.

155 **Grendel** *** MVS

220 ft./67 m. *H. Drasdo and G. Batty* *1956*

A superb route taking the left hand of the two V-grooves in the centre of the crag. Start at the right-hand end of the terrace.

1)   30 ft./9 m. Climb up to the right to the foot of the groove.   2)   100 ft./30 m. Mount a flake on the right and traverse left across the groove, and climb it to the long ledge which crosses the upper part of the crag. A superb pitch.   3)   90 ft./27 m. A short chimney leads to a higher ledge. A recess above is climbed by its right-hand corner, passing a pedestal and moving rightwards to the top of the crag.

156   **Hrothgar**   **   HVS   (4a, 5a, 5a)
295 ft./90 m.   *N. J. Soper, D. M. Dixon and C. D. Curtis   1960*
A harder sister route to Grendel taking the right-hand V-groove. The start is directly below the groove in a damp vegetated recess, reached by 150 ft./46 m. of scrambling up the right-hand end of the lower tier.
1)   55 ft./17 m. (4a) Step left and up a grassy rake to a short chimney. Climb this and move right to a good grass ledge and nut belays.   2)   140 ft./43 m. (4a) Move diagonally right, then back left up a delicate slab to gain the groove, and climb this to a big spike. Mantelshelf on to a wedged block on the left wall and continue up the groove to a good thread in a pocket. The left wall is then climbed to the long ledge.   3)   100 ft./30 m. (5a) Move up to a bilberry ledge, move to its right-hand end and make an exposed move over a bulge (crux) to easy ground.

DOVE CRAG   (376109)
This large and steep cliff is one of the most forbidding crags in the Lake District. It is finely situated at the head of Dovedale in relatively remote surroundings. Some of the best extremes in the area are found here and, rather surprisingly, a classic VS and a very good HVD. The rock needs some care and is lichenous – the routes become much harder in wet conditions and take some time to dry out after rain, although the North Buttress generally remains dry!
Approach: From the car-park and bridge at the north end of Brothers Water, follow the unmade road south past Hartsop Hall. Then take the right-hand footpath up the hillside into

Overleaf, left: Dove Crag

Overleaf, right: North Buttress, Dove Crag

159

157

OBVIOUS
FINAL
GROOVE

RAVEN'S
NEST

HANGOVER
SLAB

REST
LEDGE

157

159

Dovedale. The path continues up the valley until a short traverse left leads to the scree at the foot of the crag. About 1¼ hours. *Descent:* Cross the top of the crag and descend at the north end of the right-hand buttress.

157 **Fear and Fascination** *** E5 (6a+)
175 ft./53 m. *R. O. Graham and T. W. Birkett (shar.) 1980*
Brilliant unrelenting climbing up the most overhanging face of rock in the Lake District: the North Buttresses of Dove. Start in the centre of the face, just left of the boulders at a flake crack.
1) 175 ft./53 m. (6a) Up the flake crack to a ledge. (Belaying here will enable 165 ft./50 m. ropes to reach the top.) From the right end of the ledge pull over the bulge to an old peg. Continue up the wall to a good flake block. Continue straight up for 10 ft./3 m., then traverse right (technical crux) to a groove and step up to old peg/bolt runners and a poor rest. Move right and continue up a groove to gain a precarious ledge (rest). From the ledge, pull straight up the wall and climb for 20 ft./6 m. until a move right can be made into the final hanging groove (the obvious feature from the ground). An incredible position. Up the groove, moving right at the top and continue to belay on a large ledge.

158 **Hangover** ** HVS
235 ft./72 m. *J. W. Haggas, J. K. Booth and R. Clough 1939*
A tremendous climb – exposed and rather serious. A classic VS for many years, but pitch 2 is now 5a, following the loss of the large loose block. Start just left of a big boulder at the right-hand side of the slabs between the main buttresses.
1) 60 ft./18 m. A grassy groove leads to a tree belay in 40 ft./12 m.; then traverse right to another ledge.   2) 95 ft./29 m. (5a) Climb the corner above. At 40 ft./12 m. move left for 10 ft./3 m. then go up and right over a bulge to regain the corner. Climb the slab and short chimney above; move round the rib on the right to a stance and block belays. Care – some are loose.   3) 30 ft./9 m. Traverse right along the exposed ledge, then move up the leaning flake to a stance and small belays.   4) 50 ft./15 m. Ascend to a groove, then move right and climb the V-chimney to the top. This pitch is often rather greasy and strenuous.

Abseil from Fear and Fascination

159 **Asolo** *** E3 (5a, 5c+, 5c+)
250 ft./76 m. *T. W. Birkett, R. O. Graham (alt.) and O. Lyle 1981*
Takes the great open groove left of the North Buttress. Strenuous and spectacular. Start at the lowest point of the crag (left of Hangover) at a slab.
1) 60 ft./18 m. (5a) Climb the thin crack in the slab. 2) 90 ft./27 m. (5c+) Climb the wall directly to a bulge. Move right and over to gain a groove. Climb the groove to a junction with Hangover just below its crux. Step across the wall leftwards a few feet, then straight up a few more feet. Traverse the wall rightwards (old peg) to a ledge (and raven's nest) below the large impending groove (belay on Friends). 3) 120 ft./36 m. (5c+) Climb the groove to a sloping rock shelf on the right. Traverse right a few feet, then climb straight up the break. At the top, move right a few feet and finish using a large detached pinnacle.

160 **Extol** *** E2 (–, 5a, 5c)
350 ft./107 m. *D. D. Whillans and C. Mortlock 1960*
A magnificent climb which takes a direct line up the centre of the crag. Both impressive and serious, it is one of the classic climbs of the Lake District. Start directly below a chimney in the centre of the crag.
1) 50 ft./15 m. Broken rock leads to the foot of the chimney. 2) 150 ft./46 m. (5a) Climb the rather vegetated chimney direct. At the top, traverse right and go up the little chimney to the good block ledge on Hangover. 3) 150 ft./46 m. (5c) Move down and left, then pull on to the main wall. Climb left and up to the foot of a smooth groove. Climb this (hard if greasy) to a small ledge – a good resting place before the next section! Step right and climb the overhanging wall to a big overhang. Move right and pull into a smooth groove (crux). Continue up the groove, then the arête and mossy wall on the right to the top of the crag.

161 **Phobos** ** E2 (5b, –, 5a)
230 ft./70 m. *C. Read and J. Adams 1972/Free: P. Long and R. Valentine 1974*
A typically excellent Read/Adams climb taking a bold line up this steep wall. The climbing is serious and care should be taken

Bill Birkett on the first ascent of Asolo, top pitch

with loose rock. A rake leads round first to Phobos, then Hiraeth then Dovedale Groove to the left. Start down below some clean cracked slabs, forming the rake, beneath a striking crack cutting an overhang.

1)   100 ft./30 m. (5b) Go up to the crack, left of the overhang, and climb it to a traverse line (Hiraeth). Make the mantleshelf move and from the highest ledge climb left up the wall for 20 ft./€ m. Move right to a niche and climb up to below the overhang. Turn this on the right and belay at the foot of the terrace above.   2)   50 ft./15 m. Step right to climb a short groove to a gangway parallel to the terrace. Continue up this to a chimney leading to a stance on the right (Hiraeth).   3)   80 ft./24 m. (5a Up the short corner (Hiraeth), then move right, passing a large spike to the foot of a large corner. Climb the corner to hand-traverse rightwards along a thin crack below the roof. Then move up to easier ground and the top.

162   **Hiraeth**   E1   (5a, 5b, 5a)
250 ft./76 m.   *B. Ingle and P. Crew   1960*
An open route of great difficulty, wending its way up the steep wall between Dovedale Groove and Extol. The route is less strenuous than its neighbours. Start just right of Dovedale Groove at a shallow crack in a steep slab.

1)   100 ft./30 m. (5a) Climb the crack to a big spike, move right and step up into a niche. Traverse right on sloping holds round a large block, into a steep groove. Move up this and step left on to a grass ledge. The very steep wall and shallow groove lead to a small stance and piton belays.   2)   50 ft./15 m. (5b) Enter the groove above and continue up this with difficulty, passing a small overhang. The situation now eases and the slab is climbed to a huge block belay.   3)   100 ft./30 m. (5a) Step left off the block and climb a steep scoop on small holds to a spike on a slab. Move right to a groove, then up a steeper groove to the right to a grass ledge. Move right, and ascend delicately leftwards up the overlapping slab to the top.

163   **Dovedale Groove**   E1   (5b, 5a, −, 5a)
225 ft./68 m.   *D. D. Whillans, J. Brown and D. Cowan   1953/*
Pitches 3 and 4: J. A. Austin and N. J. Soper   1963
A strenuous route – an overhanging groove followed by an overhanging crack! Start below the obvious (and exceedingly

156

impressive) line on the left-hand buttress.

1)   75 ft./23 m. (5b) Up the groove and continue with strenuous bridging and jamming to a stance and belay below the overhanging crack.   2)   60 ft./18 m. (5a) Climb the crack to a chockstone, then gain the slab up on the left by a difficult move. Follow the slab more easily, then take a groove on the right to a grass rake. Move up this to a stance and piton belay. It is possible to leave the climb at this point along the rake.   3)   30 ft./9 m. Follow the rake up to the left for a few feet, move back right to a small stance below an undercut groove. Piton belay.   4)   60 ft./18 m. (5a) A hard move is made across the overhang to the left (the 'Western roll' technique is useful here!). Continue with difficulty up the groove to the top of the crag.

164 **Westmorland's Route**   *   HVD

320 ft./97 m.   *H. Westmorland, J. Mounsey and W. A. North   1910*
This route ascends the ridge at the left-hand end of the main face. A very good climb with some exposed situations. Start at a large boulder at the foot of the ridge.

1)   20 ft./6 m. Up either side of the boulder to some blocks.   2)   70 ft./21 m. Move right, then climb slabs which eventually lead back to the ridge. Beware of harder, direct variations.   3)   40 ft./12 m. The ridge leads to a sloping stance.   4)   50 ft./15 m. A short crack, then broken rocks to the foot of the wall.   5)   50 ft./15 m. Climb round to the right to gain a large slab. Follow this diagonally left to a good ledge.   6)   70 ft./21 m. Move up a little wall, then follow a gangway left. At the end, climb a steep wall to a large ledge.   7)   40 ft./12 m. Traverse right along the ledge, then climb a short groove, move left, and finish up the wall above.

RAVEN CRAG, THRESHWAITE COVE   (419112)

Good steep rock, facing south-east, makes this crag one of the best discoveries in recent times. All the climbs are superb and hard; the easiest is E2. It slants diagonally up the steep hillside overlooking Pasture Beck and is impressive.
Approach: From the car-park at Low Hartsop village, cross the bridge and follow the track alongside Pasture Beck. When the crag can be seen (you have to pass the crag to see it, as it faces up the valley), go steeply up to it (¾ hour).

Topography: About 300 ft./91 m. long and 120 ft./36 m. high, the crag sweeps diagonally up the hillside. On the left of the mid-section is a whitish shield-like wall, undercut at the base (this wall is taken by Top Gear), and right of this, just about centre, there is a most obvious steep crackline (Redex).

The climbs are described from left to right, descending the hillside.

Descent: Down a rake running behind and parallel to the crag.

165 **Top Gear** *** E4 (5a, 6a)

140 ft./43 m. *P. Whillance and D. Armstrong 1981*

Takes a line from right to left across the shield-like face. Bold climbing a long way from protection. Start by a ragged crack underneath the right end of the shield.

1) 30 ft./9 m. (5a) Up the crack to the big ledge below the overhang, and various belays (Friends best). 2) 110 ft./33 m. (6a) Move right and up a short flake crack right of the overhangs. Then pull left to gain a short flake crack right of the overhangs. Then pull left to gain a sloping foothold on the bottom right-hand edge of the shield. Step up (take care to arrange nut protection to Friend on right), then follow the weakness left across the face to reach a slight groove. Up this to make a final committing move on to gangway slab. Traverse right to mantelshelf on to the glacis. Step right and climb the corner to the top.

166 **Redex** ** E2 (5b, 5c)

130 ft./40 m. *C. W. Brown and T. W. Birkett (shar.) 1976*

The original climb. Start at the obvious rightward-slanting crack near the centre of the crag.

1) ft./50 m. 15 m. (5b) Climb the crack strenuously to belay at the horizontal break. 2) 80 ft./24 m. (5c) Up the continuation of the crack to a small birch tree. Step right into a groove and up this to the top.

167 **GTX** *** E3 (6a)

130 ft./40 m. *P. Whillance and R. Parker 1980*

Excellent sustained climbing. Start at a shallow scoop 15 ft./4 m. right of Redex.

1) 130 ft./40 m. (6a) Up the groove rightwards to a scoop, then step left and steeply up the wall to the obvious break. Up Redex

to the tree, then move left and climb up to an overhang. Pull over into a groove and up to a further overhang. Finger-jam over this to a ledge and finish left.

168 **Running on Empty**   ***   E4   (6a+)
120 ft./36 m.   *J. Lamb and P. Botterill   1981*
Superb climbing throughout. Takes the stepped groove right of the first section of GTX, pulling across a steep wall to a groove right of the final groove of Redex. Start at the left end of the easy ramp.
1)   120 ft./36 m. (6a+) Up the groove, moving right at the top of the first break. Pull over the overlap, gaining the wall above the spike (crux) and move up and across right to the groove. Up this to the top. Peg and block belays.

169 **High Performance**   **   E4   (6b, 6a)
140 ft./43 m.   *P. Botterill and J. Lamb   (alt.)   1981*
Down to the right in the lower wall is a thin crack. A technical and strenuous climb. Start 25 ft./8 m. left of the easy groove on the right of the crag.
1)   80 ft./24 m. (6b) Go up to a niche below and left of the thin crack. Continue to the crack: excellent runners but hard to start. Climb it to make hard final moves to belay on the slabby ledge by the side of a huge block.   2)   60 ft./18 m. (6a) Move right into the groove above the belay and traverse right to a big hold on the right edge. Step up and back left into the groove to make an exceptionally long reach to a hold high on the left (possible to flick in a nut on a sling, up to the right). Pull through the capping roof to the ledge on the left, then continue up the wall above to a stance and small nut belays.

WINTER CLIMBING

The eastern side of the Helvellyn-Fairfield chain frequently gives good winter climbing. Because of the altitude and aspect of the high corries, conditions are more reliable here than in the rest of the Lake District. On Helvellyn, Striding Edge is a good winter scramble, for which it is advisable to carry crampons. The gully just on the left of the final slopes also gives a good finish (Grade I). The slopes above Red Tarn give straightforward snow

Redex, first pitch

climbing with some steeper alternatives.

Further south in Grisedale, the crags at the head of Nethermost Cove and Dollywaggon Cove give several good gully and face climbs (Grade I/III). The gullies of St Sunday Crag also give some good routes. The high coves of Deepdale and Dovedale offer a variety of gullies, with potentially harder climbs on Hutaple Crag if conditions are very good. There are two gullies here – West Hutaple Gully which is likely to be Grade II, and Curving Gully, in the centre of the crag, which is around Grade III.

THIRLMERE

This pleasant valley is a good centre. The two crags described below can both be reached in 15 minutes, and have a large choice of hard climbs.

Access

From Penrith and the motorway, turning off down St John's-in-the-Vale. From Ambleside in the south or Keswick in the north, via the A591. There is a regular bus service through Thirlmere between Keswick and Ambleside.

Accommodation and camping

Camping and caravanning at Dale Bottom (296218) and Bracken Riggs (299205). The nearest hotels are in Thirlspot and Threlkeld, further hotels at Keswick and Grasmere. There is a YH at Stanah Cross (318190), close to the crags.

Food and drink

Only at the hotels mentioned above and at some local farms. The nearest bar is at Thirlspot (318178), normal licensing hours 11–3, 5.30–10.30 (Fri. & Sat. 11.00); Sun. 12–2, 7–10.30. There is a PO at Dale Head (317184), but the nearest shops are in Threlkeld and Keswick (early closing: Wed.). Milk and eggs can be obtained locally.

Garages and car hire

The nearest garage for petrol and repairs is at Threlkeld (tel. 649; night: Keswick 72843), which also offers a car-hire service (open 6 days a week until 6 p.m.). There is a taxi service in Keswick (tel. 72676). The nearest AA garages are in Thornthwaite, on the other side of Keswick (tel. Thornthwaite 238 or 538) or in Ambleside (tel. 33273 or 32025).

General services

Telephones at Dale Bottom (296218), and Legburthwaite (318191). Car park and public toilet at Legburthwaite (317195). There are several climbing shops in both Keswick and Ambleside.

Mountain rescue

For assistance, ring the local police, giving as much information as possible. They will contact the Mountain Rescue team which is based at Keswick.

CASTLE ROCK OF TRIERMAIN   (322197)

Castle Rock consists of two crags of excellent, steep rock facing west across the southern entrance to St John's-in-the-Vale. The

163

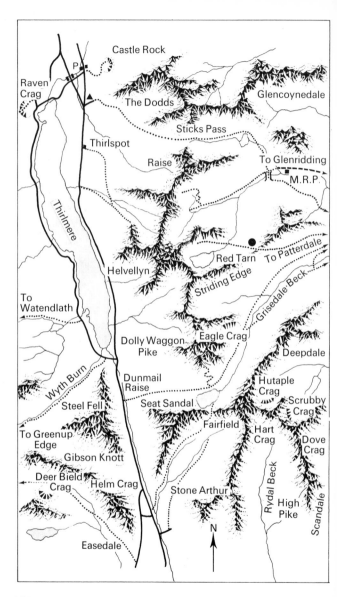

crags are well seen from the main Ambleside to Keswick road. All the climbs described are in the Very Severe category and most are located on the north crag. This crag, more than anywhere else in the Lakes, offers very steep climbing on clean rock with incut holds. Strong fingers are a distinct advantage. The crag dries quickly after rain and the overhanging nature of the routes give some protection against the elements!

Access

From the farm directly below the crag, take the gate on the right and follow a path through the fields to a bridge over a conduit (at the left-hand, north end). Continue through woods to the crag, which is reached in 10 minutes from the road.

Descent: It is probably quickest to the south – round the end of the south crag. Alternatively circle back and well round the end of the northerly crags.

170 **North Crag Eliminate**   **   E1   (4b, –, 5a, 5b)
260 ft./79 m.   *H. Drasdo and D. Gray   1952*

A superb climb, combining technical difficulty with considerable exposure. The route follows the overhanging arête at the left-hand (north) end of the crag. Start just left of the wall at the foot of a huge, open groove.

1)   110 ft./33 m. (4b) Gain the groove and follow it for 20 ft./6 m. before climbing out leftwards. Move right at the top to reach a terrace and tree belays.   2)   30 ft./9 m. Move left and climb a hidden chimney to a stance behind a large yew tree.   3)   30 ft./9 m. (5a) Climb the tree to the topmost branches! It should then be possible to reach good handholds and to swing up and right. Traverse right to a superbly exposed stance and tree belay.   4)   90 ft./27 m. (5b) Move left to the start of an impressive gangway. Runner. Climb the gangway with increasing difficulty to a very welcome large flake. Traverse left round the corner to a niche. Move delicately up and right and on to the arête which leads to the summit.

Overleaf left: Castle Rock of Triermain

Overleaf right: The final pitch of North Crag Eliminate, Castle Rock

171 **Agony** ** E1 (5b, 5b)
270 ft./82 m.   *G. Oliver and N. Brown*   *1959*
A splendid, if somewhat serious, climb comprising two long
pitches – first a steep wall, then an overhanging arête. Start at a
break just right of the wall at the north end of the crag.
1)   120 ft./36 m. (5b) Move right and climb the wall on small
holds to the break in the gangway which crosses the wall from
right to left. Traverse horizontally right for about 30 ft./9 m. then
go directly up a steep groove. Continue up the wall above to an
easy traverse line – move right to a tree belay.   2)   150 ft./46 m.
(5b) Move up into the corner above (Overhanging Bastion) then
traverse up and right, with increasing difficulty, to reach a good
ledge (runner). Move awkwardly left back on to the arête and
follow this steeply to gain a groove above. The groove leads more
easily to a huge slab: traverse this leftwards to the top.

172 **Overhanging Bastion** *** VS (5a)
270 ft./82 m.   *R. J. Birkett, C. R. Wilson and L. Muscroft*   *1939*
A tremendous and very exciting climb which follows the obvious
gangway slanting left across the main face (well seen from the
road). It is one of the best climbs at this standard in the Lake
District. Pitch 4 has been poorly protected since 1939 and should
not have peg runners placed there now! Start 70 ft./21 m. right of
the wall below a holly.
1)   40 ft./12 m. Climb to the holly and pull round it to a ledge.
Move left to some ash trees below a steep corner.   2)   60 ft./18
m. Climb the wall for 15 ft./4 m. then follow the interesting
corner to a good ledge and belay.   3)   40 ft./12 m. Follow the
slab just left of the continuing corner, until an airy move round to
the left reveals a ledge and pinnacle belay.   4)   65 ft./20 m.   (5a)
From the top of the pinnacle make some delicate moves to get on
to the gangway. Follow this more easily (runners) until it ends.
Move round left and slightly down on to a very exposed wall
which fortunately has some very good holds. Move left then go
straight up to a recess and tree belay.   5)   65 ft./20 m. Move
out of the recess on the right and follow a slab and easy wall to
the top.

Thirlmere Eliminate, Castle Rock

173 **May Day Cracks**   *   VS

205 ft./62 m.   *R. J. Birkett and L. Muscroft*   *1947*

A strenuous and sustained route up the cracks which bisect the north crag.

1)   50 ft./15 m. As for Overhanging Bastion.   2)   125 ft./38 m. From the right-hand end of the ledge, ascend the strenuous chimney (often wet) to the remains of a tree. The V-groove above is still difficult, but less strenuous, and leads to a steep wide crack. Climb this and gain a slab on the left. The continuation crack is climbed to a stance and belay.   3)   30 ft./9 m. The easier crack above to a large ledge. Scramble off to the right or finish up the big slab on the left.

174 **Thirlmere Eliminate**   ***   E1   (4c, 4c, 5b)

185 ft./56 m.   *P. Ross and P. J. Greenwood (var.)*   *1955*

A superb climb which starts below a large flake some 20 ft./6 m. right of Overhanging Bastion.

1)   50 ft./15 m. (4c) Climb the right-hand side of the flake, then from the top mantelshelf on to a small ledge. Move right and up a corner to a ledge and tree belay.   2)   75 ft./23 m. (4c) Traverse left and move up a corner until it is possible to swing left on to the arête. This is followed direct to a sloping ledge and peg belay.   3)   60 ft./18 m. (5b) The impressive corner above. Climb the overhang, then bridge up the steep corner-groove to the top.

175 **White Dwarf**   *   E2   (4c, 5c)

150 ft./46 m.   *T. W. Birkett and K. W. Forsythe*   *1978*

A steep pitch taking the obvious line up the white cone directly above the little tree belay of Thirlmere Eliminate.

1)   50 ft./15 m. (4c) As for Thirlmere Eliminate.   2)   100 ft./30 m. (5c) Up the face of the white cone to move leftwards and up into the obvious corner above its apex. Climb the corner to a gangway and continue directly up the overhanging wall above to a tree belay.

176 **Harlot Face**   *   E1   (4c, 5b, –, –,)

170 ft./52 m.   *R. J. Birkett and L. Muscroft*   *1949*

Another steep and fingery climb on excellent rock. Start some 50 ft./15 m. right of Thirlmere Eliminate at a break in the wall.

1)   50 ft./15 m. (4c) Move up to a ledge, then start up a corner

on the left. Move left on to the wall which leads steeply to a long narrow ledge. Belay at the right-hand end.   2)   45 ft./14 m. (5b) Climb the overhanging corner for 15 ft./4 m. then move round the arête on the right. A few moves lead to a large block for runner and rest. Climb the bulging corner to a ledge and tree belays.   3)   20 ft./6 m. From the top left corner of the ledge, go through a crevasse to the foot of a chimney.   4)   55 ft./17 m. Climb the chimney and continue to the top.

177 **Direct Route**   *   MVS

135 ft./41 m.   *A. T. Hargreaves and G. G. McPhee   1930*
A very enjoyable, steep route. Start just right of the lower stone wall of the south crag.
1)   35 ft./11 m. A very steep pitch with some hidden, but very good, holds. Climb straight up for 20 ft./6 m., then move left and up to a small stance.   2)   70 ft./21 m. Climb the wall to the sentry box. Step left and continue to a ledge and belay.   3)   30 ft./9 m. Over a bulge to a slab finish.

RAVEN CRAG, THIRLMERE   (304188)

A large and rather daunting crag which dominates the north end of Thirlmere lake. It possesses some fine and impressive climbs. The rock needs rather more care than, say, Castle Rock, and the crag is fairly lichenous, making the routes slippery in wet conditions and slow to dry after rain.

Access
From the little car-park at the west end of the dam, take the path through the forest about 100 yds./91 m. to the north (to Castle Crag Fort). After about 10 minutes, traverse left through the forest to the foot of the crag.

Descent: Round to the north of the crag, down a grassy gully.

178 **Genesis/Anarchist**   *   HS

275 ft./84 m.   *P. Greenwood and H. Drasdo (alt.)   1952/P. Greenwood and R. Miller   1952*
A good combination with continuous interest. Starts on the right-hand buttress, some 20 ft./6 m. right of a larch tree, and directly below a bulge and groove.
1)   35 ft./11 m. Climb the bulge and groove to a stance under an overhang.   2)   45 ft./14 m. Go up to an overhang, then move right and climb a groove and crack to a corner.   3)   30 ft./9 m.

Climb the corner crack, moving out on the right wall, to a large ledge and flake belay.   4)   40 ft./12 m. Straight up the fine wall.   5)   20 ft./6 m. Walk left to belay on an oak.   6)   50 ft./15 m. Move into the groove on the left of the grass and follow it to the start of the impressive crack.   7)   55 ft./17 m. The fine crack (rather slippery when wet) leads to the final terrace. A good pitch.

179   **Empire**   *   E3   (5a, 5b, 6a)
210 ft./64 m.   *K. Myhill and K. Jones (var.)*   *1973/Free: J. Lamb 1973*

Enjoyable and open climbing up the walls left of Anarchist. Start at the lowest point of the crag and scramble past rowan trees to a large block at the foot of a steep wall (as for Totalitarian).
1)   210 ft./64 m. (5a) (This pitch is often avoided by following easier ground to the right.) Move right to climb into a shallow groove. Up to the ledges and belay on the right.   2)   110 ft./33 m. (5b) Move up left into the niche and exit low on its right. Take the ramp rightwards then up, slightly leftwards, to a small ledge. Go up the slab above to an obvious steep groove. Up this, then left to belay on a small stance (shared with Totalitarian).   3)   40 ft./12 m. (6a) Move up to the overlap and pull rightwards (peg runner) on to the wall. Step right then up to the top.

180   **Totalitarian**   ***   E2   (5a, 5a, 4b, 5c)
270 ft./82 m.   *C. J. S. Bonington and M. Thompson*   *1964/Free: E. Grindley*

A particularly fine and varied climb following a continuously steep line. Start at the lowest point of the crag and scramble past rowan trees to a large block at the foot of a steep wall.
1)   60 ft./18 m. (5a) From the block, step left and climb a shallow groove until it is possible to pull on to a small ledge. Step left across the overhanging wall and pull into a niche. Move out right and continue to a good ledge and belay below an open groove.   2)   65 ft./20 m. (5a) Climb the groove to the bulge, then gain the slab on the right. Continue up the steep wall to the stance and belay at the end of pitch 1 of Communist Convert.
3)   60 ft./18 m. Pitch 2 of Communist Convert. Climb the

Raven Crag, Thirlmere   A = Approach to the cave

groove above leading to a good stance and peg belay below the big roof. 4) 60 ft./18 m. (5c) An impressive final pitch. Traverse right to a smooth slab, which leads up to the edge of the roof. Climb the corner on the left and move right at the top to the foot of an impending crack, which is followed to the summit.

181 **Communist Convert** ** VS

210 ft./64 m. *A. R. Dolphin, D. Hopkin and party* *1953*

So called because it goes from left to right! An enjoyable, delicate climb taking a diagonal line across the face from the cave at first. The Direct Finish is described. Start at the foot of an open corner on the right-hand side of the cave. This is reached from a point 30 ft./9 m. right of the steep grass slope on the left side of the crag. Climb a short chimney-crack then scramble up to the right. 1) 50 ft./15 m. Ascend the slabs and move right to an exposed stance and belay on the rib. 2) 60 ft./18 m. Go diagonally right to gain an open groove. This diagonal line is followed via an awkward mantelshelf to a small rock ledge and peg belay. 3) 30 ft./9 m. Cross a steep wall on the left to a rock ledge. Move down and left to belay on a grass ledge. 4) 70 ft./21 m. Climb up and right to gain a corner on the left of the big overhangs and follow this to the summit.

182 **The Gates of Delirium** ** E4 (5c+, 6a+, 4b)

200 ft./61 m. *P. Botterill and S. Clegg (var.)* *1976*

A hard climb, moving up to the cave, then moving left to climb a groove above the cave. A product of the Lakeland free-climbing renaissance. Reach the back of the cave by scrambling/easy climbing as for the Medlar. 1) 60 ft./18 m. (5c+) Up to the little cave, then traverse out left, with sundry peg runners, to a foothold stance in an intimidating position. 2) 70 ft./21 m. (6a+) Go up into the groove and climb until the left wall steepens (small wires). Make a blind move, on tiny holds, out left on to the edge, to better holds, and continue to a ledge. Step right, back above the groove line, and tackle the head wall directly to reach a grass stance. A sustained and serious pitch, with tremendous technical climbing. 3) 70 ft./21 m. (4b) Scramble left to the corner-crack and up this to the top.

Gates of Delirium traverses left from here: Chris Harper climbing

183   **The Medlar**   *   E3   (–, 6a, 4b)
200 ft./61 m.   *M. Boysen and C. J. S. Bonington   1964/Free: C. Jones   1976*

A fierce climb, both in appearance and in practice! It ascends the large corner above the left-hand side of the cave. Start at a short chimney, about 30 ft./9 m. right of the steep grass slope bounding the crag on the left.

1)   65 ft./20 m. The chimney-crack is followed by a scramble rightwards to below the centre of the cave. Climb the leftward-slanting gangway, move right and ascend to the small medlar tree at the left-hand side of the cave.   2)   95 ft./29 m. (6a) Move left and climb the wall to a good foothold below the overhang. Move left past a good thread runner, then up to a minute ledge. Climb the corner with 2 peg runners, then traverse left to where difficulties ease. Go up to a good ledge.   3)   80 ft./24 m. (4b) Ascend to a recess, then move up and left before continuing direct to a grass ledge. Climb the corner-crack above to the top.

WINTER CLIMBING

Launchy Ghyll (330158) III gives a tremendous ice climb when frozen, as do Shoulthwaite Ghyll (297196) IV and the more traditional Sandbed Ghyll (320218) II/III.

The Medlar, Raven Crag, Thirlmere

BORROWDALE

This valley has a tremendous variety of crags and climbs to offer at all standards. It is an excellent centre, as in dry weather the high crags (Scafell and Great Gable) are reasonably accessible, as well as the local crags. In wet weather (which some expect as 'typical' Borrowdale!), the valley probably has more to offer than any other, particularly on the superb rock of Shepherd's Crag. Some of the crags, but by no means all, are rather vegetated and should be avoided in wet conditions. Borrowale is often at its best in the winter months, when vegetation and tourists are at a minimum.

Access

The valley can be approached by car from Keswick in the north or from Buttermere over Honister Pass to Seatoller at the south end. The last petrol station is in Keswick. There is a regular bus service up the valley from Keswick – about every 70 minutes in the summer months; during the winter (from 1 November), 6 a day from 6.40 a.m. to 7.20 p.m., 9 p.m. on Saturday only. Borrowdale can also be reached on foot from Ambleside over Greenup, from Langdale over Stake Pass or from Wasdale over Sty Head.

Accommodation and camping

Camping is restricted to the official site at Keswick (go down the road past the bus station) and to farm campsites at Grange (see approach to Goat Crag), Stonethwaite, Seatoller and Seathwaite. There are several caravan sites in and around Keswick. The valley is well served by hotels and guest-houses. There is a good selection in Keswick and many others are scattered up the valley. Youth hostels are found at Keswick, at Barrow House (268200), at Grange (247171) and at Longthwaite (254142). There is also a hostel at the summit of Honister Pass (224135). There is an FRCC hut at Rosthwaite and a Northumbrian MC hut near the Bowderstone (255164).

Food and drink

As well as the hotels and guest-houses, there are restaurants in Keswick and one (licensed) in Seatoller. The latter is closed on Mondays and during the winter months (October to April). Cafés abound for the tourists, particularly in Grange, Seatoller and Seathwaite. There are shops in Keswick, Grange and Rosthwaite. Early closing is on Wednesday and market day on

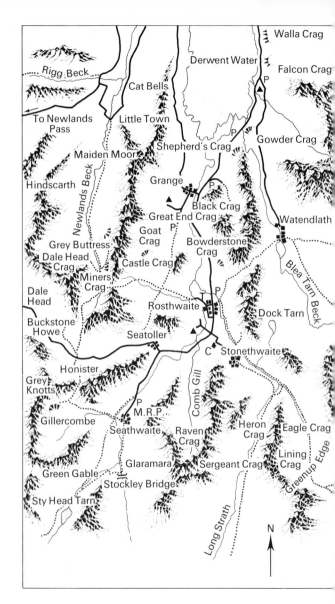

Saturday. Many of the hotels have only private bars; there are public bars in Keswick (approx. 12 around the square, plus many others) and at the Scafell Hotel in Rosthwaite (now closed Mon.–Wed. in winter). Licensing hours are 11–3, 5.30–10.30 on weekdays and 12–2, 7–10.30 on Sundays, with 11 p.m. closing on Fridays and Saturdays.

Garages and car hire

The nearest petrol is in Keswick (last pump closes 11 p.m., earlier on Sun.) For garage repairs, telephone Keswick 72064 (closes 6 p.m.) or Thornthwaite 238 or 538. Taxis in Keswick (tel. 72676). Car hire in Keswick (tel. 72064).

General services

There is a tourist information office in the Moot Hall, Keswick. Here one can hire guides for walking and/or climbing. There are public telephones at Seathwaite, Seatoller, Rosthwaite and Grange. Public toilets are at Keswick, Grange and Seatoller. Equipment shops of all kinds are found in Keswick.

Mountain rescue

For assistance, first ring the local police, giving as much information as possible. They will contact the Mountain Rescue team which is based at Keswick. Stretchers and first-aid kits are available at the following points: Seathwaite Farm (236121) and Styhead Pass (218095).

FALCON CRAGS (271205)

These impressive and deservedly popular crags have a good selection of *hard* climbs: all in the VS category and above. The crags are west facing and dry quickly (though not as quickly as Shepherd's Crag). The rock on the climbs described is generally good, but a watch should be kept for the occasional loose hold.

Approach : Park in a lay-by two miles from Keswick; the crags are clearly visible and reached by easy paths in 10 minutes. If the lay-by is full, there is a car-park a few yards up the Watendlath road on the left.

Descent : Obvious and easy grass slopes to the north of the crags.

UPPER FALCON CRAG

184 **Falcon Crag Buttress Route 1**   ***   E2   (5a, 5b, 5c+)
210 ft./64 m.   *P. Ross and P. Lockey   1958/Free: A. Parkin and P. Clarke   1975*

One of the best climbs in Borrowdale in spite of some doubtful rock. Follows a line up the centre of the upper crag via the obvious giant corner. Starts in the centre of the crag above a grassy hump where an oak tree grows.

1) 80 ft./24 m. (5a) Follow the rather loose corner up and right. Continue up a short black groove to a small ledge and peg belay on the right.   2)   70 ft./21 m. (5b) Climb a steep wall for 20 ft./6 m. to a peg runner, then traverse left and climb a strenuous overhanging crack (peg runner). Continue up the steep wall to a small stance and peg belay below the impressive final corner.   3)   60 ft./18 m. (5c+) Sustained strenuosity. Climb the corner directly with a precarious move into the final groove. (Best achieved by first moving high up the improbable-looking overhanging wall, then stepping left.)

185 **Dry Grasp**   **   E3   (5a, 5b, 6a)
195 ft./59 m.   *P. Livesey (solo)   1974*
Another good technical wall climb, taking the centre of the clean central head wall of Upper Falcons.

1)   70 ft./21 m. (5a) As for first pitch of Route 1.   2)   65 ft./20 m. (5b) Take the black groove on the left. Climb a bulge to a second bulge and over this. Up leftwards to an easy groove leading to a stance at the base of the headwall (peg belay). 3)   60 ft./18 m. (6a) Take the crack leading diagonally left to a peg runner. Now use small ramp holds to climb up the wall (crux) to reach a small ledge. Bear diagonally leftwards to a ledge. Up right to a crack and finish directly or with a step left. Belays well back.

LOWER FALCON CRAG
186 **Spinup**   **   VS
145 ft./44 m.   *P. Ross and D. Sewell   1957*
An exciting climb which starts behind a large ash tree below the left-hand corner of the lower crag.

1)   65 ft./20 m. Climb the slab leftwards, then go straight up until a gangway leads to a small stance and piton belay.   2)   80 ft./24 m. Cross the wall on the right with difficulty and climb a steep black groove for 10 ft./3 m., then step right and descend to gain an exposed traverse above the overhangs. When the traverse ends, climb straight up to the top of the crag.

Upper Falcon Crag

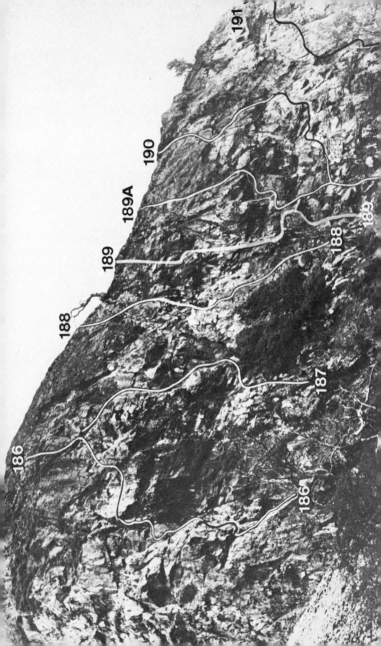

187 **Hedera Grooves** * MVS
135 ft./41 m. *P. Lockey and P. Ross* *1956*
A pleasant and quite exposed climb. Start just to the left of the
ivy mass.
1) 80 ft./24 m. Move up to a grass ledge and hawthorn bush,
then climb a short steep groove. Traverse right to another
groove; climb this then traverse left to a large, obvious holly
tree. 2) 55 ft./17 m. Climb the groove above to a tree stump.
Continue up the gangway on the left to the top of the crag.

188 **Funeral Way** HVS (5a, 4c)
165 ft./50 m. *P. Ross and P. G. Greenwood* *1956*
The route starts about 100 ft./30 m. right of the ivy mass in a
corner just right of an undercut gangway. Tree belay.
1) 75 ft./23 m. (5a) Climb on to the gangway with difficulty,
using holds on the right wall. Continue up and diagonally
leftwards to a flake crack. Climb this to a stance and belays
below a groove cutting through the overhangs. 2) 90 ft./27 m.
(4c) Easily at first then awkward bridging. At the top of the
groove, go up left along the exposed gangway to the top of the
crag, then traverse back right to belay on a large tree.

189 **Close Encounters** * E3 (6a, 5c)
170 ft./52 m. *R. O. Graham, T. W. Birkett (alt.) and R.
McHaffie* *1978*
Sustained difficulties. Start from the bay right of Funeral Way.
1) 100 ft./30 m. (6a) Climb the groove behind the tree to the
overhang; then move right and up to the peg at the start of the
traverse of the Niche. Traverse left to a groove (peg runner) and
up this to a horizontal weakness and belay (slightly
right). 2) 70 ft./21 m. (5c) Go back left, about 20 ft./6 m., to
climb a clean groove up to the overhanging wall. At the top of the
short groove, pull out left, on finger pockets, on to a slab.
Continue directly to the top.

189A **The Niche** *** E2 (5c, 5b, 4c)
175 ft./53 m. *A. Liddell and R. McHaffie* *1962/Free: J. Adams and
C. Read* *1971*
A very fine extreme with technical climbing on excellent rock.

Falcon Crag, Borrowdale

Starts 25 ft./8 m. right of Funeral Way.

1) 65 ft./20 m. (5c) Climb the bulge and the steep wall above for 30 ft./9 m., then climb a rib on the left to a peg. Move right into the Niche itself. Peg belay.   2) 40 ft./12 m. (5b) Climb up the back of the niche before traversing strenuously right to a gap through the overhang. Pull over this, then climb a gangway to a small stance and peg belay.   3) 70 ft./21 m. (4c) Continue up the gangway and wall above.

190 **Dedication**   **   E1   (4c, 5a)
160 ft./49 m.   *P. Ross and E. Metcalf   1957*
A surprisingly delicate climb, threading its way through the overhangs which guard the most formidable part of the crag. Start at the same point as the Niche.

1) 60 ft./18 m. (4c) Pull over the bulge, then move right to a small ledge. Mantelshelf, then traverse right to a ledge of shattered blocks.   2) 100 ft./30 m. (5a) From the right-hand end of the ledge, pull over a small overhang into an open groove. Climb this then step right and move up a few feet, before stepping left on to a fine gangway-corner. Up this until it is possible to move left. Finish up the continuation of the gangway.

191 **Illusion**   **   HVS   (4b, 5a)
145 ft./44 m.   *P. Lockey and P. Ross   1956*
A tremendous, classic climb with a long traverse below the huge roof. It starts near the right-hand end of the crag on a block behind a high tree.

1) 25 ft./8 m. (4b) Straight up to a stance and belays.
2) 100 ft./30 m. (5a) Climb a steep, awkward groove until it is possible to gain a huge flake up on the right. Traverse right to the first of several deep grooves. (Runners in the back of these will obviously cause rope-drag.) Continue rightwards towards the final corner under the roof. When this is reached, swing round the arête to a ledge and belay.   3) 20 ft./6 m. An easy wall above.

WATENDLATH – REECASTLE CRAG   (274176)

An excellent evening crag, 5 minutes from the road, getting the afternoon sunshine. The rock is good and very steep. The

Illusion, Lower Falcon Crag

Watendlath road (leaving the main Borrowdale road immediately after Falcon Crags) is followed for 2½ miles, until the barrel-shaped buttress of Reecastle Crag can be seen up on the left.

192 **White Noise** ** E2 (5c)
100 ft./30 m. *J. Lamb and R. McHaffie 1978*
Steep climbing, very well protected. Just right of centre is a sma hawthorn. Start about 20 ft./6 m. left of the hawthorn at a large block below an impending scoop.
1) 100 ft./30 m. (5c) Climb up strenuously to gain a thin, slightly leftward-slanting crack in a whitish ramp. Continue up this to a bulge (rather mossy) and straight on over to nut belays

193 **Rack Direct** ** E2 (5c)
120 ft./36 m. *S. O. Miller and R. Parker 1977*
Sustained difficulties and strenuous. Start immediately right of White Noise.
1) 120 ft./36 m. (5c) Climb the steep wall to the obvious break Go straight up to a large tree at the top of the crag.

194 **The Rack** ** HVS (5a)
130 ft./37 m. *R. McHaffie and party 1973*
An early route up this bulging crag – a good climb. Starts 12 ft./ m. left of the hawthorn and climbs the steep wall, finishing up a crack slightly to the left.
1) 130 ft./37 m. (5a) Up the steep wall to move on to a sloping ledge. Go right and up to a further ledge; then climb the impending wall to a rest on the left. Move up and diagonally lef to a sloping ledge. Descend to a line of holds leading to the crack Up this and a widening groove to a flake and ledge on the right. Up the rib to a tree belay.

195 **The Gibbet** E1 (5b)
100 ft./30 m. *P. Ross, A. N. Boydell and F. Briant 1964/Free: D. Armstrong and R. Parker 1978*
Start right of centre below a gangway slanting to the right.
1) 110 ft./30 m. (5b) Go diagonally left, then right to below th overhanging wall below the start of the gangway. Pull on to the

Reecastle Crag, Watendlath

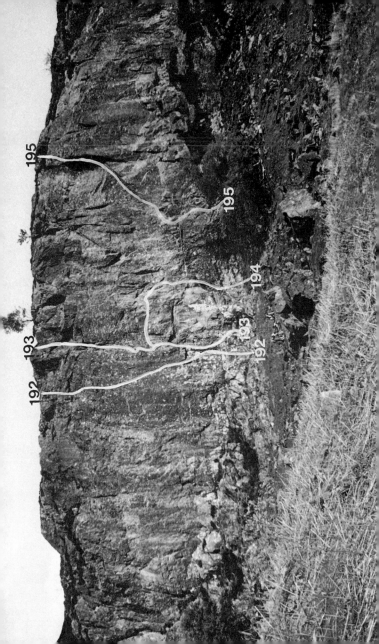

gangway and follow it to a steep groove. Climb this until it is possible to move out right and on up to the top.

GOWDER CRAG   (266187)

An impressive buttress clearly visible from the road near the Lodore Hotel. It is approached via the tourist path from the hotel to the waterfall, or by a path a few hundred yards to the north which skirts the hotel grounds (and avoids payment of the toll!). The rock is good but, once again, a watch should be kept for loose blocks. The route described faces the afternoon sun and dries quickly.

196 **Fool's Paradise**   **   MVS
315 ft./96 m.   *P. W. Vaughan and J. D. J. Wildridge   1951*
A long varied climb with good situations. Start by scrambling up for 25 ft./8 m. to a tree just right of the ridge running down to the lowest point of the crag.
1)   40 ft./12 m. Follow the corner over blocks to belay on a tree under an overhang.   2)   40 ft./12 m. Traverse delicately left on to the ridge and climb this to a large ledge and belay.   3)   65 ft./20 m. Descend a little on the right to gain a traverse across the slabs. Follow this for some 65 ft./20 m. then climb up to a crack. Make a difficult move right, then find a belay by a block on the right, or continue up the next pitch.   4)   50 ft./15 m. Move left into the obvious groove and climb this, taking the left-hand branch to a terrace and tree belays.   5)   50 ft./15 m. Traverse right along the terrace to the foot of a deep chimney.
6)   70 ft./21 m. Climb the chimney and pull over the overhang. Go up the wall to the final chimney, which is awkward to start. A good pitch.

SHEPHERD'S CRAG   (264185)

A unique climbing ground! The buttresses provide good pitches for both beginner and tiger, and dry very quickly after rain. The rock is generally excellent.

Access to the crags is particularly easy as they are next to the road at a point 4 miles from Keswick, just pass the Lodore Hotel.

There are a great many climbs here apart from the ones described; most of these would be obvious on further exploration.

White Noise, Reecastle Crag

The climbs are described from left to right and are reached by a short walk through the wood from the top of the little hill 100 yds/84 m. south of the Lodore Hotel.

197 Brown Crag Wall   *   HS

190 ft./58 m.   *R. Wilkinson and K. C. Ogilvie   1950*
A good climb on the wall at the north end of Shepherd's Crag. It starts on polished holds about 75 ft./23 m. right of the fence and about 20 ft./6 m. left of a very steep groove (conclusion: E1 (5b)).
1)   50 ft./15 m. Climb up into a slippery little corner then move out right and up steeply to a ledge and peg belay.   2)   70 ft./21 m. Traverse left for 10 ft./3 m. then go up the fine wall, slightly left, until it is possible to traverse 20 ft./6 m. right to a tree belay.   3)   70 ft./21 m. Climb the steep but pleasant scoop running diagonally left to the top of the crag.

198 Brown Slabs Arête   *   D

150 ft./46 m.   *C. D. Frankland and Bentley Beetham   1922*
On the slabs just round the corner from Brown Crag Wall are three popular climbs. This one starts near the left-hand end of the slabs and goes up and diagonally left for 50 ft./15 m. to a conspicuous notch, then climbs the ridge in two pitches.

199 Brown Slabs Direct   VD

130 ft./40 m.   *Bentley Beetham   1948*
This climb starts about 20 ft./6 m. right of the Arête climb and goes directly up the slabs in three pitches.

200 Brown Slabs   D

130 ft./40 m.   *Bentley Beetham   1946*
Starts about 30 ft./9 m. left of the very polished corner-crack. It goes up a fault past two trees, then takes the easiest line up the upper slab to belay on the top.

201 Ardus   ***   S

120 ft./36 m.   *V. Veevers, H. Westmorland and P. Holt   1946*
Walk south from Brown Slabs along the path until a large buttress is reached. Ardus climbs the wide couloir/gully on the

Ardus, Shepherd's Crag

193

left of the main wall, finishing up an exciting slab. Start by moving up from the path to a ramp going diagonally right.

1) 55 ft./17 m. Climb across the ramp rightwards, then go up to belay in the gully below a huge block. 2) 30 ft./9 m. Climb over the block and continue direct to a large ledge and belays. 3) 35 ft./11 m. Traverse left across the exposed slab and climb the first crack reached to the top. The second crack, 10 ft./3 m. further left, is slightly easier. Tree belay.

202 **Aaros** * E1 (5b)
120 ft./36 m. *R. O. Graham, T. W. Birkett (var.), R. McHaffie and K. Forsythe 1978*
A surprisingly worthwhile climb directly up the wall left of Ardus. Start just right of Ardus.
1) 120 ft./36 m. (5b) Climb a short wall and cross Ardus to gain a shallow sentry box. Step right and climb straight up a steep wall until the angle eases. Climb directly up to the Ardus traverse and move right along this to a thin crack in the steep headwall, 10 ft./3 m. left of the corner (Ardus Direct). Climb the thin crack directly to the top (crux).

203 **Eve** ** VS
155 ft./47 m. *W. Peascod and B. Blake 1951*
Starts about 50 ft./15 m. right of Ardus behind a tree and beside a split block.
1) 40 ft./12 m. Climb a slab and steep crack to a ledge and block belays. 2) 65 ft./20 m. Up into the corner, then make a long stride left on to the rib. Go diagonally left across the big slab, with an awkward mantelshelf *en route*, to a small stance and nut belays. 3) 50 ft./15 m. Climb up the rib steeply, then go right following the obvious crack with good handholds and lots of exposure to the top of the crag.

204 **Adam** ** HVS (4c, 5a)
135 ft./41 m. *P. Ross and R. Wilkinson 1955*
A steep pitch, one of the best hereabouts, with good holds. Start in a corner some 20 ft./6 m. right of Eve.
1) 35 ft./11 m. (4c) Climb the crack on good jams to the large ledge and block belays. 2) 100 ft./30 m. (5a) Move up a polished wall on the right to a large runner. Then go left and up to gain a steep crack. Climb this, then move right steeply to

194

reach the holly tree. Climb up behind the tree (or the groove on the right) into a corner. Pull out left and climb the steep wall above to finish at the same point as Eve.

205 **Kransic Crack Direct**   HVS   (5a)
100 ft./30 m.   *G. B. Fisher, D. Oliver and F. Bantock (without direct finish)   1952*
The path south from the start of Adam arrives after several hundred yards at a steep, obvious crack forming the left-hand side of a huge flake.
1)   100 ft./30 m. (5a) Climb the excellent jamming crack to the top of the large flake. Traverse right along the flake, then across a steep wall. Then move up and back left on to the wall above the flake and climb this directly to the top. (The groove on the left of Kransic Crack is Fisher's Folly – VS. Climb the groove to a ledge and belay. Then make a long traverse right to finish at the same point as Kransic Crack Direct.)

206 **The Grasp**   E1   (5a+)
80 ft./24 m.   *D. McDonald, R. McHaffie and R. Robinson   1978*
A pleasant and popular extreme. Start below the right-hand side of Kransic Crack flake.
1)   80 ft./24 m. (5a+) Climb up to the obvious black bulge and pull over leftwards from the right-hand side (a long reach). Continue up the steep wall above and then take a slightly leftward-slanting gangway to the top.

207 **Little Chamonix**   *   VD
205 ft./62 m.   *Bentley Beetham   1946*
A deservedly popular climb. About 70 ft./21 m. right of Kransic Crack there is a chimney with an oak growing from it. Start about 20 ft./6 m. right of this chimney.
1)   25 ft./8 m. Climb a short crack to a ledge.   2)   65 ft./20 m. Move on to a corner on the left, then go up to gain a ramp leading up diagonally left to a large grassy terrace.   3)   40 ft./12 m. Scramble rightwards to a corner below impressive grooves.   4)   40 ft./12 m. Up the left-hand groove and climb over the block in a sitting position! Traverse the slab on the right and go up the arête to belays.   5)   35 ft./11 m. Climb the steep wall to a pinnacle, then make an exposed move right to reach a chimney which leads easily to the top. Tree belays.

BLACK CRAG (263174)

This superb large crag dominates the tiny valley of Troutdale and provides excellent climbing at all standards on good rock. It is divided into two buttresses by a vegetated gully. The right-hand buttress provides wall, groove and slab climbing and all the routes in the lower grades. Troutdale Pinnacle has tremendous variety and is one of the best climbs in Borrowdale. The left-hand buttress is steeper, with a band of overhangs, and several hard climbs.

Approaches: There are two. The easiest is from Derwent View (midway between the Borrowdale Hotel and Grange). A narrow lane leads left from the double bend into Troutdale, from where a path leads directly up to the crag. About 20 minutes. Cars should be left on the main road 100 yds./91 m. south of the lane entrance. Alternatively, from the Bowderstone car-park (253168), follow paths north-east over a little col into Troutdale. About 30 minutes to the crag.

Descent: From the top of the climbs, traverse the top of the crag to the south to join a good path descending from the col diagonally back to the foot of the crag.

208 **Troutdale Pinnacle**   ***   MS

360 ft./110 m.   *F. Mallinson and R. Mayson   1914*

This well-established classic climb starts where the footpath meets the foot of the crag, either at a broken chimney or up a crack on the right. It is rather harder, but still enjoyable, on a wet day.

1)   25 ft./8 m. The chimney or crack leads to a ledge with a belay at the right-hand end.   2)   45 ft./14 m. Climb a wall and a shallow groove to a large block belay.   3)   45 ft./14 m. Follow polished holds up a groove on the right on to the slabs. Climb these rightwards to belay below a short corner.   4)   35 ft./11 m. Move up the corner, then left on to a higher slab. Small stance and thread belay.   5)   70 ft./21 m. Traverse left, across and down the slab to the wall impasse (small stance and belay possible on the slab a few feet down). Climb the short, steep section on polished but good holds. Easier ledges soon lead to good belays.   6)   30 ft./9 m. The wall above to the top of the Pinnacle.   7)   60 ft./18 m. Ascend the corner up the steep ridge

Steve Hubbard on the Grasp, Shepherd's Crag

with good protection, finishing with an exciting move left to high footholds. Easily thereafter to a ledge and belays.

209 **Troutdale Pinnacle Superdirect**   HVS   (4a, 4b, 4a, 5a, 5a, −)

365 ft./111 m.   *P. Ross and D. Oliver   1954*

A fine varied climb which starts at the centre of a slab 20 ft./6 m. left of the previous climb.

1)   40 ft./12 m. (4a) Climb the slab to a large ledge and belays.   2)   75 ft./23 m. (4b) The steep crack above leads to a narrow ledge. Traverse right to a large block belay.

3)   80 ft./24 m. (4a) Climb the wall above, moving left occasionally, to a small ledge and belays below a superb-looking crack.

4)   75 ft./23 m. (5a) The fine steep crack.   5)   35 ft./11 m. (5a) Move up into a polished groove, then gain with difficulty an obvious finger-traverse on the right. Those with thin fingers have a distinct advantage on this traverse, which is followed to an easier groove leading to the top of the pinnacle.   6)   60 ft./18 m. As for last pitch of previous route.

210 **Prana**   *   E3   (5c)

140 ft./42 m.   *P. Gomersal   1977*

Takes a worthwhile line up the walls of the left buttress. Start just left of the tree-filled gully below slabs. Scramble up these (invariably wet) to a ledge and tree belay.

1)   140 ft./42 m. (5c) Climb a dark streak leading to the half-way roof. Pull directly over (small holds), then climb straight up the wall until a step left on to a ledge is made (junction with Grand Alliance). Straight up the bulging wall above to where the angle eases. Step left then, up to the top.

211 **Vertigo**   *   E2   (−, 5a, 5c, 5b)

260 ft./79 m.   *P. Ross and W. Aughton   1958/Free: P. Whillance and D. Armstrong   1977*

A highly enjoyable climb taking the obvious break in the overhangs on the left-hand buttress. Start below the centre of the buttress.

1)   40 ft./12 m. A grassy scramble and some wet ledges lead to a

Black Crag, Borrowdale

199

belay on a yew tree below the steep wall.   2)   50 ft./15 m. (5a)
The steep break on the left is climbed directly to the traverse line
across the wall. Move left to a peg belay below the huge
roof.   3)   40 ft./12 m. (5c) Move back right to below the break
in the overhangs. Gain the crack by means of a mantelshelf and
follow it, moving out right at the top, over the overhang, on to an
exposed ledge. Peg belay.   4)   130 ft./40 m. (5b) Climb the
steep wall and move left on to the rib. Follow this more or less
directly to the summit. This could be a hard pitch in greasy
conditions.

212   **Grand Alliance**   **   E3   (4c, 5b, 5c+, 4a)
230 ft./70 m.   *R. Matheson and E. Cleasby   1976*
An exceptionally fine main pitch. Starts up an arête to the right
of the corner of the Shroud.
   1)   35 ft./11 m. (4c) Follow the blunt arête to a block belay.
   2)   50 ft./15 m. (5b) Go across right to twin blocks. Move up
into the overhung corner, then pull out right to climb the wall
above. Block belay.   3)   105 ft./32 m. (5c+) Up towards the
break (as for Vertigo), then break out right beneath the roof.
Continue traversing with difficulty until it is possible to pull up
to small ledges. (Good diagonal nut slot above on the left.) Climb
the wall, trending leftwards to some undercuts. Step right and
make some technical moves up the wall to better holds. Easier
climbing leftwards then leads to a large block belay.
   4)   40 ft./12 m. (4a) Take the rib on the right to the top.

213   **The Shroud**   VS
240 ft./73 m.   *P. Ross and P. Lockey   1958*
A varied climb which is, however, rather mossy and slow to dry.
Starts at the foot of a steep groove at the northern end of the
left-hand buttress.
   1)   40 ft./12 m. Climb the fine groove to a ledge and belay on
the right.   2)   50 ft./15 m. Follow a shallow groove on the left
to an overhang. Move right and up to the peg belay under the
large overhang.   3)   70 ft./21 m. Traverse left for about 25 ft./8
m., then go straight up over a small overhang. Continue steeply;
pass another small overhang on the left and climb a short groove
to a grass ledge and peg belay.   4)   80 ft./24 m. Gain a rib on
the right and follow slabs and grooves rightwards to a bulge.
Move right and continue more easily to the top.

GRANGE CRAGS (258117)

These are a series of recently discovered/gardened crags, starting immediately above the Black Crag car-park on the double bend before Grange Bridge. They can be reached in seconds from the car-park, are quick to dry and offer extremely good rough rock (possibly the best in Borrowdale). The crags themselves belong to the National Trust but the land below is private. At the time of writing, climbers are using the crags with access only from the car-park, traversing along underneath the crags on the obvious worn path. Meanwhile the BMC are trying to resolve access problems.

CAR-PARK CRAG

This buttress lies immediately behind the car-park. Where a wall and wire fence abut the crag, there is an obvious groove to the left – this is Desmond Decker. The routes are described from left to right.

214 **First Contact** VS

40 ft./12 m. *R. McHaffie and P. Taylor 1984*

The short arête left of Desmond Decker.

215 **Desmond Decker** E2 (5c)

50 ft./15 m. *C. Downer, C. Bacon, R. McHaffie and P. Taylor 1984*

Take the obvious groove, hard to start, left of the wire fence.

216 **Fender Bender** E3 (5c)

70 ft./21 m. *C. Downer and R. McHaffie 1984*

Take the grooved arête directly above the wire fence.

216a **Mercedes** VS

60 ft./18 m. *R. McHaffie and C. Downer 1984*

The chimney groove right of the wall/fence, starting from the left.

Another dozen routes have been climbed to the right (VS-E2).

NAGG'S BUTTRESS

Really two buttresses separated by a dirty gully, they lie a few hundred yards over to the left of Car-park Crag, where the path

201

hits the crag, and are the biggest and best areas of rock on Grange Crags. The routes are described from right to left (as approached).

RIGHT-HAND BUTTRESS

217 **Red Neck**   E1   (5b)
100 ft./30 m.   *C. Downer and C. Bacon   1983*
The first route up the obvious wall. Climb the wall direct until forced rightwards on to the arête. Up the steep corner crack above.

218 **Sudden Impact**   *   E2   (5c)
100 ft./30 m.   *C. Downer and T. Watts   1983*
Climb the steep greenish wall up to a small roof. Pull over this on to a ledge. Gain the clean corner and follow it to the top.

LEFT-HAND BUTTRESS

219 **Rough Justice**   **   E2   (5c)
100 ft./30 m.   *C. Downer and P. Lee   1984*
Follow a curving crack to the right to enter a niche. Go up on to a ledge on the right and follow the crack on the left until forced across the wall to the right arête. Up this, then on to the top.

220 **Pressure Drop**   *   E2   (5c)
100 ft./30 m.   *C. Downer and P. Lee   1984*
From the same point as Rough Justice, go left of the crack to a vague scoop and up right to a ledge. Then go back left, using a short ramp to pull on to a ledge. Follow the corner above to the top.

221 **Sleeping Partner**   HVS   (5a)
110 ft./33 m.   *C. Downer and C. Bacon   1984*
Climb the obvious niche and pull out left up a steep juggy wall to an enjoyable slab finish.

GREAT END CRAG   (260170)
This crag, which was once heavily vegetated, has been the scene of several large fires. The centre of the crag has recently been

scoured of vegetation, cleaned and brushed to yield several new climbs. Some rock hereabouts needs care, but the climbs are good.

Approach: From Troutdale, using either of the approaches to Black Crag. Go directly up the hillside to the foot of the crag. Time 30 minutes.

Descent: A good path leads down through the trees on the east (Black Crag) side.

222 **Nagasaki Grooves** *** E4 (5b, 6b, 4b)
300 ft./91 m. *C. Read and J. Adams 1974/Free: P. Livesey (solo with back rope) 1974*

A good route, sustained at a reasonable standard, but with a distinct crux.

Start, as for Banzai Pipeline, at a pinnacle at the base of the crag (left of the biggest open corner).

1) 105 ft./32 m. (5b) As for Banzai Pipeline, pitch 1, to belay below the distinct jamming crack. 2) 150 ft./46 m. (6b) A long, absorbing pitch. Take the slab on the left leading into a series of grooves directly above. Balance up slightly right to the base of a smooth groove. Up this (crux), with a high step, to good holds below a bulge. Continue over this to another overlap and on directly up the groove to a ledge. 3) 45 ft./14 m. (4b) Up the crack at the back of the recess to the top. Flake belay back 15 ft./4 m.

223 **Banzai Pipeline** ** E1 (5b, 5a, 5a, 4c)
305 ft./93 m. *D. Nicol, C. Downer, H. Cobb and C. Bacon (alt.) 1977*

Another good route, with a first pitch that is bold and requires a cool approach. Start at a pinnacle at the base of the crag, left of the largest open corner, at the foot of the central pillar.

1) 105 ft./32 m. (5b) Move up a shallow white corner then left, over an overlap, to the foot of a clean corner. Climb the corner, then move left and ascend the next corner (crux) to a slab. Belay. 2) 50 ft./15 m. (5a) Take the jamming crack to a ledge. 3) 50 ft./15 m. (5a) Continue up the chimney-crack above to a ledge. 4) 100 ft./15 m. (4c) Go left to stand on a spike. Swing left into a slanting groove (Nagasaki Grooves), then climb the cleaned walls to the top.

224 **Great End Corner**   ***   HVS   (–, 4c, 5a)
250 ft./76 m.   *D. S. Nichol, C. Downer, I. Conway and A. Hellier   1975*

A good route, well protected. Starts below the corner in the centre of the crag.

1)   50 ft./15 m. Climb the corner to a ledge on the left. Tree root belay.   2)   150 ft./46 m. (4c) Climb the bed of the corner to a short smooth groove. Climb the groove (delicate), or the crack on the left wall, to a line of large flakes. Continue up the corner to a ledge. Piton belay.   3)   50 ft./15 m. (5a) Move left into the undercut groove and after a difficult pull continue more easily to the top.

225 **No Holds Barred**   E1   (5b, 4c)
220 ft./67 m.   *C. Downer and S. Kysow   1982*

Again, a worthwhile route dug from the vegetation. Start at the Corner.

1)   150 ft./46 m. (5b) Move right to climb the weakness up the wall, parallel to the corner, to gain an obvious traverse line.   2)   70 ft./21 m. (4c) Continue up a vertical corner to a grassy ledge, whence scrambling leads to the top.

BOWDERSTONE   (254164)

Reached from the Bowderstone car-park (10 mins.), this huge block of rock, its top overhanging its base, offers a wide variety of bouldering. The hardest, up the overhanging ladder face, are desperate and remain dry even during the wettest Lakeland summers. Recently certain climbers have been known to visit the Lake District purely to climb on the Bowderstone.

EAGLE CRAG   (277122)

This is the steep crag facing north across Greenup Ghyll, with an impressive profile well seen from Stonethwaite and the main Borrowdale road. The steepness and exposure, together with the excellent nature of the rock compensate for its dark aspect. All

Great End Crag, Borrowdale

Overleaf left: Al Phizacklea on the Bowderstone; Wall Direct above the Crack

Overleaf right: The Bowderstone

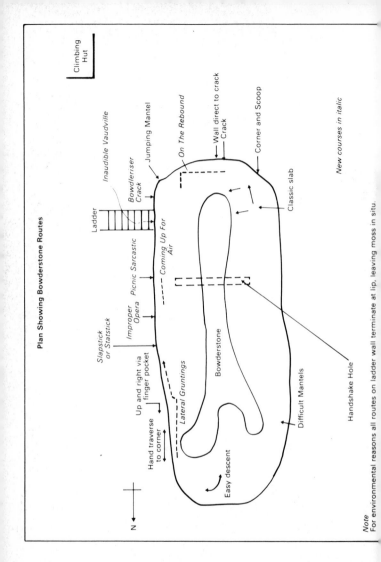

Plan Showing Bowderstone Routes

Climbing Hut

Inaudible Vaudville

Jumping Mantel

Bowdleriser Crack

On The Rebound

Wall direct to crack

Crack

Corner and Scoop

Ladder

Coming Up For Air

Classic slab

Picnic Sarcastic

Improper Opera

Slapstick or Statstick

Up and right via finger pocket

Lateral Gruntings

Bowderstone

Handshake Hole

Hand traverse to corner

Difficult Mantels

Easy descent

N

New courses in italic

Note
For environmental reasons all routes on ladder wall terminate at lip, leaving moss in situ.

Eagle Crag, Borrowdale

208

the routes here are in the VS category or above.

Approach: From Stonethwaite, cross the bridge and follow the Greenup path along the north side of the river. Leave the path near some sheep-folds, then cross the stream and go diagonally rightwards across the fellside to the foot of the crag.

Descent: Round the east end of the crag and down the true left bank of a wide grassy gully. There is another relatively small crag on the east side of the gully.

226 **The Great Stair** MVS

260 ft./79 m. *W. Peascod and S. B. Beck 1946*

At the east end of the crag, a short rake ascends from left to right. Start about 25 ft./8 m. up the rake.

1) 50 ft./15 m. Climb the wall past the tree to a ledge. Go straight up the second wall for a few feet, then diagonally right to a second small ledge and belay. 2) 35 ft./11 m. Diagonally left up the third wall to a large grass platform. 3) 55 ft./17 m. A steep wall with small holds leads to a ledge. Follow a diagonal line left to a grass terrace with a thread belay on the left arête. 4) 55 ft./17 m. A smooth wall is climbed rightward to turf ledges which lead to the foot of a fine chimney. 5) 65 ft./20 m. The pleasant chimney leads to the top.

227 **Falconer's Crack** ** VS

220 ft./67 m. *W. Peascod and S. B. Beck 1946*

A classic climb – at the top of the grade – involving a strenuous crack and delicate wall climbing. Start on the left of some steep corners left of the centre of the crag.

1) 25 ft./8 m. The crack has good holds and leads to a ledge and belay. 2) 35 ft./11 m. The narrow 'two step' crack is climbed over a bulge. 3) 30 ft./9 m. The groove above leads to a niche and belay near a peregrine's nest. 4) 60 ft./18 m. Move 15 ft./4 m. left to gain a rib, then climb the wall beyond. Easier climbing then leads to a belay below the chimneys of Great Stair. 5) 70 ft./21 m. Climb the face on the right of the chimney, finishing up a slab.

228 **Daedalus** ** E2 (5c, 5a)

160 ft./49 m. *P. Nunn, B. L. Griffiths and P. Ross 1965/(since climbed free)*

A steep, impressive climb with considerable difficulties. Start

210

below a very steep chimney in the steep corners to the right of Falconer's Crack. The route follows a thin crack up the green wall before finishing up the steep final wall.

1)   100 ft./30 m. (5c) Gain a ledge below the chimney. Climb the chimney and the ramp above to a tree. Ascend a bulge into a steep groove. Climb the groove, then go up the wall above, moving right to good holds. Climb diagonally rightwards to a triangular ledge and peg belay.   2)   60 ft./18 m. (5a) Step left and climb the steep wall to a slight groove. Continue up the groove to the top.

229 **Post Mortem**   *   E3   (5a, 6a)
140 ft./43 m.   *P. Ross and P. Lockey*   *1956*
Although not a long climb, Post Mortem is notorious as one of the most strenuous climbs in the Lake District. There are probably more tales of jammed knees, upside-down moves and involuntary descents associated with this climb than with any other! Start directly below the overhanging crack.

1)   80 ft./24 m. (5a) Follow a flake rightwards, then continue to a large ledge and tree belay.   2)   60 ft./18 m. (6a) The Crack. After the initial 20 ft./6 m., pass the chockstone, to continue strenuously, by layback at first, up the fine crack to the top.

230 **Inquest Direct**   **   E2   (5c, 4b)
180 ft./55 m.   *J. Lamb and W. Freelands*   *1977*
An excellent little route, taking an impressive natural line on the right-hand edge of the Post Mortem wall. Start immediately below the obvious niche underneath the groove line.

1)   120 ft./36 m. (5c) Into the niche, and pull out over the roof into the steep crack above. Up this to a rest on the edge. Step right and up to the overhang. Gain the steep groove on the right with difficulty. Up this, past a tall spike, to make an exit on the top right to a stance and belay.   2)   60 ft./18 m. (4b) Continue easily from the right end of the ledge until possible to move left a few feet. Climb to the top via a wide crack and easier ground.

BLEAK HOW CRAG   (274122)

This recently 'discovered' crag of superb rock is situated on the east side of Langstrath, above the entrance to this valley. From the car-park at Stonethwaite, follow the footpath, on the west side of the river, to a small wooden bridge. The crag can be seen

above, directly up the hillside. Best reached from the bottom left of the vegetated foot of the crag and up to gain the Assembly Block – the rock promontory below the crag. (30 minutes.)

231 **Brush Off** ** HVS (5a)
100 ft./30 m. *C. Downer, C. Bacon and S. Kysow* *1984*
Thinly protected and exciting climbing up the slab left of the obvious arête (Fancy Free).
1) 100 ft./30 m. (5a) From the top of the earth mound, climb up and leftwards to a leftward-slanting crack. Move up rightwards, then straight up (left of vegetation) to a ledge. Up the wall above to the top.

232 **Fancy Free** * HVS (5a)
100 ft./30 m. *C. Downer, C. Bacon and S. Kysow* *1984*
Takes the fine arête above the Assembly Block.
1) 100 ft./30 m. (5a) Up the arête, deviating slightly to the left, to the sloping break at mid-height. Pull on to the upper part of the arête directly over the overlap and continue up the arête, rightwards, to the top.

233 **Bleak How Buttress** *** E2 (5c)
120 ft./36 m. *D. Hellier* *1983*
A very good route on excellent rock. Start 30 ft./9 m. to the right of the Assembly Block, below a steep slab about 10 ft./3 m. higher.
1) 120 ft./36 m. (5c) Up to the slab and climb it (crux) up the centre to a good hold. Move left to the arête, then up a short steep groove to an overlap. Climb the overlap to a slanting gangway, then move right on to a slab. Follow up the slab, trending leftwards, to finish up the easier wall above.

234 **The Reiver** * HVS (5a)
120 ft./36 m. *C. Downer* *1984*
Superb positions. Start as for Bleak How Buttress.
1) 120 ft./36 m. (5a) On to the slab then move right to climb up the juggy wall to a ledge. Continue on up, moving slightly left, on more awkward holds, to end up a short crack.

Bleak How Crag

RAVEN CRAG   (248114)

A large, rather broken crag in a good situation facing north-east over Combe Ghyll. It offers one of the best climbs of 'Difficult' standard in the Borrowdale valley.

Approach: From Mountain View cottages, where the main road crosses the river, follow the Thornythwaite Farm road. After about 100 yds./91 m., cross a stile on the left and follow the good path. At the entrance to Combe Ghyll, a fainter path goes left and leads diagonally across the fellside to the foot of the crag. Total time: 45 minutes.

Descent: Follow a grass ramp behind a stone wall and the subsequent path round the south-east end of the crag.

235   **Raven Crag Gully**   **   VD

510 ft./155 m.   *W. Wilson and J. W. Robinson   1893*

The most obvious feature of the crag is a classic gully, usually wet, providing strenuous climbing and (for an enthusiastic party) much enjoyment. Note that in wet weather the Severe alternative to pitch 8 would almost certainly have to be taken. The gully is at its very best in a hard winter (up to Grade IV).
1)   75 ft./23 m. Moderate climbing on the right to a cave under a chockstone, which is climbed on the right.   2)   70 ft./21 m. A groove on the right side of the gully is climbed for 55 ft./17 m., then traverse across the gully to its left side.   3)   65 ft./20 m. Up the groove on the right wall, then easy climbing on the left.   4)   45 ft./14 m. Scrambling.   5)   70 ft./21 m. A rib on the right of the gully is followed to a cave at 40 ft./12 m. Pass this on the right to a belay.   6)   100 ft./30 m. Scrambling, apart from a 15 ft./4 m. wall.   7)   50 ft./15 m. Up the right wall to a chockstone, then traverse awkwardly right to a belay.   8a)   35 ft./11 m. Climb up a few feet, then traverse into gully below the Capstone, which is climbed on the left to the top.   8b)   30 ft./9 m. Severe. Climb the steep rocks direct from belay.

236   **Corvus**   ***   D

450 ft./137 m.   *Bentley Beetham   1950*

A very good, continuously interesting climb. From Raven Crag Gully, in the centre of the crag, find the second gully to the left (south) and start a few feet left of this.

The hand-traverse on Corvus (pitch 6) Raven Crag, Comb Ghyll

1) 60 ft./18 m. Straight up the slabs for 50 ft./15 m., then move right around the corner to a good belay in the gully. 2) 30 ft./9 m. Climb the left wall of the gully to belay on a good ledge. 3) 35 ft./11 m. Traverse left along the broad ledge to the foot of a groove. 4) 80 ft./24 m. Climb the corner on good holds, then go up the steep chimney. Finally, ascend easily rightwards to a good stance. 5) 95 ft./29 m. Move 20 ft./6 m. right, then climb a rib on good holds to belay at the foot of a wall. 6) 25 ft./8 m. Traverse left across the steep wall on flake handholds to a big ledge. Belay. 7) 45 ft./14 m. A short wall then easy rocks to a terrace. 8) 40 ft./12 m. The rib above to a belay below a scoop. 9) 40 ft./12 m. Continue up the scoop to the top of the crag.

GILLERCOMBE (221124)

The combe contains a relatively large crag and the pleasant buttress route is traditionally used as an aproach to routes on Gable Crag.

Approach: From Seathwaite, cross the river and go up the steep fellside on the left of Sourmilk Ghyll. Continue into the combe when the crag appears on the far side to the north-west. Time: approx. 1 hour. A faster approach begins at Honister summit. Follow an indefinite path diagonally leftwards to a shallow col on the skyline. The crag is then straight ahead and is easily reached in 30 minutes.

Descent: Skirt around either end of the crag.

237 **Gillercombe Buttress** *** MS

360 ft./110 m. *H. B. Lyon and W. A. Woodsend 1912*

A pleasant and popular climb. Start just to the right of an obvious gully near the centre of the crag.

1) 45 ft./14 m. Climb up steeply to a square recess on the left. Continue up the right wall to a stance and belay. 2) 45 ft./14 m. Ascend to the left of belay for 20 ft./6 m., then traverse up right across a mossy slab to a belay. 3) 35 ft./11 m. Traverse left for 20 ft./6 m., then climb easy rocks to a belay on the left. 60 ft./18 m. of scrambling leads to the start of the next pitch. 4) 35 ft./11 m. Go left to the foot of an open chimney. 5) 60 ft./18 m. Climb the chimney, then go up to the right to a stance. 6) 35 ft./11 m. Ascend a short steep corner to a large ledge. Another bout of scrambling leads in 80

ft./24 m. to a large bilberry corner.   7)   30 ft./9 m. Step left
from a flake of rock and climb a groove to a ledge. Belay on the
left.   8)   50 ft./15 m. Climb slabs to the foot of a small chimney.
Belay on the right.   9)   25 ft./8 m. Continue up the slabs on the
right of the chimney to the top of the crag.

GOAT CRAG (NORTH)   (245165)

Few large crags were 'discovered' as recently as the northerly
end of Goat Crag. The routes were literally dug out of vegetation
following Les Brown's discovery of Praying Mantis in 1965.

The crag is very large but still holds quantities of vegetation.
Where this has been removed, the routes are generally of very
good quality. The crag faces north and the routes dry relatively
slowly.

Approach: Easily seen from Grange, the crag is best reached by
following an unsurfaced road south-west from the café at Grange
for ½ mile to a campsite (249168). Cross the campsite (west) to a
stile, then follow a narrow path along the top of the woods until
the crag can be approached directly. Only 15 minutes from the
campsite. Most of the climbs start from a rocky rake slanting up
below the crag.

Descent: Descend easy rakes to the south and skirt below all the
crags – rather long if the party is returning for another climb. On
some routes it is quicker to descend by abseil and this is the
norm.

238   **The Peeler**   *   VS

270 ft./82 m.   *B. Henderson, D. McDonald and J. Cook   1965*

An enjoyable climb up a prominent crack and groove on sound
rock. Start by scrambling up left from the ramp to a prominent
yew tree belay at the foot of the obvious crack.

1)   100 ft./30 m. Move left from the yew tree into the crack.
Follow this to a good stance and tree belay.   2)   70 ft./21 m.
Ascend the cleaned corner groove until a break left can be made
to a holly tree. Belay. The best climbing ends here and it is
possible to descend by abseil from this point.   3)   40 ft./12 m.
Climb a corner over perched blocks to a large flake; go up this to
belay.   4)   60 ft./18 m. Easy climbing and scrambling leads to
the top.

239 **DDT**   *   HVS   (5a, 4c)

220 ft./67 m.   *J. Lee, A. Jackman and P. Ross   1965*

Much further up the ramp from the foot of the Peeler is an impressive corner to the right of an undercut buttress. DDT follows this corner.

1)   120 ft./36 m. (5a) Climb the corner and turn a bulge on the right. Continue up the groove and fine crack to a ledge and piton belay.   2)   100 ft./30 m. (4c) Move right up a short wall into the deep groove. Follow this to a steeper section which leads on to an upper slab. Go diagonally left to tree belays. Continue by long heathery scrambling, or abseil off using convenient trees. (Abseil is best.)

240 **Tumbleweed Connection**   ***   E2   (5c, 5b)

190 ft./58 m.   *P. Botterill and D. Rawcliffe   1976*

Starts immediately left of the distinct corner groove (Praying Mantis), then gains the steep wall to the left – fine climbing.

1)   90 ft./27 m. (5c) Follow the hand-traverse left to the edge, then pull straight over into a shallow scoop. Move up (tree runner high on right), then across and down left, using a crack (runners). Move up to a small roof, then left to the obvious weakness leading straight up the wall to a peg runner. Go right, stepping low, to gain a groove on the edge and climb it to a tree belay (junction with Praying Mantis).   2)   100 ft./30 m. (5b) Follow the break leftwards until, above the traverse, a shallow groove leads up the wall. Follow the continuation of the groove leading to the overhang. Move leftwards through the overhang to the arête and climb the slab above.

241 **Praying Mantis**   ***   HVS   (5a, 4c, 4a, 4c)

260 ft./79 m.   *L. Brown and J. S. Bradshaw   1965*

A really splendid climb with a tremendous variety of climbing and some of the best situations in Borrowdale. The route is strenuous at first, but as the exposure increases, it becomes more delicate. Start in a groove some 50 ft./15 m. right of the corner followed by DDT.

1)   75 ft./23 m. (5a) Move up to a large flake. Climb the crack and groove with difficulty to a narrow niche. Step left on to a slabby wall and gain the slab above by a step to the right. Climb

Goat Crag

the slab to a tree belay.   2)   50 ft./15 m. (4c) Follow the grass
rake up to the left, then cross a smooth wall into a groove. Go up
this for 15 ft./4 m. until a step right leads to a good stance and
peg belay on the face of the buttress.   3)   25 ft./8 m. (4a)
Traverse right to a small exposed stance and peg
belay.   4)   110 ft./33 m. (4c) Climb the wall diagonally right
for a few feet to a good thread runner. Ascend directly up the
steep wall above, eventually stepping left on to the final slab.
Follow this to a heather terrace and tree belay.

Footless Crow : Important Note
*The top undercut flake (with the important Friend protection) has now
disappeared, and there have so far been no known re-ascents without it. The
climb will now be considerably more difficult and the following description
is included for its historical interest only.*

242   **Footless Crow**   ***   E5   (6b)
180 ft./55 m.   *P. Livesey   1974*
A tremendous modern route. Start in the centre of the Great
Buttress, 20 ft./6 m. right of Praying Mantis, by scrambling 25
ft./8 m. to a shallow groove.
1)   180 ft./55 m. (6b) Up the groove to where it bulges. Pull into
the niche and straight up to gain a rightward-sloping ramp.
Continue along this, then up to reach a cluster of bolts (possible
stance here) below the overhangs. Up to the left there was a flake
with a bashed-over peg, above this gain an undercut, then a
further undercut (Friend 2½ placement on its left-hand side). *This
has now disappeared.* Move down left from this (low left foothold)
to make a long reach to a vital layaway hold beneath an overlap
(crux). Step left again until a crack provides an excellent hold and
good protection (Friend 1). Step left, then up the green wall to
reach overhangs (no further protection above). Pull leftwards
through these and up the slabby wall. Move left to cleaner rock
on the left and finish up a shallow groove and wall to heather
ledges and tree belay high up.

243   **Bitter Oasis**   ***   E3   (5c, 5c)
150 ft./46 m.   *P. Livesey and party   1975*
This magnificent and difficult route goes up the wall to the right
of Praying Mantis. The difficulties are sustained throughout.

Praying Mantis, Goat Crag

Start about 40 ft./12 m. above and right of Praying Mantis behind a tree.

1)   90 ft./27 m. (5c) Step off the tree and go up to a peg runner. Pull on to a little slab on the left, then move right to an undercut hold. Enter the groove above and climb this to another peg runner. Continue awkwardly to a bulge and climb this, using the only jugs on the route, to gain a slab which leads with surprising difficulty to a small haven on the right edge of the buttress.   2)   60 ft./18 m. (5c) Move up slightly, then traverse left to a downward-pointing spike. Move round this and up groove above to a bolt runner on the left. A hard move up short wall above leads to a few feet of easier climbing and the top.

244   **Monsoon**   VS
210 ft./64 m.   *G. Oliver and C. Griffiths · 1966*
This is the chimney-groove bounding the main buttress on the right.

1)   80 ft./24 m. Scramble up ledges to the right of Bitter Oasis to a stance below the chimney.   2)   130 ft./40 m. Climb the chimney to the overhang, step right and continue to the same line until a traverse right leads to a rib. Go up this for a few feet then back left to a narrow slab which completes the climb.

WINTER CLIMBING

GREAT END   (227085)
This is the most accessible high crag and is approached directly up Grains Ghyll from Seathwaite. The traditional gullies give very good winter climbs. Care should be taken to establish that conditions are good, and that there is no avalanche danger in Central Gully. The best descent (particularly in the dark!) is to skirt round all the crags eastwards towards Esk House.

Cust's Gully   Grade I
200 ft./61 m.
The right-hand (westerly) gully gives a straightforward slope, with possibly one small ice pitch, under an impressive wedged chockstone arch.

Great End, showing Central and South-east Gullies

Central Gully   Grade I–II

600 ft./183 m.   *W. P. Haskett Smith*   *1882*

A fine winter climb. Follow the gully to a definite fork. The right branch (normal route) usually has a short, steep ice pitch followed by a slope of hard snow. The left fork can offer a good long ice pitch (sometimes Grade III).

South-east Gully   Grade I–II

600 ft./183 m.   *W. P. Haskett Smith*   *1882*

Rather less obvious than Central Gully; on the left of the latter. Start easily on snw slopes to an ice pitch at about 200 ft./61 m. This is usually turned on the right. Traverse back into the gully and continue, usually on steep snow.

Buttresses

In suitable conditions, the buttresses of Great End can offer exciting climbs. When the gullies are full of people, try for example the buttress on the right of Central Gully at about Grade I/II.

GABLE CRAG   (213105)

This is easily accessible from the top of Honister Pass along the slopes of Brandreth, and is often in good condition. The crag is described in the Wasdale section.

OTHER CLIMBS

The next highest winter-climbing ground is Gillercombe, where slight gullies at around Grade I are the usual order of the day. In hard winter, an entertaining approach via Sourmilk Ghyll could be made. All other crags in Borrowdale are distinctly low for winter climbing and a hard winter is required. (If in doubt – Derwentwater should be frozen solid!) Then Raven Crag Gully becomes a superb ice climb (Grade III/IV) with three big pitches. Sergeant Crag Gully also presents a challenging climb. Further exploration is left to the reader in a suitable winter.

Jack Carswell below the main pitch, Central Gully, Great End

BUTTERMERE AND NEWLANDS

This area gives a varied selection of climbs of all grades (except the highest) on mountain crags set in beautiful surroundings. Few climbers visit the area, which is relatively remote, and with the exception of Buckstone How, it is still unusual to share a crag with another party. In poor conditions the higher crags can be rather greasy and slow to dry, and protection is not always adequate, making the climbs a serious proposition. However, climbers can easily reach the more sheltered crags of Borrowdale over Honister Pass.

Access

To Buttermere, by road from Keswick and Borrowdale via Newlands or Honister Pass, or from the West Coast via Crummock Water. The crags at the head of the Newlands valley are quickly reached from the top of Honister Pass, or by driving and walking up the Newlands valley from Stair. The Mountain Goat minibus runs over Newlands Pass to Buttermere village four times a day (April to end of Sept.) An alternative approach is to take the bus from Keswick to Seatoller and walk over Honister Pass (5 miles to Buttermere village). The nearest railway station is at Workington, 18 miles away.

Accommodation and camping

The most convenient campsite for the crags is at Gatesgarth Farm (194149) at the foot of Honister Pass, but for those who prefer to camp nearer the pub, there are sites in Buttermere village. There are two hotels in Buttermere village and several farms and guest-houses in the area offering accommodation. There is also a youth hostel in the village and one on the summit of Honister Pass, and an FRCC climbing hut at Hassness (186158). In the Newlands valley there are several hotels and guest houses at Braithwaite, Stair and Swinside.

Food and drink

The two hotels in Buttermere village serve meals, drinks and bar snacks, and several of the farmhouses sell teas and snacks. The Fish Hotel and the Bridge Hotel in Buttermere both close during the winter months. The Swinside Inn (Newlands) does not. The Kirkstile Inn at Loweswater (142210) is worth a visit. Real-ale enthusiasts may care to try the Wheatsheaf Hotel, Lorton. Licensing hours 11–3, 5.30–10.30 (Fri., Sat. 11.00); Sun. 12–2, 7–10.30. The nearest shop is in Lorton (162255) although there

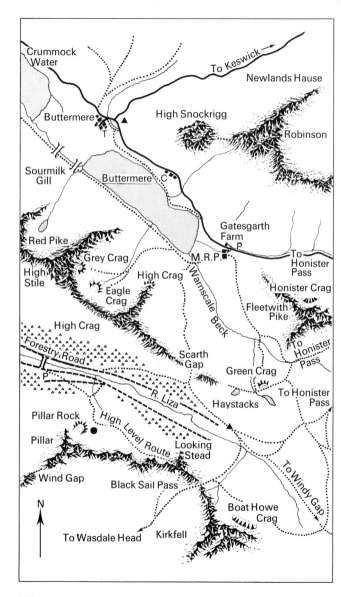

is a PO in Buttermere village and both the farm at Gatesgarth and the snack-bar at Buttermere sell milk and eggs. For Newlands, there are shops in Braithwaite, Portinscale and Keswick.

Garages and car hire

There are some petrol pumps in Buttermere village, but the nearest breakdown and repair services are in Keswick (see preceding chapter) or over Whinlatter Pass in Thornthwaite (tel. 238 or 538).

General services

Mostly poor: there is a telephone in Buttermere village but Keswick is the nearest place with climbing shops.

Mountain rescue

For assistance, ring the local police (999) or go to the MR post at Gatesgarth Farm (194149; tel. Buttermere 256).

BUCKSTONE HOW   (223143)

This crag, with its sunny aspect and short approach, is one of the most popular crags in the area. The routes vary in length from 150–300 ft./46–91 m., but all are hard. The rock is steep and the holds frequently suspect or alarmingly smooth, which makes for an unusually serious feeling on most climbs. In compensation, the protection is usually quite good and the rock dries rapidly after rain.

Approach: Park at the top of Honister Pass, and take an old quarry track which leads NW to a quarry spoil heap and old cableway. Cross these and descend slightly to the foot of the crag. 10 mins.

Descent: Traverse right and descend the slanting rake which forms the top edge of the crag. Much loose material lies on this rake and great care must be exercised to avoid dislodging stones on to parties on the cliff below.

245   **Groove Two**   *   VS

150 ft./46 m.   *W. Peascod and S. B. Beck   1947*

About 70 ft./21 m. left of the extreme right of the crag is a pair of clean cut grooves, set one above the other and separated by a

Overleaf left: Buckstone How from Honister Crag, Buttermere

Overleaf right: Cleopatra, Buckstone How

large terrace. The rock is sound but the climb is harder than it looks!

1) 60 ft./18 m. The first groove leads to the terrace. Belay by a birch tree.   2)   90 ft./27 m. Climb the right wall of the groove for a few feet until a subsidiary groove on the left can be entered. Climb this until a very awkward move enables the main groove to be regained. Continue up this (still interesting) to the large rake.

246 **Cleopatra** *** HVS (4c, 5a, 4c)
230 ft./70 m. *W. Peascod and B. Blake 1949*
This fine climb is one of the best of its standard in the area. It combines steep climbing on reasonably sound rock with good protection, fine situations and sustained interest. About 80 ft./24 m. left of Groove Two, a grassy gangway slants up to the left below the large overhangs. Start just right of this up a broken rib.
1) 80 ft./24 m. (4c) Climb the rib to a runner then go diagonally rightwards over the overhang on to a gangway. Follow this up to the left to a crack which is followed for a few feet until an airy traverse on pockets can be made across the wall on the right to a large stance. Piton belay recommended.
2) 65 ft./20 m. (5a) Make an awkward move up the rib on the left, then traverse left into the left-hand of two grooves. Climb this using a dubious spike and step left to a good belay but poor stance.   3)   85 ft./26 m. (4c) A difficult move over the overhang on the right is followed by easier climbing up the groove above to the top of the crag.

247 **Honister Wall** ** HS
285 ft./87 m. *W. Peascod and S. B. Beck 1946*
A good climb, although care is needed with some of the holds. The route starts up a clean wall just right of a large block on the path at the foot of the crag, some 60 ft./18 m. left of Cleopatra.
1) 60 ft./18 m. Climb the wall, stepping right at any difficulties, to the rake below the overhangs to a stance and various doubtful belays.   2)   85 ft./26 m. Traverse left across a steep open groove and climb a steep arête to a niche. Step right and continue directly via a short groove to a large recess.   3)   40 ft./12 m. The Black Wall. Climb the corner to a good runner, then traverse strenuously right to the rib and move up to a belay on the right.   4)   60 ft./18 m. Climb diagonally leftwards under a small

overhang, and up broken ground to a stance and poor belays. 5) 40 ft./12 m. Climb diagonally rightwards to the top of the crag.

248 Sinister Grooves ** VS
250 ft./76 m. *W. Peascod and S. B. Beck 1948*
A climb of great character up the highest part of the crag. Start some 35 ft./11 m. left of the large block directly below a conspicuous and deeply cut V-groove at 100 ft./30 m.
1) 80 ft./24 m. A steep wall and shallow groove lead with increasing difficulty to a good stance below the groove. 2) 40 ft./12 m. The smooth groove is climbed with some difficulty to a stance on the left. 3) 40 ft./12 m. The loose rib above is climbed to a large recess and good belay below a line of cracks and chimneys. 4) 90 ft./27 m. The easy-looking crack proves smooth and quite strenuous. After 20 ft./6 m., the chimney is entered and followed steeply, but on good holds, to the top of the crag.

EAGLE CRAG (172145)
Standing in a commanding position at the head of Birkness Combe is Eagle Crag, the largest cliff in the area. The rock is perfect, but as the crag faces north, it is rather slow to dry. This means the climbs can be very greasy, and although Eagle Front can be done in the rain, it is generally advisable to pick a dry day to visit this excellent crag.
Approach: From Gatesgarth Farm, a level track across the fields is followed through a gate. A few yards up the hillside, the Birkness Combe path branches off to the right below a small broken crag and slants up into the Combe itself. The path follows the general line of the stream which drains the Combe, until a final scree slope leads to the foot of the crag (1½ hours).

249 Carnival ** HVS (−, 5a, 5a, 5a, 5b, 4c, 4a)
500 ft./152 m. *N. J. Soper, J. A. Austin and I. Roper 1965*
A poorly protected climb of great character. The climb takes a line of cracks and grooves immediately right of Central Chimney (VS) and commences up broken rock some 80 ft./24 m. left of the point where the crag bends round into the deep scree gully, which bounds it on the right.
1) 100 ft./30 m. Easy scrambling left leads to a recess below an

impending crack.   2)   45 ft./14 m. (5a) The crack is climbed
with difficulty, finishing with a short layback, to a block belay
below a shallow groove.   3)   70 ft./21 m. (5a) Step down to the
right and traverse delicately to the foot of a discontinuous flake
crack. Climb this for 30 ft./9 m., passing some wedged flakes, to
the foot of a V-groove which leads more easily to a stance and
thread belay at the left-hand end of the long terrace.   4)   85
ft./26 m. (5a) Move up to the left then down round a rib to a
ledge, then make an ascending traverse to a chockstone belay in
Central Chimney.   5)   55 ft./17 m. (5b) Move round to the
right to a ledge below a smooth groove. Climb the right wall for
10 ft./3 m. then traverse right again (crux) to reach a square-cut
groove. Continue up this and step right to a ledge and
belay.   6)   95 ft./29 m. (4c) The cracked rib on the left is
followed by easier rock to a good stance below a grassy
groove.   7)   50 ft./15 m. (4a) Pleasant climbing up the left wall
of the groove to the top of the crag.

250 **Eagle Front**   ***   VS
495 ft./151 m.   *W. Peascod and S. B. Beck   1940*
This splendid climb takes a meandering but logical route up the
front of the buttress. In dry conditions, the climbing is pleasant
and sustained: in wet conditions, the route becomes a major epic.
Starts up a rib about 60 ft./18 m. left of the corner of the crag.
1)   60 ft./18 m. The rib is followed by a short traverse right to
a good belay.   2)   95 ft./29 m. Climb the groove until it is
possible to traverse right at the earliest opportunity to the foot of
a gangway sloping up to the left. Follow the gangway (often wet)
to a steep groove. This is climbed, using sloping holds on the left
wall, to a small ledge and good runner. Move right, then back left
underneath a bulge on to some slabs, then follow a line of flakes
back right to an overhung ledge.   3)   60 ft./18 m. Pull into a
shallow groove above the right-hand end of the ledge, step right
and ascend easily to the Terrace.   4)   75 ft./23 m. The Terrace
is traversed to the left, passing a small slab, using a doubtful
undercut flake, to a stance and a small thread belay immediately
left of the slab. Piton belay recommended.   5)   45 ft./14 m.
Move left to a higher ledge, then climb the steep wall above on

Eagle Crag, Buttermere
C = Central Chimney VS. Easy descent via gully on right

awkwardly spaced holds until a delicate move can be made into an open groove on the right. This is climbed to a bulge, when a sloping ledge with poor belays is reached by another step right. Piton usually in place.   6)   65 ft./20 m. Traverse right in a fine position at the foot of a clean slab (often wet). Climb this with difficulty to a ledge and chockstone belay.   7)   60 ft./18 m. The fine crack in the corner is a great deal easier than its appearance would suggest. Step right at the top to reach a magnificent stance and belay.   8). 35 ft./11 m. Finish up easy rock.

GREY CRAG   (172148)

This crag lies just to the west of Eagle Crag and, being of south-easterly aspect, is altogether a drier and sunnier place. It consists of four rather broken buttresses of grey rough rock: in ascending altitude Harrow Buttress, Mitre Buttress, Chockstone Buttress, and Oxford and Cambridge Buttress (see photograph). The climbs are shorter and less serious than the routes on Eagle Crag, with more routes in the lower grades. By joining routes on the buttresses, a long climb can be made, leading to within 100 yds./91 m. of the summit of High Stile.
Access: As for Eagle Crag, then climb the scree to the foot of the crag.
Descent: By scree gullies on the left of the crags or heather slopes on the right (east).

251   **Harrow Buttress**   D
130 ft./40 m.   *W. Bishop and W. A. Woodsend   1912*
A short but popular route. Start just left of the lowest point of the crag. Combined with Rib and Wall, over 400 ft./122 m. of excellent climbing can be had.
1)   30 ft./9 m. The arête is climbed on good holds to a belay on the right.   2)   40 ft./12 m. Continue up the chimney then traverse left to a rock ledge below a broken groove.   3)   60 ft./18 m. The groove and easy rock lead to an overhung corner. Move left and continue to the top of the buttress. The start of Rib and Wall is 80 ft./24 m. down the rake on the left.

252   **Mitre Buttress Direct**   *   VD
235 ft./72 m.   *A. C. Pigou and party   1915*
A rather broken route with one very good pitch up the wall to the right of the cave. Starts at the foot of a subsidiary buttress below

Grey Crag, Buttermere

237

the main buttress. A pleasant way of reaching this point is to climb Harrow Buttress, then scramble down the gully on the left.
1) 40 ft./12 m. Climb the subsidiary buttress with a steep initial wall. 2) 45 ft./14 m. Climb the wall by an awkward pull-up, then scramble to the right to the foot of the face proper. 3) 70 ft./21 m. Ascend direct to a ledge and continue to a narrow mantelshelf. Traverse left to the edge of the buttress, then follow a scoop on the left to the foot of the prominent cave. 4) 40 ft./12 m. Climb the wall on the right of the cave. The wall is exposed and looks extremely blank from below, but after an initial awkward move, there are very good holds. 5) 40 ft./12 m. Traverse left to a steep crack and follow this to the top.

253 **Rib and Wall** D

290 ft./88 m. *W. Peascod and G. G. MacPhee 1945*
An obvious rib between Mitre and Harrow Buttresses gives the first pitch of this varied climb. Easily reached from the top of Harrow Buttress.
1) 45 ft./14 m. The rib is climbed to a recess. 2) 30 ft./9 m. Continue on good holds to a good block belay. 3) 20 ft./6 m. Climb the blunt nose above with difficulty to a bridged block which joins the rib to the main face. 4) 45 ft./14 m. Above is a wall of wedged blocks. Climb these, trending rightwards, to the foot of a V-groove. 5) 35 ft./11 m. An awkward move round to the right gives access to a narrow ledge, which is traversed until a short ascent can be made into a deep recess. 6) 35 ft./11 m. The wall and crack on the right. 7) 80 ft./24 m. Slabs of beautifully rough rock lead to the top.

254 **Slabs West Route** HS

165 ft./50 m. *W. Peascod and A. Barton 1942*
This route lies on the slabs, on the left side of Chockstone Buttress, which rise from the scree gully between Harrow Buttress and Chockstone Buttress. The start is at a point some 15 ft./4 m. left of an obvious rightwards traversing line. The climb is a delightful exercise in technique, with minimal protection.
1) 95 ft./29 m. Move diagonally right, then directly up to a good resting place. Go back leftwards until you can go straight up the slab to a terrace. 2) 70 ft./21 m. From the pile of blocks, climb up to a niche on the left. Step out right and continue directly to the terrace below Oxford and Cambridge Buttress.

255 **Oxford and Cambridge Direct Route** * MS

125 ft./38 m. *H. V. Reade 1914*

A good continuation to the Slabs West Route. It takes the edge of
the Oxford and Cambridge Buttress. Start just right of the arête.
1)   45 ft./14 m. Climb up to an overhang and step left and up to
a rock ledge and good belays.   2)   50 ft./15 m. A short bulging
crack on the left proves awkward. Move right and climb the arête
delicately to the top of the crag.

256 **Suaviter** * MS

135 ft./41 m. *W. Peascod and S. B. Beck 1941*

A short but interesting route up the line of a crack which splits
the left end of Grey Wall. Grey Wall is the wall of perfect rock on
the right side of Chockstone Buttress. Start at a large bollard in a
shallow corner below the left end of a long ledge.
1)   20 ft./6 m. Climb the bollard and the corner until it is
possible to move right and climb the face to the ledge.   2)   50
ft./15 m. From the left end of the ledge, move down and make a
delicate traverse across the steep wall to a thin crack in the centre
of the slab. Climb the crack to a ledge with doubtful blocks and a
higher ledge on the left.   3)   65 ft./20 m. Climb the ridge above
and a 20 ft./6 m. chimney to the top.

257 **Fortiter** * MVS

145 ft./44 m. *W. Peascod and S. B. Beck 1941*

15 ft./4 m. right of Suaviter is a long crack bisecting some small
roofs, and this provides the line of this exhilarating little climb.
1)   20 ft./6 m. Good holds lead to the right-hand end of the long
narrow ledge.   2)   70 ft./21 m. The thin crack in the wall above
is started from the right. The crack has good holds until a more
awkward move over the overhang can be made. Step right into
another crack and up this to a good stance and belay.   3)   55
ft./17 m. The corner crack and arête above lead to the top.

GREEN CRAG (201131)

This is the recently developed crag at the head of Warnscale
Bottom. In general it is heavily vegetated, but it has several
climbs of character in the upper grades. The three climbs
described here are typical of the crag. Being more popular than
the rest, they have now become thoroughly defoliated and rank

with the best climbs in the area. Unfortunately the crag is very slow to dry.

Approach: The cliff face north-west and can be reached in ¾ hr. from Gatescarth along the Fleetwith Quarry track. Where this starts to rise from the valley floor, the stream is crossed and a pleasant zig-zag path is followed up the tongue between the streams to the foot of the crag. The cliff can be reached in a slightly longer time from Honister Pass by following the old Drumhouse track over the col. The top of the crag is in an area of rocky knolls, reached by a short descent and crossing the stream.
Descent: To the south of the crag by scrambling down broken ground overlooking the ravine of Black Beck.

258 **Paper Tiger**   MVS
270 ft./82 m.   *J. A. Austin and N. J. Soper   1966*
The climb makes an impressive ascending traverse into the centre of the crag, starting at a holly below the right hand of two big green corners. This corner is Thorgrim, a wet HVS.
1)   110 ft./33 m. A short cleaned groove and slab are followed by steep grass, which is climbed to a dead tree up to the left, level with the foot of the corner.   2)   80 ft./24 m. The large overhang 60 ft./18 m. up to the left is gained by a long ascending traverse (no protection). Climb the overhang, which proves less alarming than appearances would suggest, to a good stance and piton belay.   3)   80 ft./24 m. The steep wall above is climbed, zigzagging right or left when difficulties appear, to the top of the crag.

259 **Saraband**   *   HVS   (−, 5a, 5b, −)
275 ft./84 m.   *J. A. Austin and T. Sullivan   1967*
This route turns the overhangs to the left of Paper Tiger by slab climbing of great elegance. Start at a deep vegetated groove directly below the left end of the overhangs, and about 60 ft./18 m. right of a tree-topped pedestal.   1)   25 ft./8 m. Scramble up the groove to a piton belay.   2)   80 ft./24 m. (5a) Climb the steep slabs, trending slightly leftwards to a small stance 15 ft./4 m. below the large overhangs. Peg belay.   3)   110 ft./33 m. (5b) Climb up to the overhang, then traverse left into a green groove. This is climbed to a resting place just above a small overhang. Step left to a good foothold on the edge of the slab and climb this on dwindling holds, until forced to step round the

240

arête on the left into a groove (often wet). Up this to a stance and piton belay on the left. A sustained pitch.   4)   60 ft./18 m. Easy rocks to the top.

260   **The Wray**   *   E1   (5a, 5b, 4b)
260 ft./79 m.   *M. G. Mortimer and R. F. Allen   1974*
A good route – somewhat harder than Saraband. Start below the peg belay of Saraband, some 110 ft./33 m. below the large overhang.
1)   100 ft./30 m. (5a) Climb the steep wall directly to belay below the overhang.   2)   120 ft./36 m. (5b) Traverse right to reach the foot of a short gangway leading leftwards through the overhang. Follow this to a steep slab overlooking Saraband and climb to where it steepens into a small pillar. Move right into a short groove and then transfer to the arête on the right. Climb steeply into another groove, which leads more easily to a stance and belay.   3)   40 ft./12 m. (4b) Move right and climb the wall above to the top.

HIGH CRAG   (183145)
The rocky northern face of High Crag steepens directly above Gatescarth Farm into a steep pillar of sound clean rhyolite, which yields several good routes.
Approach: Either directly up the hillside or, longer but less laboriously, by following the Birkness Combe track to the old wall at the entrance to the combe, then striking back leftwards to the foot of the crag.
Descent: Well to the left (east)

261   **Samson**   **   E1   (−, 5c, −)
230 ft./70 m.   *O. Woolcock and R. D. Brown   1964*
Ascends the steep, smooth wall on the east side of the main buttress. A magnificent second pitch. Start on the Rock Table Ledge – a little way up on the left.
1)   70 ft./21 m. From the blocks, follow a rib on the right, then grass, to a large ledge.   2)   110 ft./33 m. (5c) Make an ascending traverse right, above the overhang, to gain the thin crack in the centre of the wall. Piton runner. The crack is climbed with difficulty to easier ground. Continue to a block belay.   3)   50 ft./15 m. Easy slabs to the top.

262 **The Philistine** *** E1 (5b, −)
175 ft./53 m. *E. Cleasby and T. W. Birkett. 1975*
Clean, airy climbing up the glaringly obvious arête. Start right of
Samson, below the overhang.
1) 125 ft./38 m. (5b) Climb to the overhang, then step round to
the right to a thin crack. Up the crack, then move delicately left
to gain the arête. Continue directly up the arête to a
belay. 2) 50 ft./15 m. Continue straight on to finish.

263 **High Crag Buttress** ** HVS (−, 4c, 5a, 5a)
190 ft./58 m. *L. Kendal and R. McHaffie 1963*
A short but very fine route, of a high standard of difficulty and on
perfect rock. The climb commences directly below the crack line
which passes between a pair of prominent niches, or 'eyes'.
1) 15 ft./4 m. Easy climbing to an ash. 2) 40 ft./12 m. (4c)
Climb on to a pedestal behind the ash and continue up the crack
above to the left-hand cave. 3) 50 ft./15 m. (5a) Climb the
overhang between the caves and continue up the fine chimneys
to another niche and chockstone belay. 4) 80 ft./24 m. (5a)
Climb the right-hand arête to a good thread runner, then make
an extremely delicate ascending traverse to gain an easier-angled
area up to the right. The groove above leads without further
difficulty to the top.

264 **Delilah** ** MVS
165 ft./50 m. *W. Peascod and B. Blake 1951*
Follows a fine groove up the right-hand side of the buttress. Start
just left of the foot of the chimney bounding the buttress on the
right-hand side.
1) 55 ft./17 m. Gain a higher ledge, then move up to a narrow
rock ledge. Traverse right and climb a thin crack to a stance and
belay. 2) 110 ft./33 m. Climb up and left into the groove,
which is followed directly to the top.

DALE HEAD CRAG (225156)

This cliff is finely situated at the head of Newlands valley, on the
north face of the fell of the same name. The rock is good but
rather vegetated and slow to dry.
Approach: From Honister Pass, the Dale Head path leads off

Samson, High Crag

243

directly northwards to Dale Head Tarn. Pass to the left of the tarn, contour the northern flank of the fell and trend downwards to pass below a rock rib. The crag is then reached up a steep scree slope (approximately ¾ hr.).

Descent: Cross the knife-edge then descend a gully on the right.

265 **Dale Head Pillar**   VS

260 ft./79 m.   *W. Peascod and G. Rushworth   1948*

A classic climb, steep and exposed in the upper section. Start just right of the Pillar, which is itself on the left of the main face. Scramble 15 ft./4 m. to a grassy corner below a crack.

1)   80 ft./24 m. Follow the crack to a ledge and belay.   2)   40 ft./12 m. Climb the wall on the left of a grassy groove, until a traverse left can be made to a large ledge on top of the Pillar.   3)   60 ft./18 m. Ascend the steep and exposed groove on the right. Exit on the left and climb a slab to a recess and thread belay.   4)   80 ft./24 m. A short wall leads to a ledge; then climb a bulging wall starting on the right. An open groove and easier climbing leads to the top.

266 **Mithril**   HVS   (4c, 5a, 5a, 4c, –)

300 ft./91 m.   *N. J. Soper and A. Wright   1963*

The start is at a rightward-facing cracked groove, about 25 yds./23 m. right of the corner of the crag.

1)   55 ft./17 m. (4c) Climb the crack and step left into a shallow groove. Move up to a grass terrace.   2)   70 ft./21 m. (5a) Above are two grooves. Enter the left one and climb it and the left arête until a leftward traverse can be made to a crack. Climb this to a forbidding recess. Good belays.   3)   50 ft./15 m. (5a) Climb the overhanging crack to gain an overhung gangway on the right. Follow this and make an exposed move over the bulge into a niche. Peg belay.   4)   65 ft./20 m. (4c) Traverse left, below another overhang, to gain easier grooves leading to an iron spike. Belay.   5)   60 ft./18 m. Easy rocks lead to the crest of the crag.

MINER'S CRAG   (232158)

This pleasant and unfrequented crag lies on the east side of the head of Newlands valley, conveniently opposite Dale Head Crag.

High Crag, Buttermere

245

It faces south-west and dries quite quickly, so is a useful alternative to Buckstone Howe and the Borrowdale Crags.

Approach: The quickest approach is usually from the top of Honister, as for Dale Head Pillar, but keeping to the right side of Newlands Beck. Alternatively, cars can be driven up the valley from Little Town as far as Castle Nook. Follow the good track until level with Dale Head Pillar. Miners' Crag is the last crag on the left.

Topography: The lowest section of the crag is a flat buttress between a gully on the left (Newlands Gully, VD) and broken ground on the right. Higher up on the right is a series of steep slabby grooves and ribs, giving the climbs described below, and ending on the Quartz Rake. Above and to the right is another steep but shorter wall.

Descent: The climbs described below finish on the Quartz Rake. Descend this to the right.

267 **Miners' Grooves** * MVS

245 ft./75 m. *G. Rushworth, W. Peascod (alt.) and G. G. MacPhee 1948*

A good groove climb, well protected but with some suspect rock in the upper section. Starts at a slab below a steep V-groove, near the left end of the south-west face.

1) 40 ft./12 m. Easy slabs lead to the foot of the groove. 2) 90 ft./27 m. Ascend the groove for 45 ft./14 m. to a stance below the steep upper section. Swing left on a good hold to the arête, then climb the arête and the shallow gully above to a belay. 3) 60 ft./18 m. Climb the main groove in the wall above. Belays on the right. 4) 60 ft./18 m. Easy but loose ribs lead to the Quartz Rake.

268 **Corkscrew** HS

210 ft./64 m. *G. Rushworth and W. Dennison 1948*

A good route up the slabs and ribs to the right of Miners' Grooves. Starts 30 ft./9 m. to the right of that climb, below the left end of a prominent slab.

1) 50 ft./15 m. Climb a rib to a niche at the left edge of the slab. Belays up on the left. 2) 80 ft./24 m. Ascend a steep little crack on the left, and continue up the groove above. Traverse

Mithril, Dale Head Crag

right into another groove and climb this to an exposed stance. Move back left across the top of the groove and go up easily to a stance and spike belays below a sweep of slabs and a steep corner above.   3)   80 ft./24 m. Cross the slabs to the ridge on the right. Climb the airy exposed arête, the hardest part of the climb, then the easier ridge above to the Quartz Rake.

WINTER CLIMBING

Much of the Buttermere and Newlands area is too low and near the sea for good winter climbing. Birkness Combe can offer a variety of winter routes; Birkness Chimney and Birkness Gully give excellent climbs with a broken region of crags and gullies to the east offering easier routes. Central Chimney on Eagle Crag could give a superb and difficult winter climb. In a hard winter, the north-facing gullies in Warnscale Bottom occasionally come into condition and give difficult climbs. Finally, Grasmoor has a large crag in its northern combe (Dove Crag – 179204). This is reached in about 1½ hours from Lanthwaite Green. There are three gullies giving good and often hard climbs.

When the Buttermere crags are out of condition it is worth remembering that Gable Crag is usually better and only an hour's walk from the top of Honister Pass (see Wasdale section).

Buttermere in winter. High Crag, Eagle Crag and Grey Crag are visible in Birkness Combe

ENNERDALE

The main attraction of this quiet afforested valley is the towering bastion of Pillar Rock, a unique geological feature which inspired the beginnings of the sport of rock climbing in Lakeland. The crag offers a wide variety of excellent routes at all standards of difficulty, with the added attraction that the climbs are not usually crowded. In bad weather, however, the Rock becomes very greasy, and even routes of Difficult standard can become major epics. At a lower altitude, pleasant climbing can be found on the crags on Bowness Knott (111155) and on Anglers' Crag (099151). There is a public car-park at the foot of Bowness Knott, at the start of the Forestry Commission road. The upper part of the valley is shown on the Buttermere map.

Access

The entrance to the valley is conveniently reached by road from Cockermouth, Whitehaven and Calder Bridge. Unfortunately for the climber, the Forestry Commission has imposed a ban on unauthorized vehicles using the unmetalled road which runs up the valley from the car-park at Bowness Knott. An agreement between the Forestry Commission and the British Mountaineering Council allows a limited number of vehicles to drive as far as Gillerthwaite. The procedure is: 1) collect a numbered permit from either Colin Warnham, Dower Cottage, Pardshaw Hall, Cockermouth (tel. Cockermouth 3531), or Peter Moffat, Cross Lanes, Seascale (tel. Seascale 230); 2) inform the Head Forester (tel. Lamplugh 275) before using the road; 3) display the permit and park in the car-park at Gillerthwaite. The valley can also be reached by long but pleasant walks:

a) from Wasdale via Black Sail Pass.
b) from Buttermere over Scarth Gap Pass.
c) from Borrowdale – from the top of Honister Pass via a good track leading first west, then south-west over the slopes of Brandreth to the head of Ennerdale.

The nearest public transport to the valley is an infrequent bus service to Ennerdale Bridge from Whitehaven.

Accommodation and camping

Accommodation in Ennerdale is sparse: incredibly, the Anglers' Hotel was demolished to allow the level of the lake to be raised – a plan which has now been shelved! Several of the farms at the lower end of the valley and around Ennerdale Bridge offer accommodation and will allow camping. There are two youth hostels in the valley: the famous Black Sail (194123) hostel at the head of the valley, and another at Gillerthwaite (142141) near the head of the lake.

The variety of insect life in the Ennerdale forest is an active discouragement to low-level bivouacs, but high campsites and fair-weather bivouacs can be found below Pillar Rock.

Food and drink

Many of the farmhouses in the region serve excellent teas, and there is a café in Ennerdale Bridge. The nearest restaurants are in Cleator Moor and Whitehaven. Fortunately, there is a pleasant pub in Ennerdale Bridge, the Fox and Hounds, which serves bar meals as well as Lion Ales. Licensing hours are 11.30–2.30 p.m. and 5.30–10.30 p.m. on weekdays and 12–2 p.m. and 7–10.30 p.m. on Sundays, with 11 p.m. closing on Fridays and Saturdays. There are two small shops in Ennerdale Bridge and larger stores in Cleator Moor and Whitehaven (early closing day: Wednesday).

Garages and car hire

There are service stations in Cleator Moor and Whitehaven, and the nearest breakdown-recovery services are in Whitehaven (tel. 3694) or Workington (tel. 66655). Taxis are available in Cleator Moor (tel. 811695 or 811806) or in Whitehaven (tel. 2511 or 63959). Car hire is available in Whitehaven (tel. 66611 or 65281).

General services

There is a public telephone in Ennerdale Bridge. There are also public toilets there. The nearest mountaineering shops are in Whitehaven and at Wasdale Head.

Mountain rescue

There is a mountain rescue post at Ennerdale youth hostel, Gillerthwaite (142141; tel. Lamplugh 861237), and an unmanned post (172124) at the foot of Shamrock, Pillar Rock (40 yds./36 m. east of the foot of Walker's Gully). There is also a first-aid post at Black Sail youth hostel (GS stretcher; hostel open Easter – 31 October only; no telephone; grid ref. 195123). Otherwise phone 999 as usual.

Pillar Rock, from the foot of the firebreak

PILLAR ROCK (172123)

This superb crag has a number of long and excellent routes of all grades of difficulty. The rock is sound and gives good friction in dry conditions, but in wet weather the altitude and aspect of the crag produce a greasy coating which can increase the severity of the climbs considerably. In high summer, the north-east face of the Rock catches the early morning sun and can dry fairly quickly, whereas the west faces will generally dry in the afternoon.

Approach: The shortest approach to the Rock is still from Ennerdale, despite the recent restrictions on the use of Forestry Commission roads. Obtain a permit as explained in the section on access, then drive to Gillerthwaite. Walk up the road for about 1½ miles, then take a right fork to reach a bridge across the Liza (165135). Turn left after the bridge and after about 100 yds./91 m., a sign marking the start of the path to the Rock will be seen. This leads diagonally through the trees to the combe below the Rock. Total time to the foot of the Rock, about 1½ hours. The approach from Wasdale Head is a long but pleasant walk (2 hours). From the Wasdale Head Hotel, follow the well-marked path to Black Sail Pass until just after crossing Gatherstone Beck a path branches left up to the ridge. Follow the ridge towards Pillar until, just at the start of the steep part, a good path on the right (cairn) leads round the north-east flank of the mountain. This is the famous High Level Traverse and leads to Robinson's Cairn and the east side of the Rock.

From Borrowdale, it is possible to start from the top of Honister Pass and traverse the slopes of Brandreth, then follow a path below Gable Crag and Kirkfell to the top of Black Sail. A long walk – about 3 hours to the Rock. From Buttermere, ascend Scarth Gap Pass, then traverse right for ¼ mile and descend a diagonal path through the forest. This leads to the River Liza at the new footbridge and a path ascending to the Rock. About 2 hours.

Topographical: The structure of Pillar Rock is somewhat complicated, and deserves some study in advance. Descent routes are not straightforward, and many seemingly obvious descents lead to vertical gullies. *In mist or bad weather getting off the Rock safely can take considerable skill and experience:* more parties have been forced to bivouac on Pillar than on any other crag in Lakeland. A plan of the Rock is given opposite. The crag is

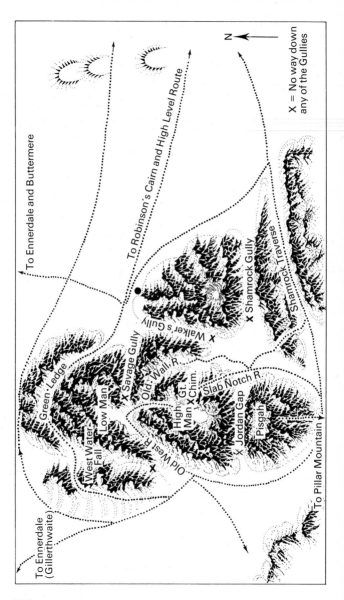

N

X = No way down
any of the Gullies

To Ennerdale and Buttermere

To Robinson's Cairn and High Level Route

To Ennerdale
(Gillerthwaite)

Green Ledge

West Water
Fall

Low Man

Old West R.

X Savage Gully

Old Wall R.

High
Gt.
Man

Gt. Chim.

X Walker's Gully

X Shamrock Gully

Shamrock Traverse

Slab Notch R.

X Jordan Gap

Pisgah

To Pillar Mountain

conical in appearance, the top being named High Man, whilst a subsidiary shoulder on the valley side is called Low Man. The south side of the Rock is short and separated from the main mass of Pillar Mountain by a rift (Jordan Gap) and a subsidiary peak, known as Pisgah. The north and west faces of the Rock are long and give the best climbing. At the corner of the north and west faces is a deep gully, the Waterfall, and above lies the West Cove. The east edge of the Waterfall gives a polished route of moderate standard (harder when wet), whilst the buttress on the right gives easy scrambling except for a 20 ft./6 m. chimney near its foot. Along the base of the north face is a large terrace, the Green Ledge, and below this is a subsidiary belt of slabs. To the east of the north face lies the buttress of Shamrock, separated from the Rock by the famous cleft of Walker's Gully (VS). High up the north-east side of Shamrock is a wide rock ledge, the Shamrock Traverse. This provides an easy route to the south and west faces of the Rock from Robinson's Cairn. Follow the traverse then go behind Pisgah and down scree to the west faces. The Shamrock Traverse also provides an excellent descent route, although note that the traverse lies *above* the top of Shamrock Gully and care should be taken not to confuse the two in descent.

SHAMROCK

Shamrock is the first part of the crag to be reached on the approach from Wasdale, and a prominent landmark is the blue stretcher box at its base. The main part of the crag is split by a diagonal ramp, the Great Heather Shelf, rising from left to right. Because of this and other large ledges, the climbs are more broken than elsewhere on Pillar, but the individual pitches are as good as any on the Rock. Photon, Eros and Thanatos are the quickest routes to dry after rain.

Descent: From the tea-table block at the top of Shamrock, scramble down for some 30 ft./9 m. to the col at the top of Shamrock Gully. Do NOT attempt to descend this, but scramble up the grassy gully on the right for 150 ft./46 m. to gain the Shamrock Traverse footpath. Follow this leftwards off the crag.

Pillar Rock, The Shamrock
GHS = Great Heather Shelf

269 **Photon** MVS

490 ft./149 m. *W. A. Barnes and party 1967*

A long route with varied climbing, well protected and with large
stances. The rock is clean and the climb dries relatively quickly
as it catches the early morning sun. Start at the foot of the
obvious, cleaned groove reached by scrambling up the left side of
the Great Heather Shelf for 200 ft./61 m.

1) 80 ft./24 m. Climb the groove to a ledge. Piton
belay. 2) 100 ft./30 m. Move right and climb the slabby
corner to where the groove steepens. Climb the corner to below a
bulge. Fix protection in the crack on the right, then climb this by
a layback move. Continue up the crack to reach a good ledge on
the left. 3) 40 ft./12 m. Climb the corner formed by a large
chockstone, then move right to a grassy bay. 4) 100 ft./30 m.
Climb straight up the pleasant slab on the left to a ledge
overlooking Shamrock Gully, below the final square tower.
Scramble up to the left for 20 ft./6 m. to a belay on the edge of the
gully. It is possible to escape from this point up the easy upper
section of Shamrock Gully. 5) 70 ft./21 m. The open groove
on the left of the tower is climbed, passing a block, to the crest of
the ridge above the tower. 15 ft./4 m. above is another ledge and
belay. Alternatively take the groove on the left, immediately
above the belay: steeper and more strenuous but with better
protection. 6) 100 ft./30 m. Easier scrambling along the
alpine-style ridge leads to the tea-table block at the top of
Shamrock.

270 **Eros** * E2 (5b, 5c, 5b)

270 ft./82 m. *W. S. Lounds and J. C. Eilbeck (alt.) 1968*

A series of eliminate variations on Photon, giving good sustained
climbing with little protection. Starts as for Photon, or, better, by
climbing Thanatos and walking left across the Great Heather
Shelf.

1) 80 ft./24 m. (5b) Climb the rib on the right of the cleaned
groove. The final 20 ft./6 m. is very delicate, up the centre of a
mossy triangular slab with an awkward grassy landing. Piton
belay, as for Photon. 2) 110 ft./33 m. (5c) Climb the steep rib
directly above, to the left of the slabby groove of Photon. The
angle eases at 60 ft./18 m., but the slab above is still delicate and
unprotected. Finally a ledge is reached and a traverse can be
made to the left to a grassy bay and belay. 3) 100 ft./30 m.

(5b) The overhanging groove above is the next obstacle. The blank middle section has been climbed free, but most parties will be forced on to the steep bounding rib on the right. Continue to a ledge above (belay). Step back left across the groove and climb the left edge of the slab, and the broken rib above, to join Photon at the top of pitch 4 of that climb.

271 **Thanatos/Electron**   ***   HVS/VS
533 ft./162 m.   *J. C. Eilbeck and W. S. Lounds   (alt.)   1968/A. G. Cram and J. C. Eilbeck   1966*
A very good combination, sustained at VS standard, with the crux of Thanatos being slightly harder. Thanatos can be avoided, if necessary, by scrambling up the left side of the Great Heather Shelf (which splits the two climbs) for 200 ft./61 m. to the foot of an obvious corner some 70 ft./21 m. of Photon. Electron dries rather slowly after heavy rain. Start 20 ft./6 m. right of the conspicuous blue stretcher box at the bottom of Shamrock, below the big corner capped by two overhangs.
   1)   80 ft./24 m. (4b) Climb a slab and up to a corner. Ascend this, with an exit on the slab on the left, and continue up bilberry ledges to a belay beneath the corner proper.   2)   100 ft./30 m. (5a) Climb the corner (the right-hand of two grooves) to the large overhang. Traverse left round the rib into the second groove and bridge up this until the good ledge on the left can be gained (crux).   3)   20 ft./6 m. of climbing. The easy corner above leads to the Great Heather Shelf. Scramble across this, slightly down to the left, to the bottom of a big corner, which is the first pitch of Electron.   4)   85 ft./26 m. Climb on to the higher grass ledge and continue up the square corner. A bulge proves awkward at mid-height, and further up, another problematical move is overcome before the holds improve and a good grass ledge is reached.   5)   80 ft./24 m. Continue up the groove for 40 ft./12 m., then go right across a ledge to a short wall, which leads to a large block belay below and to the left of a fine layback crack.   6)   70 ft./21 m. A good pitch. Climb the crack to a resting place and good runner at 40 ft./12 m. Continue up the final steeper section to a belay on the slab above.   7)   100 ft./30 m. The difficulties and angle now relent. Climb the grey arête above, move right and follow a second arête to the tea-table block at the top of Shamrock.

Shamrock Tower   *   MVS

550 ft./168 m.   *S. H. Cross and party   1940*

A classic mountaineering route despite the large field at mid-height. The rock is good but becomes very greasy in the wet. Start 20 ft./6 m. right of the stretcher box at the foot of Shamrock.

1)   60 ft./18 m. Climb an easy-angled cleaned slab and scramble up a few feet to the foot of a corner. Follow this for a few feet until it is possible to break out left up a steep slab to a ledge. Belay on another ledge a few feet higher.   2)   70 ft./21 m. Step round the rib on the right and ascend steeply for 20 ft./6 m. Traverse right and climb a small awkward corner to a ledge and large block belay.   3)   80 ft./24 m. Traverse left from the block and balance into a V-groove. Climb this, moving right, and then go up diagonally on the right to grass. Move back left to a block belay.   4)   130 ft./40 m. Move right and ascend grooves to the Great Heather Shelf. Cross this diagonally to the right to a large flake belay.   5)   30 ft./9 m. Ascend a few feet, then traverse right to a sitting belay.   6)   120 ft./36 m. Climb the corner on the right for 20 ft./6 m., then move right to gain the long corner, which gives very pleasant crack and chimney climbing. At the top, exit right to a belay.   7)   60 ft./18 m. Continue up the easier broken ridge above to the top of Shamrock.

Walker's Gully   ***   HS

390 ft./119 m.   *O. G. Jones, G. D. Abraham and A. E. Field   1899*

One of the most famous of the classic gullies. Start at the foot of the deep cleft between Shamrock and the north face of Low Man. There is some danger of stonefall if there are parties on the scree fan above the gully.

1)   50 ft./15 m. An easy pitch, then scree to the foot of a high, green chimney.   2)   30 ft./9 m. The right wall of the chimney to a belay.   3)   40 ft./12 m. An exposed groove with poor holds leads past the first chockstone.   4)   80 ft./24 m. Scrambling up the gully bed.   5)   30 ft./9 m. Rocks on the left to a wet cave.   6)   30 ft./9 m. Climb up behind, then over the first chockstone. Bridge the gully to a sloping chockstone, then gain good holds over the upper chockstone.   7)   30 ft./9 m. Easy ground to a cave with a window.   8)   15 ft./4 m. A strenuous

The long corner of Electron, Pillar Rock

struggle through the hole. 9) 55 ft./17 m. An easy through-route or a staircase on the right leads to big boulders. Go over these to a cave below the huge capstone of the gully.

10) 30 ft./9 m. Move across the right wall on sloping holds. A tall man can then back-up with his back on the left wall. Otherwise continue rather strenuously up the right wall to the amphitheatre.

NORTH FACE OF LOW MAN

This fine face gives some of the longest and most exposed routes on the Rock. All the routes start from the Green Ledge, though some pitches on the slabs below can be found. Grooved Wall is the only route hereabout which dries quickly. A good combination is to start with a route here and continue up the west face of High Man – a total of about 700 ft./213 m. of climbing.

Descent: It is best either to continue up well-scratched rocks to High Man and descend from there, or to descend the Old West Route: from the top of Low Man, traverse round to the right (west) on a good path which becomes an easy scramble and leads diagonally to the West Cove. It is possible to traverse east to the top of Walker's Gully, but as this route is rather loose, it is not recommended.

274 **Grooved Wall** *** VS
280 ft./85 m. *H. M. Kelly, H. G. Knight and W. G.*
Standring 1928

An excellent route, taking a series of grooves up the right (true left) wall of Walker's Gully. Start just to the right of the gully, 50 ft./15 m. of scrambling above the path.

1) 60 ft./18 m. Climb awkward grassy ledges to a wide chimney, which leads to the top of a large flake. 2) 60 ft./18 m. Ascend the groove above to a ledge on the right. 3) 60 ft./18 m. The groove above is barred by an overhang which forms the hardest part of the climb. Fortunately some good protection can be arranged in the crack leading over the overhang. Continue up the groove to a belay. 4) 60 ft./18 m. After some initial steepness, the angle eases and the groove is

Pillar Rock, north face
GL = Green Ledge. 273 = Walker's Gully. ST = Shamrock traverse

followed to a ledge and belay. 5) 70 ft./21 m. The final groove is not easy. Above the groove, some ledges lead to a stance and belay. Scramble up until the scree on the left can be gained above Walker's Gully, taking care not to bombard possible parties below. The Shamrock traverse lies about 300 ft./91 m. above.

275 **North-east Climb** * HVD

420 ft./128 m. *G. D. and A. P. Abraham 1912*

A fine climb which becomes considerably harder in wet or greasy conditions. Start as for the North Climb.

1) 100 ft./30 m. The first pitch of the North Climb (q.v.). Then climb 65 ft./20 m. up the second pitch to belay above a chimney. 2) 30 ft./9 m. Move a few feet up the gully, then traverse across the rib on the left. A 10 ft./3 m. chimney leads to a small stance and belay. 3) 25 ft./8 m. Move left round the rib then across a slab to grassy ledges. 4) 35 ft./11 m. Two chimneys with a difficult finish. 5) 40 ft./12 m. Climb a short slab on the left then walk left to the foot of a long V-groove on the wall of Walker's Gully. 6) 80 ft./24 m. Ascend the groove. 7) 60 ft./18 m. A mossy wall on the right then a vertical chimney and easier rocks. 8) 50 ft./15 m. A steep chimney and grassy ledges lead to the top. From here traverse, with care, either left to the amphitheatre above Walker's Gully or right to Low Man.

276 **North Climb** ** HD

320 ft./97 m. *W. P. Haskett Smith, G. Hastings and W. C. Slingsby 1891*

A popular classic, with good belays and short pitches making the climb suitable for large parties. The final pitch is Mild Severe unless the alternative finish, involving an abseil, is taken. In wet weather, the polished nature of the holds makes the climbing somewhat harder. Starts at the left-hand end of Green Ledge, at a short wall below a large ledge.

1) 35 ft./11 m. An easy mantelshelf and a slab trending left lead to a ledge at the foot of an obvious gully line (Savage Gully). 2) 95 ft./29 m. Climb the line of the gully for three short pitches to the foot of a deep twisting chimney on the right. At this point the gully steepens and twists to the left. 3) 40 ft./12 m. Squirm up the twisting chimney to a good ledge and

North-west Climb, Pillar Rock

belay.   4)   45 ft./14 m. Climb the open V-chimney slanting up to the left, then move right to a good ledge.   5)   45 ft./14 m. On the right wall of the corner above is a slanting chimney crack (the 'Stomach-Traverse'). Climb this to a large ledge.   6)   20 ft./6 m. Climb the cave pitch in the corner. Above this, a short walk leads to the massive 'Split Blocks'.   7)   20 ft./6 m. Climb the chimney between the blocks to their top.   8)   20 ft./6 m. Traverse to the left to a good ledge below and to the right of the projecting Nose. The first few feet (the Strid) are awkward and exposed.   9)   25 ft./8 m. The Nose (MS). From the corner on the right-hand side of the Nose, traverse out on a good flake foothold. At this point, a good side hold for the left hand can be reached, and by pulling on this and using a hidden foot (or knee!) hold round the corner, the Nose can be surmounted. From the top of the Nose, an easy (but loose) gully leads to the top of Low Man.

Alternative finishes: 9a)   25 ft./8 m. The Hand-Traverse (HS). From the right end of the ledge ascend the steep wall for 10 ft./3 m. until a good flake can be reached. Hand-traverse to the left to gain the top of the Nose.   9b)   130 ft./40 m. Descent into Savage Gully (HD). From the ledge below the Nose, abseil down on the left into Savage Gully and traverse to the left, round the corner, to the foot of a V-chimney. Climb the chimney without difficulty, then traverse up to the right for 60 ft./18 m. to the ledges above the Nose.

277   **Scylla**   *   VS

440 ft./134 m.   *A. G. Cram and W. Young   1963*

The climb takes the impressive crack splitting the large wall set in the centre of the north face. Unfortunately, the introductory pitches are rather scrappy, but the main pitches give excellent sustained climbing at the upper limit of its grade. The obvious Direct Finish is E2 (5c). Starts in a small grassy bay to the left of the Nor'-nor'-west Climb, directly below the obvious crack pitch high above.

1)   90 ft./27 m. Scramble up into a corner. Climb the corner on the right, then move right and scramble up ledges and over a large boulder to the foot of a wide square chimney.   2)   90 ft./27 m. The chimney is awkward to start, but soon relents and leads to a large ledge. Continue up in the same line, or move left and climb a groove, to reach the foot of a steep wall. Belay on the

266

left.   3)   110 ft./33 m. Climb the fine crack splitting the wall.
The first 40 ft./12 m. are the hardest, but frequent runners and
good jams help to relieve the tension. At the top, pull out left to a
good ledge. Large but dubious block belays or a piton.   4)   90
ft./27 m. Climb steep wall behind belay until the right-hand end
of a horizontal break can be reached. Make a long stride to the
left and pull round on to a ledge with difficulty. Continue
traversing round to the left, with an awkward balance move at
the end, to reach a V-groove. Jam up the groove until the top of
the pinnacle which forms its left side can be reached. Cross the
steep wall on the right and pull round to easy ground. Scramble
up to a stance and belay.   5)   60 ft./18 m. Easier but looser
climbing on the right leads to the summit of Low Man.

278   **Puppet**   *   E1   (5b, 4b, 5b)
440 ft./134 m.   *A. G. Cram and B. Whybrow   1966*
An alternative way up the large wall taken by the crack of Scylla.
The climbing becomes better and harder as height is gained,
pitch 5 being particularly exposed and exciting. The start and
the first two pitches to the foot of the steep wall are the same as
those given for Scylla (q.v.).   3)   60 ft./18 m. (5b) Ascend the
crack of Scylla for 20 ft./6 m. to a good runner. Traverse right
across the wall (steep and delicate) to the foot of a deep groove.
Climb the groove or the arête on the right to a small stance and
belay.   4)   60 ft./18 m. (4b) Take the corner and vague rib
above until a few moves right lead to a small stance below the
steep wall above. Piton belay.   5)   70 ft./21 m. (5b) Climb the
steep shallow groove above, and continue up the impending wall
above on widely spaced holds, which improve, to a good
ledge.   6)   80 ft./24 m. Move left and climb easier rocks to the
top of Low Man.

279   **Nor'-nor'-west Climb**   **   VS
450 ft./137 m.   *A. T. Hargreaves and G. G. Macphee   1932*
The upper half is particularly fine and exposed. A delicate and
classic climb. Start at the right-hand side of a large grassy bay in
the corner under the bounding buttress.

1)   100 ft./30 m. After the initial slab, trend away from the wall
for 40 ft./12 m., then back towards a wide crack.   2)   30 ft./9
m. Climb up to a large block and turn it on the left.   3)   40
ft./12 m. Up the slab trending left to a ledge. Climb the corner on
the right to the large ledge on top of the buttress (junction with

NW Climb). 4) 30 ft./9 m. A V-groove just left of the glacis. 5) 50 ft./15 m. An exposed traverse left, slightly down at first, crosses the top of a crack near the finish and ends on a sloping ledge and belay. 6) 60 ft./18 m. Climb up for some 15 ft./4 m. then move on to exposed arête on the left. Ascend this to the overhang, whee a few moves right lead to a small stance and peg belay. 7) 35 ft./11 m. Traverse right to small ledges. 8) 55 ft./17 m. Climb a 10 ft./3 m. crack on the left, then follow a ledge up and leftwards to a belay. 9) 50 ft./15 m. The arête on the left leads to the summit.

280 **North-west Climb** *** MVS

445 ft./136 m. *F. W. Botterill and party 1906*

A fine climb on clean rock, enjoyable even in wet weather. Starts at the right-hand end of Green Ledge below a short gangway leading to the right.

1) 70 ft./21 m. Climb the gangway to a ledge, then a 30 ft./9 m. chimney followed by a traverse across a slab on the left. 2) 55 ft./17 m. A chimney leads to a corner and belay. 3) 50 ft./15 m. Ascend the short buttress on the left, then a crack to easier ground. Go right across the large platform to a large easy-angled slab. 4) 30 ft./9 m. Climb the slab and a corner, then traverse left to a belay. 5) 60 ft./18 m. Traverse round a corner on the left, then ascend a bulge and two ledges to reach a recess. Leave this on the right, with an awkward move, to reach a grass ledge. Continue up to a higher ledge and belay. 6) 20 ft./6 m. Climb the corner, then left to a delicate nose of rock which leads to Block Ledge. 7) 80 ft./24 m. Step left and ascend ledges to a short V-chimney. Bridge up the chimney, then make a long stride back across the top of the chimney and climb mossy rock, with poor holds, to some small grassy ledges. 8) 20 ft./6 m. Traverse right and climb to the foot of a steep chimney. Good belay but poor stance. 9) 60 ft./18 m. Oppenheimer's Chimney. The start is hard but protected by a good runner. At the top of the chimney 20 ft./6 m. of scrambling lead to the summit of Low Man.

281 **Charybdis** ** HVS (–, 4c, 4c, 5a, 5a, 4b, 5a)

435 ft./132 m. *A. G. Cram and W. Young 1964*

The route follows a series of imposing cracks and grooves up the north-west arête. Start from Green Ledge as for the North-west Climb.

268

1)   50 ft./15 m. Climb the gangway and the 30 ft./9 m. chimney.   2)   100 ft./30 m. (4c) Continue up the same chimney, then climb a wall split by cracks to a large platform.
3)   70 ft./21 m. (4c) Move right to a glacis. Climb this and the corner above to belay below the deep, overhanging groove.
4)   50 ft./15 m. (5a) Climb into the groove (runner). Move down on to the left wall and ascend a layback flake. Return to the groove along an awkward gangway and move up to a sloping stance and thread belay.   5)   40 ft./12 m. (5a) Climb the green groove above. Move left at the top to a stance and belay.   6)   50 ft./15 m. (4b) The groove on the right (or the fine arête on the right of the groove) to a large block belay.   7)   75 ft./23 m. (5a) Climb the shallow groove above (20 ft./6 m. right of Oppenheimer's Chimney). Move right over the bulge then follow a slanting crack up the wall to the top.

WEST FACE OF LOW MAN

This wall of excellent, clean rock catches the afternoon sun and offers relatively short climbs in the lower grades. They can, however, be followed by a route on the west face of High Man, after a short descent down the Old West Route.
Descent: At the top of the climbs, traverse right to reach a good path (the Old West Route) which becomes an easy scramble and leads diagonally down to the West Cove.

282 **The Appian Way**   **   HS
215 ft./65 m.   *H. M. Kelly and R. E. W. Pritchard   1923*
A particularly fine wall climb with impressive situations. Start by a large block on a terrace, reached by scrambling across from the chockstone at the head of the waterfall.
1)   60 ft./18 m. Climb up on the left of a mossy chimney for 15 ft./4 m. then step back right across the corner. Continue up corner to a stance and flake belay.   2)   50 ft./15 m. Climb the thin crack in the corner and at the top traverse delicately across the wall on the left to a fine, airy spike for a belay. (The traverse line is lower than that shown in the photograph.)   3)   40 ft./12 m. Move left and ascend a series of steep ledges to grass ledge with a large block leaning against the wall. Thread and spike belays.   4)   70 ft./21 m. Ascend the impending crack on the left of the block and continue up slabs to the top.

Left: Pitch 6 of Charybdis, Pillar Rock

Above: Pillar Rock, west face of Low Man
OW = Old West Route

West Wall Climb   **   VD

210 ft./64 m.   *H. M. Kelly and party   1919*

A pleasant climb on good clean rock. Good belays are frequent, and all the pitches given below can be split if desired. Starts 40 ft./12 m. above the chockstone at the top of the waterfall.
1) 30 ft./9 m. Climb a mantelshelf to a ledge, then ascend a V-shaped chimney. Belay on the left.   2) 50 ft./15 m. Straight up steeply to a sloping ledge, then a short traverse right followed by more steep climbing to a glacis. Belay in the corner.   3) 60 ft./18 m. The crack on the right wall is followed to a good ledge. Traverse up to the left for 40 ft./12 m. to a pile of blocks.   4) 70 ft./21 m. Climb the blocks to a good stance and belay. Continue up a short exposed groove, then easier climbing leads to the Old West Traverse near the top of Low Man.

WEST FACE OF HIGH MAN

A superb face which catches the afternoon sun, and gives a variety of sustained routes on excellent rock. There are several good slab climbs, which are among the first on the Rock to dry after rain.

Descent: A tricky problem on the first occasion! The best descent from the top of High Man is to descend the Slab and Notch Climb (Moderate). A few yards north of the summit cairn, a wide chimney descends on the east side (right). Descend this for 20 ft./6 m., then descend well-scratched slabs on the right (looking out) for some 50 ft./15 m. until an easy traverse right leads to the Notch. Descend a short polished corner, then cross the huge slab to the final short step leading into the amphitheatre. (*NB* – It is necessary to climb *up* the amphitheatre to reach either the Shamrock traverse or the scree gully leading back to the foot of the west face. The scree slopes of the amphitheatre lead down into Walker's Gully – HS). An alternative descent is to abseil or climb down the crack (Difficult) below the summit to Jordan Gap. Then descend slightly to the east to gain the amphitheatre.

The descent on well-scratched rocks to Low Man is graded Moderate. This could then be followed by the Old West descent.

Appian Way, Pillar Rock

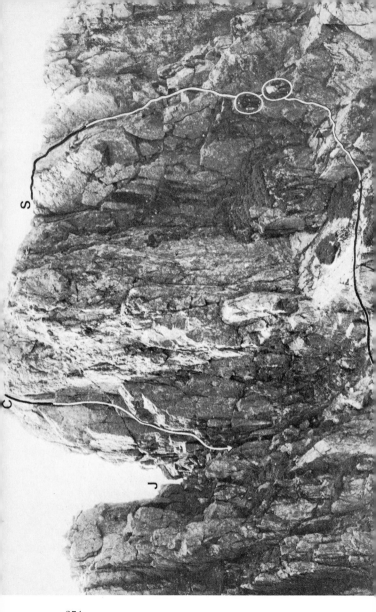

284 **Gondor** ** E2 (4a, 5b, 5c)
250 ft./76 m. *A. G. Cram and K. Robson* *1967*
The climb takes an improbable line up the bulging arête to the
left of the prominent groove of Gomorrah. Probably the most
technically difficult climb on the Rock, but difficulties are well
protected. Starts as for Gomorrah.
  1)   100 ft./30 m. (4a) As for Gomorrah, the relatively easy lower
section of the ridge to a ledge and belay below a steep
groove.   2)   60 ft./18 m. (5b) Climb the groove in the arête to a
bulge. Move out right across the steep slab to a good foothold.
Climb the square-cut overhang above. Continue up the steep
wall above with difficulty to a small stance and piton
belay.   3)   90 ft./27 m. (5c) Two alternatives are available to
start the pitch. The first possibility is to climb the overhanging
arête on the right above the belay for 8 ft./2 m. using hidden
holds round the corner, then move right on to the wall. The
second way is to descend slightly, traverse right round the
corner, and ascend the steep wall directly. The second possibility
is perhaps more difficult, but has the advantage that it is possible
to see the holds (if the light is good!). From the centre of the wall,
zigzag left, then continue up the centre to an easier groove.
Climb this to a large ledge and belay.

285 **Gomorrah** ** VS
285 ft./87 m. *H. M. Kelly and C. F.Holland* *1919*
A fine climb taking the big groove on the left side of the face. The
route is well protected and of a reasonable standard if the normal
finish is taken. Starts some 70 ft./21 m. along the Old West
Route, 20 ft./6 m. left of the grassy groove which terminates in a
prominent large triangular overhang.   1)   100 ft./30 m. Follow
the line of the ridge above, passing a grass ledge at 35 ft./11 m.,
to a ledge and belay below the steep buttress on the left of the big
groove.   2)   80 ft./24 m. Move right and slightly down across a
slab into the bay beneath the groove. Gain a wide crack on the
right which becomes the groove higher up. Climb the groove to a
stance on some cracked blocks below a roof. Nut belay. The

*East side of Pillar Rock, from the Amphitheatre, showing Jordan Gap (J)
and the descent routes
S = Slab and Notch (Moderate)
C = Central Jordan climb (Difficult)*

variation finish goes left from here.   3)   55 ft./17 m. Climb the
steep slabby wall forming the left side of the groove, past the roof,
to where the groove steepens. Step into the crack and climb this
for 20 ft./6 m. Traverse out right to a small stance and belay on
the rib.   5)   50 ft./15 m. Return to the chimney and climb this,
or more pleasantly take the rib behind the belay: both lead to the
top of High Man.

Alternative finish: Takes the upper half of the buttress to the left of
the final groove. Harder than the original route, giving sustained
climbing in superb positions.   3a)   70 ft./21 m. From the belay,
traverse left with difficulty to gain the foot of a steep crack. It is
wise to arrange protection here before moving on. Climb the
crack to a resting place below a slabby groove. Pull into the
groove, and climb this, exiting on the left into another groove,
which leads to a good ledge and belay.   4a)   30 ft./9 m. Easy
climbing leads to the top of High Man.

286   **Vandal**   **   HVS   (4c, 4c, 4c)
250 ft./76 m.   *G. Oliver, J. M. Cheesmond and L. Willis   1959*
A justifiably popular climb. Starts directly below the large
triangular roof which is a prominent feature of the west face.
1)   80 ft./24 m. (4c) Scramble up the grassy corner to a stance
15 ft./4 m. below the roof. Move right across the wall and climb
up to a small ledge. Continue up a steep crack on the right with
an awkward landing to a stance and belay.   2)   120 ft./36 m.
(4c) Climb the crack on the right to a small overhang at 40 ft./12
m. From here make a long step left and climb the steep wall, or
alternatively continue up the corner, starting with a long reach.
Either way leads to a fine slab which is climbed to a grass stance.
Continue up for 20 ft./6 m. to a belay below the final rib of
Gomorrah.   3)   50 ft./15 m. (4c) Climb the rib to the top of
High Man.

287   **Rib and Slab Climb**   ***   S
300 ft./91 m.   *C. F. Holland, H. M. Kelly and C. G.
Crawford   1919*
Fine open climbing, on superb rock; one of the best slab routes of
its standard in the Lakes. Starts level with the embedded block at

West Face of High Man, with Jordan Gap and Pisgah on the right

the foot of the New West Climb and about 40 ft./12 m. to the left of it.

1)   30 ft./9 m. Easily up to a grass ledge on the left.   2)   80 ft./25 m. Step right on to a steep rib and climb this on good holds until some small ledges on the left can be reached. The steep slab above is bounded by a groove on the left. Climb the slab with difficulty, or the slightly easier rib on the right, to a ledge. The groove above is gained by an awkward move and leads to a stance and belay.   3)   40 ft./12 m. Climb the steep rib, on the left of the polished groove of the New West, to a stance and belay.   4)   70 ft./21 m. The route now takes the fine slab on the right. Traverse right, following a line of small incut holds, until it is possible to strike straight up the centre of the slab. At the top, the traverse line of the New West is gained, with a good block belay on the right.   5)   80 ft./24 m. Move up right for a few feet, then climb straight up the incredibly rough slab on the left to reach the top of the crag.

288   **New West Climb**   ***   HD

290 ft./88 m.   *G. D. and A. P. Abraham, C. W. Barton and J. H. Winger   1901*

An excellent route with varied climbing and good belays. The rock is clean but very polished, so the climb becomes a grade harder in poor conditions. Starts just above a large block embedded in the scree a few yards to the left of the deep gully (West Jordan Gully). The pitches described below can be further split if desired.

1)   70 ft./21 m. Slant left on easy rocks, followed by a rib to a small corner. Continue up a steep staircase to a good ledge.   2)   35 ft./11 m. A wide chimney leads to a small platform, then a short traverse left is followed to a good belay.   3)   55 ft./17 m. Climb an awkward groove, then a short slab and a delicate step left leads to the foot of a

Opposite : West Face of High Man and Low Man, Pillar Rock

Overleaf left: A typical situation on the west face of High Man, Pillar Rock

Overleaf right: South-west Climb, Pillar Rock

chimney.   4)   60 ft./18 m. Climb the chimney with difficulty –
a strenuous thrutch! The angle eases at 30 ft./9 m., good belay
but poor stance. From this point traverse horizontally right
round the arête, then ascend a pile of blocks to a large
belay.   5)   40 ft./12 m. Follow a difficult slab, trending right, t
a corner and stance with belay 6 ft./2 m. above.   6)   30 ft./9 m
High Man is reached by a short chimney.

289 **South-west Climb**   **   MVS
215 ft./65 m.   *H. R. Pope and W. B. Brunskill   1911*
A superb slab climb with small but positive holds. Starts just left
of the bottom of West Jordan Gully, the deep cleft separating the
west face of High Man from Pisgah, and takes the slabs which
bound the right-hand edge of the face.
1)   30 ft./9 m. Climb easy rocks to a grass ledge below a
slab.   2)   85 ft./26 m. Climb the slab, slanting up to the right,
on small but good holds. A short steep section at 40 ft./12 m. is
overcome by a pull on excellent handholds, and leads to a small
ledge and belay. It is usual to continue up the slab above for
another 40 ft./12 m. to another ledge and belay.   3)   100 ft./
30 m. Traverse left for 15 ft./4 m. until it is possible to climb the
slab up to the right on small holds. Move left under a large block
and climb steep rib to the summit of the Rock.

WINTER CLIMBING

Although Pillar Rock does face north, good snow and ice
conditions are fairly rare. However, the gullies in the high corrie
beside the Rock regularly give pleasant Grade I/II snow climbs.
In hard ice conditions, Walker's Gully can give a ferocious climb
of Grade IV standard. Other climbs (such as the Old West
Route and the other gullies) can give good climbs, but are very
infrequently in condition.

SOUTH LAKES

CHAPEL HEAD SCAR (SD443862)

This limestone cliff, lying on the southern fringe of the Lake District, offers warm sunny climbing when the rest of the area is impossibly wet. It is sheltered, faces SW and is a sun-trap. The rock is good steep limestone and all the routes are hard and strenuous.

The following agreement has been reached by the BMC, and to protect our environment and ensure access, MUST be strictly adhered to.

RESTRICTIONS

1) No climbing from 1 March to 1 August, to prevent disturbing nesting birds.
2) Use marked paths only for access to and from crag.
3) The climbing area is restricted to the right of the large central gully.
4) No gardening.
5) Descend by abseil – fixed ring right of Cyborg buttress – or path at RIGHT end of crag.

Access

The crag lies on the Whitbarrow Escarpment directly above Witherslack Hall (4 miles east of Newby Bridge).

From the entrance to the Hall, take the tack on the right, past buildings, to a kissing-gate giving access to a field. Follow the path leftwards to enter the woods by a stile next to a gate. Continue on the track for 200 yds.v183 m., until a sign-posted path leads to the crag up the scree. Where the path hits the crag is Moonchild.

290 **Sun God** HVS (5a)

100 ft./30 m.   *D. and L. Cronshaw   1973*

The steep, most obvious flake-crack just left of where the path joins the crag.

1)   100 ft./30 m. (5a) Up the flake (harder than it looks) to the dead tree and continue up the steep crack to the yew. (Abseil from this yew.)

peg runner, to first thread. Move right into a shallow groove
(Rock 4 placement at the top.) Up and then left to a second
thread. Climb the wall above, just to the right of a very faint
groove (Rock 1), to a good hold (Rock 7 in the break). Move up
and traverse left to a larger groove (Rock 1 & 2) with a good
crack in it. This leads to the left end of the long roof. Move up
over the roof to gain a ledge. Hand traverse right (peg runner) to
big holds. Move up to the hanging stance. (A 165 ft./50 m. rope
will lower you to the ground.)

295 **Android**   ***   E4   (5c)
   150 ft./46 m.   *E. Cleasby and P. McVey   1979/Free: D. Knighton*
   Start 35 ft./11 m. right of Wargames and 20 ft./6 m. left of a large
   yew growing at the base of the crag, by a smaller tree. Superb
   climbing.
   1) ` 150 ft./46 m. (5c) Climb the tree (peg runner under overlap)
   and step off a branch leftwards (poor thread). Make an awkward
   move to a scoop and make a delicate traverse left for 20 ft./6 m.
   (high peg runner). Then move up the steep wall (peg runner)
   until it eases. Make a hard move up to a yellow flake and carry
   on up the wall, then move right to gain a groove through a little
   overlap. (Abseil sling to right.)

296 **Superdupont**   *   E5   (6c)
   150 ft./46 m.   *P. Cornforth   1985*
   15 ft./4 m. right of Android.
   1)   150 ft./46 m. (6c) Climb the wall from a sapling (with first a
   knife blade and then 4 *in-situ* bolts for protection) to a rest. Pull
   out left through the overhang to gain a ledge. Move up the wall
   to clip last, distant bolt. Continue up the wall above then trend
   right to abseil slings beneath the roof.

Paul Cornforth on Wargames

LIST OF CLIMBS

WASDALE

Scafell Crag

Scafell East Buttress

GREAT LANGDALE

White Ghyll Crag

96	**	MVS	Slip Knot	1
97	*	HVS	Laugh Not	1
98	*	E1	Man of Straw	1
99		S	Hollin Groove	1
100	*	MVS	White Ghyll Wall	1
101	**	VS	Gordian Knot	1
102	***	VS	Haste Not	1
103	**	E2	Haste Not Direct	1
104	**	E3	Paladin	1
105	*	S	White Ghyll Chimney	1
106	*	S	White Ghyll Slabs	1

Pavey Ark

107		M/D	Crescent Climb/Gwynne's Chimney	1
108	**	HVS	Arcturus	1
109	***	E2	Cruel Sister	1
110	*	HVS	Golden Slipper	1
111		VD	Cook's Tour	1
112	**	D	Rake End Chimney	1
113	**	VS	Rake End Wall	1
114	*	E2	The Brackenclock	1
115	**	HS	Stoat's Crack	1
116	***	E3	Brain Damage	1
117	***	E2	Astra	1
118	**	E4	Fallen Angel	1
119	**	HVS	Cascade	1

Gimmer Crag

120	*	VD	Gimmer Chimney	12
121	*	HS	Bracket and Slab Climb	12
122	**	MS	'B' Route	12
123		E1	Crystal	12
124	**	HVD/S	Ash Tree Slabs/'D' Route	12
125	***	HVS	Intern/Kipling Groove	12
126	**	VS	North-west Arête/'F' Route	12
127		E1	Springbank	12
128		E1	Whit's End Direct	12
129	**	E4	Midnight Movie	12

Dale Head Crag

Miner's Crag

ENNERDALE

Pillar Rock

Chapel Head Scar

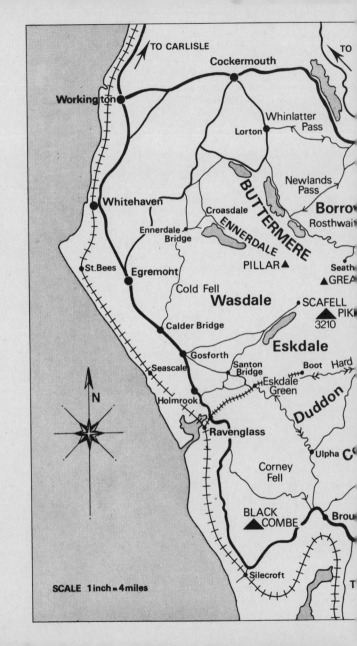